ט"ו סיון תשע"ב

בברכת התורה,

איתן

GENDER EQUALITY AND PRAYER IN JEWISH LAW

GENDER EQUALITY *and* PRAYER *in* JEWISH LAW

by

ETHAN TUCKER

and

MICHA'EL ROSENBERG

מכון הדר

MECHON HADAR

KTAV PUBLISHING

Gender Equality and Prayer in Jewish Law

ISBN 978-965-524-198-3

Typeset by Ariel Walden

Printed in USA

KTAV Publishing
527 Empire Boulevard, Brooklyn, NY 11225
Tel. 718-972-5449, www.Ktav.com

Names: Tucker, Ethan, 1975– author. | Rosenberg, Micha'el, 1978– author.
Title: Gender equality and prayer in Jewish law / Ethan Tucker, Micha'el Rosenberg.
Description: Brooklyn, NY : Ktav Publishing, [2017]
Identifiers: LCCN 2017038892 | ISBN 9789655241983 (hardback)
Subjects: LCSH: Women in synagogues. | Jewish women—Religious life. | Sex role—Religious aspects—Judaism. | Jews—United States—Social life and customs. | Women (Jewish law) | Women in Judaism. | BISAC: RELIGION / Sexuality & Gender Studies. | RELIGION / Prayer.
Classification: LCC BM726 .T83 2017 | DDC 296.4/5081—dc23 LC record available at https://lccn.loc.gov/2017038892

Contents

Acknowledgments

THIS book has been more than a decade in the making. We began teaching the material at the heart of this book in various settings that were grappling with a way to integrate gender egalitarian practice around prayer with a robust commitment to the discourse and practice of Jewish law (*halakhah*). The earliest presentations took place during the founding stages of Kehilat Hadar and the DC Minyan, both prayer spaces and communities that have embodied the values of this book for years. It quickly became clear that what began as sessions in independent *minyanim* and university settings needed to become an accessible resource for many more people than we could reach in person.

As is the case with all such projects, our voices and insights here channel the wisdom of our ancestors, our teachers, our colleagues, and our students. We begin with thanks to our parents, who have, each in their own ways, supported our journeys in *talmud torah* and who remain a source of inspiration to us as models of committed Jewish life. Ethan would like to thank his father and teacher, Rabbi Gordon Tucker, for teaching him Torah from his earliest years: Abba, thank you for giving me this gift of access to, and love of, Jewish texts.

Our teachers are many and we proudly stand on their shoulders. We both benefitted from an extraordinary undergraduate Jewish experience that was centered around Harvard Hillel. The dynamic vision of that institution, which allowed for a deep and meaningful interchange of ideas between the kinds of Jews who too rarely learn from each other, was essential to who we have become and the kinds of teachers we strive to be. Dr. Bernie Steinberg directed an extraordinary Jewish community, and a rich variety of undergraduate *minyanim* enabled us to imagine a world in which Jews practicing differently could nonetheless share core values and speak a shared language. In particular, the

Orthodox and Student Conservative *minyanim* were, for us, models of commitment and respect that continue to inspire us until today.

We are also both proud to be alumni of the Wexner Graduate Fellowship. The Wexner Foundation's investment in both of us, including support for complex training that combined rabbinic ordination in Israel with doctoral studies in the United States, made the scholarship at the heart of this book possible. We are also deeply indebted to the Wexner Foundation for connecting us with colleagues from across the spectrum of Jewish belief and practice. Our experiences with them helped inspire us to believe that it is possible to construct shared and respectful discourse around even the most contentious issues.

Many teachers over the years have encouraged, prodded, and challenged us, both generally and in particular with regard to the texts and arguments in this book. Some of them will agree with our conclusions and others will not, but we hope that they will all appreciate the extent to which our work reflects our debt to them. Our years studying at Yeshivat Ma'ale Gilboa were particularly precious to us. In that special *beit midrash* on a remote hilltop in northern Israel we encountered a passion for Torah, a thoroughgoing intellectual openness and a conviction that the eternal word of God must speak to our contemporary challenges. We are particularly thankful to R. David Bigman and R. Elisha Ancselovits, each of whom invested deeply in our education and supported our journeys towards *semikhah* with the Chief Rabbinate of Israel. While our analysis and conclusions are our own, we nonetheless owe them a deep debt for the culture of *talmud torah* they build and sustain on a daily basis. From R. Bigman we learned to listen carefully to every voice in every layer of our rich tradition. The values-based discourse of *halakhah* that we learned from R. Elisha informs every page of this book. We are proud to call ourselves their students.

We are both proud alumni of the Graduate School of the Jewish Theological Seminary, where we both received doctorates in Talmud and Rabbinics. While this is not an academic work, the reader will see the influence of contemporary scholarship throughout this book. We thank JTS for its investment in our education and for the access we received to outstanding scholars in rabbinics during our years there.

Our colleagues are many. We want to express deep gratitude to the board, faculty, staff and supporters of Mechon Hadar, where we have both taught over the years and which has been Ethan's professional home for the last decade. This extraordinary institution and the extraordinary people who work there is the living instantiation of the theoretical model we sketch out throughout this book. It is one thing to talk about gender-equal *minyanim* in theory, it is quite another to attempt to make that vision a reality. The *beit midrash* at

Mechon Hadar has been a central incubator for these ideas. Thank you to our colleagues, Rabbi Elie Kaunfer, Rabbi Shai Held, and Rabbi Avital Hochstein, who have supported this project since its inception. We are also grateful to the full-time faculty of Mechon Hadar, Rabbi Aviva Richman, Dena Weiss and Rabbi Jason Rubenstein, who have all been critical dialogue partners through the years. Supporters of Mechon Hadar have also been passionate about the need for this book and have made its publication possible. We are particularly grateful to David Andorsky, Dov Grossman, David Hiltzik, Yair and Stephanie Listokin, Sally Mendelsohn and David Lowenfeld, David Morris and Elisheva Urbas, Ron Moses, Jeremy Pava, Marc Schiller and Karyn Turecki Schiller, Jorian Schutz, and Yuval Segal, who offered targeted support for this project. Thank you for stepping up and believing in the power of *halakhah* to address our contemporary challenges.

For the last four years, Micha'el has been fortunate to work in the wonderfully supportive environment of Hebrew College, a pluralistic setting that honors personal commitments while forcing those of us who work there to sharpen our thinking. In particular, the leadership of Rabbis Art Green and Sharon Cohen-Anisfeld has helped create an atmosphere in which creative and careful thinking can thrive.

The substance of this book is the result of many years of shared learning and discussion. Pride of place goes to our friend and colleague Aryeh Bernstein. It is virtually impossible to conceive of this book without him. He worked tirelessly on much of the drafting and redrafting of this discussion, helping us to put oral teachings into written form so that they could reach a larger audience. Aryeh's efforts to turn a set of *shiurim* into prose form helped launch this book and formed its initial kernel. Even as our presentation of the material has changed somewhat over the years, his impact remains throughout. Even more important, Aryeh has been an indispensable thought partner, always pushing us to sharpen our formulations and to be sensitive to hear the truth even when it is hidden. His love for Torah, its cosmic significance and its stubborn focus on human needs has been a guiding light for us. We are honored to call him a colleague and a friend.

We would also like to thank R. Aryeh Klapper, who has engaged us on these issues over the years, ever since our shared time at Harvard Hillel. He has always offered sharp critiques and criticisms, while constantly encouraging us to tighten our analysis and follow through the ramifications of every step of the argument. It has been a privilege to learn from him and with him on this and other matters. R. Yossi Slotnik also read drafts of this analysis in its entirety and his critiques led to significant revisions that strengthened our analysis considerably. We are grateful to have him as a colleague, supportive critic and friend. Friends and mentors who have challenged us, allowing us the chance to sharpen our learning and teaching, are always preferable to those who simply offer support for what we already believe.

We are also deeply grateful to Sally Mendelsohn, Raphael Magarik and Dena Weiss, who read the manuscript in its entirety, reviewing its language and structure. Their insights strengthened it tremendously. No detail was too small to catch their eye; of course, any errors are our own.

Our students, both at Mechon Hadar and at Hebrew College, have been constant sources of energy and strength for us. Over 500 alumni of Mechon Hadar alone have learned this material in depth over the years; their questions and challenges have left a deep impact on the work. Watching new scholars of Torah emerge is one of the greatest joys of teaching. And it is humbling and rejuvenating to be challenged by those who encounter for the first time sources that we have been turning over for decades. If our Torah has remained fresh, it is thanks to them.

Our families have provided incredible support during this process. Our children have had to tolerate long conversations over Shabbat meals about the Rambam's view of obligation in prayer. Our spouses, Ariela Migdal and Miriam-Simma Walfish, have been invaluable conversation partners and have helped the seeds of these ideas flourish into a full presentation. Our own conviction that *halakhah* must address contemporary issues of gender are inspired and guided in no small part by their wisdom and model. We hope our children will all live in a world that affords them a sense of full citizenship in and responsibility for Torah and *mitzvot*. If this book can play a small part in making that world a reality, that is sufficient reward for the work.

Last in word but first in thought—we recognize our debt to the One who gives Torah, who has blessed us to be among those who sit in the *beit midrash* so that we may discover the wonders of these teachings. We pray that this book will be worthy to be a חלק בתורתך.

Introduction[1]

SINCE the middle of the last century, various communities of Jews, initially in the United States and subsequently elsewhere in Israel and throughout the Jewish world, have questioned, advocated for, argued over, and implemented adoption of equal roles for men and women in Jewish communal prayer services. Different communities have taken on varying degrees of gender egalitarian practice, some removing gender as a consideration in any aspect of communal ritual, others continuing to count only men for the *minyan*, even as women equally read from the Torah, while others have adopted other versions of partial egalitarian practice. Some have incrementally moved toward egalitarian practice over time. Some communities have instituted these practices in consultation with organized movements and rabbinic bodies and others have acted independently and with reference to their own grassroots views, sometimes articulated in halakhic language and sometimes not. Though the halakhic questions regarding egalitarian *minyanim* have earned a fair amount

1. Many have addressed this topic before. See: א. פרימר, "מעמד האשה בהלכה: נשים ומנין", *אור המזרח* לד (תשמו): 69–86; Mayer Rabinowitz, "An Advocate's Halakhic Responses on the Ordination of Women," in *The Ordination of Women as Rabbis: Studies and Responsa*, ed. Simon Greenberg, JTSA, New York, 1988; Joel Roth, "On the Ordination of Women as Rabbis," ibid.; A. Frimer, "Women and Minyan", *Tradition* 23, 4 (1988): 54–77; ד. גולינקין, "נשים וקריאת התורה בציבור", *תשובות ועד ההלכה* ג (תשמח) (http://www.responsafortoday.com/vol3/2.pdf.); J. Hauptman, "Women and Prayer: An Attempt to Dispel Some Fallacies," *Judaism* 42,1 (1993): 94–103; M.J. Broyde and J.B. Wolowelsky, "Further on Women as Prayer Leaders and their Role in Communal Prayer," *Judaism* 42,4 (1993): 387–395; J. Hauptman, "Some Thoughts on the Nature of Halakhic Adjudication: Women and 'Minyan'," *Judaism* 42, 4 (1993): 396–413; ד. גולינקין, "נשים במנין וכשליחות ציבור", *תשובות ועד ההלכה* ו (תשנז): 59–79 (http://www.responsafortoday.com/vol3/2.pdf); A. Frimer and D. Frimer, "Women's Prayer Services – Theory and Practice," *Tradition* 32, 2 (1998): 5–118; M. Shapiro, "*Qeri'at ha-Torah* by Women: A Halakhic Analysis," *Edah* 1, 2 (2001) – see also the follow-up comments by Y.H. Henkin and M. Shapiro in the same issue (http://www.edah.org/backend/coldfusion/displayissue.cfm?volume=1&issue=2);

of literature, there is still a need for a comprehensive treatment of the issue that seeks to understand the underlying concerns and issues of the different positions taken. This problem is most acutely felt by members of independent prayer communities who care about observing *halakhah* properly, but who are not affiliated with an organized denomination whose standards they can adopt or whose central rabbinic body they can trust without understanding the halakhic issues themselves. Further, many Jews seek a thorough personal understanding of their Jewish lives in their halakhic expression and will be served by an accessible, thorough treatment of this topic, which, though minor in its legal prominence, is quite significant in contemporary personal experience.

METHOD AND SCOPE

It is our intention here to submit the major questions of gender and public prayer to a thorough, transparent, and accessible analysis. We will aim to survey sources that are relevant to the questions we raise as we identify differing approaches. Our goal will always be to understand the positions we discover on their own terms, as we attempt to articulate the values that underlie various approaches.

Two overarching methodological concerns generally guide us. First, any idea and any position that claims a coherent reading of earlier sources is worthy of being taken seriously and understood. We try to avoid crushing the legitimacy, authority or viability of rulings based on the nature of their authors or how widely they were accepted when they were proposed. The position of every sage and *posek* is worthy of consideration and is a theoretically viable pathway for thinking about the proper application of *mitzvot* to our lives.

Second, cherry-picking positions in order to make a halakhic argument is not only tendentious, it is also often unwise.[2] As important as it is to un-

---

D. Sperber, "Congregational Dignity and Human Dignity: Women and Public Torah Reading," *Edah* 3, 2 (2003) (http://www.edah.org/backend/JournalArticle/3_2_Sperber.pdf); א. שוחטמן, "עליית נשים לתורה", סיני קלה–קלו (תשסה): רעא–שמט; G. Rothstein, "Women's *Aliyyot* in Contemporary Synagogues," *Tradition* 39, 2 (2005): 36–58; ד. שפרבר, דרכה של הלכה: *קריאת נשים בתורה, פרקים במדיניות פסיקה*, ירושלים תשסז; S. Riskin and M. Shapiro, "Torah *Aliyyot* for Women – A Continuing Discussion," *Meorot* 7:1 (2008); א. ב. הלבני, *בין האיש לאישה*, ירושלים תשסז; A. and D. Frimer, "Partnership *Minyanim*," in *Text and Texture*, found at: http://text.rcarabbis.org/partnership-minyanim-by-aryeh-a-frimer-and-dov-i-frimer/. We have drawn on much material found in these various publications. Our analysis here was significantly influenced by an unpublished article on egalitarian minyanim by R. Shai Wald. While R. Wald's argument was not fully fleshed out and seems never to have been intended as anything more than a private response to a private inquiry, he suggested several creative new lines of thinking that guided our analysis here.

2. In the words of Tosefta Eduyot 2:3: לעולם הלכה כדברי בית הילל והרוצה להחמיר על עצמו לנהוג כחומרי בית שמאי וכחומרי בית הילל על זה נאמ' הכסיל בחושך הולך התופס קולי בית שמאי וקולי בית הילל רשע אלא או כדברי בית שמאי כקוליהון וכחומריהון או כדברי בית הלל כקוליהון וכחומריהון: A person should strive for

derstand every possible position, it is equally important to understand the basis of the opposition, particularly when it is broad and reflected among the majority of a person's contemporaries. Minority views can be critical for reopening conversations, but they should not be favored at the cost of the wisdom of the majority. Ideally, a halakhic argument inspired by a minority position should make the case as to why conditions have changed such that the erstwhile minority would command majority support in the present moment.

Both of these principles aim to maximize wisdom and reflect two different messages that emerge from Tosefta Eduyot 1:4:

תוספתא עדויות א:ד

לעולם הלכה כדברי המרובין לא הוזכרו דברי היחיד בין המרובין אלא לבטלן
ר' יהודה אומ' לא הוזכרו דברי יחיד בין המרובין אלא שמא תיצרך להן שעה ויסמכו עליהן

Tosefta Eduyot 1:4

The *halakhah* always follows the majority. The words of the minority are only recorded alongside those of the majority in order to reject them.
R. Yehudah says: The words of the minority are recorded alongside those of the majority so that if they are needed at a later time, people can rely on them.

Minority views, says R. Yehudah, are theoretically as valuable as any other and must be studied carefully, since they may prove to be critical religious pathways at a later point in time.[3] But the primary, anonymous voice in the Tosefta reminds us that minority views must be kept in perspective. They were considered and rejected. To the extent one is inspired by the perspective of such a view, one must account for the majority's opposition and explain how that same majority might view things differently through the lens of a later, different experience of the issue.

Our focus on ideas and values also means that we do not claim to cite every potentially relevant source on the topic. We will often be content to cite enough material to outline a basic approach, with a particular focus on earlier sources that lay the groundwork for the contours of all subsequent conversations. In many cases, we examined sources that we felt essentially replayed prior arguments and elected not to engage them in deeper analysis.

---

intellectual and religious integrity when studying *halakhah* rather than engaging in a haphazard search for opinions – whether lenient or stringent – on which to hang one's hat.

3. This is a remarkable passage, in that R. Yehudah's very words seem to be cast as a minority view!

We welcome the insight and wisdom of readers to add to our framework with other positions we may not have yet fully considered.

Regarding scope, we will address two major questions:

1) The role of gender in selecting a *Sheliaḥ Tzibbur* (prayer leader) for public prayer. The question of Torah reading has been dealt with at length in other articles and responsa;[4] we will build on that literature to consider the more general question of leading rituals that require a *minyan* of ten.
2) The role of gender in counting the *minyan* of ten for public prayer and other associated rituals.

Our primary goals here are several:

1) To clarify misconceptions and dismiss red herrings that often cloud discussions on this topic;
2) To provide a sound basis for understanding the halakhic consequences of various positions related to gender and prayer;
3) To provide a unifying discourse that can make sense of both egalitarian and non-egalitarian practices in Jewish prayer and enable proponents of both to be able to share a unified halakhic conversation despite their divergent practical conclusions.

There are a range of issues we will **not** address, not for their lack of importance, but in order to focus our discussion. The first group of these is practices that are gendered in classical rabbinic sources, but that do not involve power issues with regard to female participation in parts of the service. For instance, women were classically exempt from reading the *Shema*, but individuals in many contemporary congregations never have their obligations fulfilled by the leader in this regard. Nor does the leader perform this function with regard to the blessings surrounding the *Shema*, where, in many (mostly Ashkenazi) congregations, he or she recites the bulk of the blessing silently, only cueing the congregation regarding pace by reciting the very end of the blessing, which is not sufficient for discharging another's obligation.[5] Similarly, women

4. See Shapiro, "*Qeri'at ha-Torah*," Sperber, "Congregational Dignity," שוחטמן, "עליית נשים לתורה"; Rothstein, "Women's Aliyyot"; *שפרבר, דרכה של הלכה*; Riskin and Shapiro, "Torah *Aliyyot* for Women"; all are referenced above.

5. See Mishnah Berurah 59:15 and Beur Halakhah 59 s.v. *benaḥat* for recognition of the fact that congregants are no longer careful to listen to the *Sheliah Tzibbur* (*Sha"tz*) during the blessings of *Shema*, instead saying those blessings themselves. As a further extension of this trend in many

were classically exempt from *Hallel*. However, the way we recite *Hallel* today features all individuals reciting the entire text on their own, including the opening *berakhah*.[6] In both these cases, the character of the leader should not make a difference. Whenever rituals like the *Shema* and *Hallel are* recited in a way that is intended to enable congregants to fulfill their obligations through the leader, it is not tenable to have someone who is exempt from these rituals fulfill the obligations of others in them. Only a paradigm shift in thinking about gender and ritual obligations – which we discuss at several points – could alter this analysis with respect to female leadership.[7]

---

communities today, not even the leader says the words loud enough for anyone to follow them. The notion that the leader of the blessings surrounding Shema no longer fulfills the obligations of congregants seems to be assumed by R. Yosef Karo in his defense of minors who lead *Arvit* on Saturday nights. We will explore this case in depth below, Part One, nn. 124–129.

6. Women's exemption from *Hallel* seems to flow from Mishnah Sukkah 3:10. That mishnah states that when an adult male leads *Hallel* for others, the respondent only needs to answer הללויה at various intervals, relying on the leader to say the core of the text for him. But when a woman, slave or minor leads *Hallel*, adult males must repeat the entire text word-for-word after them. Rashi Sukkah 38a s.v. *makrin* explains this as being based on an early custom, in which the communal prayer leader would fulfill others' obligation in *Hallel*. He says that women, slaves and minors are all exempt from *Hallel*; this exemption is what triggers the respondent's obligation to repeat after them rather than relying on their recitation. Tosafot Sukkah 38a s.v. *mi* also infers from this Mishnah that women are generally exempt from *Hallel*. In our settings, where all individuals say all of *Hallel* personally without being prompted by the *Sha"tz* (and the *Sha"tz* in most communities does not even say all of *Hallel* out loud, such that individuals could not choose to rely on the *Sha"tz* even if they wanted to), considerations of obligation would not be relevant. The Mishnah proceeds to curse a man who finds himself in a situation where he needs to be cued by a woman slave or minor, even if he says all the words himself. (Rashi and Tosafot explain the concern behind this curse differently, see there.) When a woman is *not* cueing those present, both because the leader does not say all the words of *Hallel* aloud and because those present have the text in front of them in the *siddur*, there is a strong case to be made that the curse should not apply. For this sort of analysis, see: ד. קורן, "כולם בקיאים בהלל", *מלין חביבין* ב (תשסו): ג–י. Aryeh and Dov Frimer in "Partnership Minyanim" disagree, arguing that having a leader who is not obligated in *Hallel* may itself be the source of the curse and/or may produce a problem of *kevod haztibbur*. The notion that someone of lesser obligation might be unfit for leadership of the service even when they are *not* fulfilling the obligations of others is not an argument without merit and is not to be dismissed lightly. Nonetheless, to the extent that is a concern, it is not specific to *Hallel* and relates to broader issues of honor and dignity we will address below. Note also that it might be possible to read Mishnah Sukkah 3:10 as stemming from concerns other than obligation. The exemption of women from *Hallel* is not directly noted anywhere in rabbinic sources and it is strikingly absent from Rambam's Mishneh Torah. Rambam codifies Mishnah Sukkah 3:10 at Hilkhot Megillah VeḤanukkah 3:14, but merely prescribes the Mishnah's protocol without mentioning the curse or even suggesting that there is anything wrong with appointing a woman, slave or minor as the leader as long as one does not rely on their recitation in place of saying *Hallel* oneself. He nowhere suggests that these figures are exempt, as is his normal practice. The concern might have to do with social status and the general impropriety of placing oneself in a ritually dependent relationship with such figures. We hope to return elsewhere to a careful reading of Rambam on this issue.

7. Such a paradigm shift is most obviously required in order to argue for a gender-blind practice surrounding the sounding of the *shofar* on Rosh Hashanah. The gender gap in rabbinic sources is clear and power issues are very much in play, given that one person blows the *shofar* for the entire community. In keeping with Mishnah Rosh Hashanah 3:8, the one who blows the *shofar* must be obligated in order to discharge the obligations of others. Validating a woman as an

Second, we will not systematically address overarching concerns of sexuality that may or may not recommend that women and men in various circumstances be separated or integrated. These issues are centrally important and also notoriously variable across communities and societies. More to the point, they tend to be comprehensive in ways that overwhelm the details of specific rituals and practices. To the extent that the mixing of men and women in a room is improper (whether in the context of sacred spaces or more generally), a broad regime of gender separation is necessary. To the extent that a given community displays no such concerns in mixed-gender settings, those concerns may be irrelevant. To the extent that gender segregation heightens sexual energy in a sacred space, such separation may itself be problematic. To the extent that individuals experience mixed-gender prayer settings as inappropriately sexualized, those individuals have an imperative to avoid such settings. These are all serious questions and concerns but beyond the scope of our analysis.[8] While we engage the possibility of mixed-gender prayer practices and quorums throughout, we also intend our analysis to be sound for communities where full gender segregation during prayer is the norm and perhaps even the recommended ideal. Most concretely, nothing we say in our analysis takes a position one way or the other on the question of *meḥitzah*, the physical barrier between men and women that has also often functioned as an ideological barrier between different segments of the Jewish community. It is our conviction that it is possible to have separate conversations about gender equality on the one hand, and gender blindness, on the other.

Our overarching hope is that the reader will emerge not only wiser, but more committed to the wisdom and richness of *halakhah* as a whole.

---

effective *shofar* blower for men would require claiming that contemporary women are maximally obligated in *mitzvot*, including those from which they were traditionally exempt. The notion of such a paradigm shift will periodically resurface throughout our discussion and is most directly addressed in Part Two, n78 and onward.

8. Others have thoughtfully addressed these sorts of issues, though we hope to have more to say about them in another context. For now, readers can see: R. Saul Berman, "Kol 'Isha," in *Rabbi Joseph H. Lookstein Memorial Volume*, Ktav 1981, 45–66; R. Yehuda Herzl Henkin, *Equality Lost*, Urim, 1999; Ibid., *Understanding Tzniut: Modern Controversies in the Jewish Community*, Urim, 2008; ר' דוד ביגמן, "עיון מחודש ב'קול באשה ערוה'", באתר קולך: http://www.kolech.com/show.asp?id=28988. See also Responsa Piskei Uzziel Bisheilot Hazman #44 and Responsa Yeḥaveh Da'at 4:15 for two important responsa on these sorts of issues.

PART ONE

Serving as *Sheliḥat Tzibbur* – Communal Prayer Leader

THE prayer leader (*Sheliaḥ Tzibbur,* or *Sha"tz*) performs a number of functions, including helping the community keep a uniform pace. Two functions are particularly critical for determining someone's eligibility to serve as a *Sha"tz*:

1) The prayer leader's fulfillment of the obligations of those assembled in some aspect of the service. We will focus on this issue in the context of the public recitation of the *Amidah* at *Shaḥarit, Minḥah, Musaf* and *Ne'ilah.*
2) The leading of those parts of the service known as *devarim shebikdushah* – *Kaddish, Barekhu* (at *Shaḥarit* and *Arvit*), and *Kedushah* (at *Shaḥarit, Minḥah, Musaf* and *Ne'ilah*). These elements are only said in the presence of a quorum of ten.

We will devote the first section of our discussion to analyzing both of these modes with respect to gender.

I. RECITING THE *AMIDAH* ALOUD AT *SHAḤARIT, MINḤAH, MUSAF,* AND *NE'ILAH*

One of the central roles of the public recitation of the *Amidah* has traditionally been to enable those in the community who do not know how to pray to have their obligation in prayer fulfilled, as we see in the Shulḥan Arukh's ruling:

שולחן ערוך או"ח קכד:א

לאחר שסיימו הצבור תפלתן, יחזור ש"צ התפלה, שאם יש מי שאינו יודע להתפלל יכוין למה שהוא

אומר, ויוצא בו; וצריך אותו שיוצא בתפלת ש"צ לכוין לכל מה שאומר ש"צ מראש ועד סוף; ואינו מפסיק; ואינו משיח; ופוסע ג' פסיעות לאחריו, כאדם שמתפלל לעצמו.

Shulḥan Arukh OḤ 124:1

After the community finishes their prayers, the *Sha"tz* repeats the prayer, so that if there is someone who does not know how to pray, he may have intention to what the leader is saying, and discharge [his obligation] through it. The one who is discharging [his obligation] through the prayer of the *Sha"tz* must have intention for all that the *Sha"tz* says, from beginning to end, and may not interrupt, nor speak, and takes three steps backwards, like a person who is praying oneself.

The **Mishnah** establishes the principle that only one who is obligated (in a *mitzvah*) may fulfill another person's obligation toward it:

משנה ראש השנה ג:ח

זה הכלל כל שאינו מחויב בדבר אינו מוציא את הרבים ידי חובתן.

Mishnah Rosh Hashanah 3:8

This is the principle: Anyone who is not obligated in a matter cannot discharge the many of their obligation.

Therefore, since *Shaḥarit*, *Minḥah*, *Musaf* and *Ne'ilah* all feature a public recitation of the *Amidah*, it would seem that one would have to be personally obligated in that prayer in order to serve as a *Sha"tz*. In order to allow for gender neutrality around leadership of the *Amidah* in a mixed-gender space one would minimally have to show that **either**: (1) obligation is no longer relevant for leading the *Amidah*; **or** that (2) the obligation in the *Amidah* is gender blind/equal.

A. The Argument that Obligation is No Longer Relevant

One can argue that in most contemporary communities the leader is usually *not* fulfilling the obligations of those unable to pray on their own. It is a well-established principle that one who knows how to pray cannot fulfill one's obligation in prayer by listening to the *Sha"tz*.[1] This principle is generally adhered to uncompromisingly; those who know how to pray are expected to do so on their own and cannot rely on the leader to discharge this obligation

1. The source for this ruling is found on Talmud Bavli Rosh Hashanah 34b–35a and is incorporated into the conclusions of Shulḥan Arukh OḤ 124.

for them.[2] If an entire community were to be comprised of knowledgeable Jews, various regulations surrounding the public *Amidah* might not be in full force. This type of situation and its legal consequences was already highlighted by **Magen Avraham** (Poland, 17th c.):[3]

מגן אברהם נג:כ

... ונ"ל דדוקא בזמניהם שהיה הש"ץ מוציא הרבים י"ח בתפלתו... משא"כ עתה שכלם בקיאין רק הש"ץ הוא לפיוטים.

Magen Avraham 53:20

... It seems to me this was specifically in their times, when the *Sha"tz* discharged the masses of their obligation in prayer ... which is not the case now, when all are literate, and the *Sha"tz* is only for liturgical poems.

Indeed, **R. Ben Zion Uzziel** (Israel, 20th c.) affirmed that in any context in which all congregants are praying individually, the *Sha"tz*'s sole function is in organizing the service, i.e., keeping everyone together at the same pace. He adds that even people otherwise considered peripheral members of the public prayer community ought to be able to serve in this role, explicitly mentioning children and women:[4]

שו"ת משפטי עוזיאל ג, מילואים ב

... במקום שהשומעים אומרים מלה במלה אחרי המברך והקורא אינו אלא מקריא לפניהם הדברים, הרי שהם יוצאים ידי חובתן בברכת עצמם והקורא אינו אלא מסדר הדברים פותח וחותם כל ברכה. וכן בקדושת השם פותח דברי קדושה והקהל עונים אחריו שפיר יכול המקריא להיות קטן או אשה...

Responsa Mishpetei Uzziel III, *Miluim* 2

... In a place where the listeners say each word after the one making the blessings, and the reader is only reading the words before them, they fulfill their obligations with their own blessings and the reader only sets the pace by reciting the beginning and end of each blessing. So is it with the *Kedushat HaShem* –he opens the words of *Kedushah* and the community answers after him – so the reader could properly be a minor or a woman.

2. See, for example, Mishnah Berurah 124:1: אבל הבקי אינו יוצא אפילו בדיעבד בתפלת הש"ץ/"But a literate person does not fulfill [the obligation] even *post facto* with the prayer of the *Sha"tz*."

3. The context here is the *halakhah* allowing an individual to prevent another individual from being appointed *Sha"tz*. The Magen Avraham argues that this law applied only when the job of the *Sha"tz* was to fulfill everyone's obligations, since no one should have to be represented by someone objectionable.

4. R. Uzziel's responsum addresses the question of children leading a children's service, e.g., in elementary school, but for which a *minyan* of adults is present.

According to this approach, in communities where all have access to a *siddur* and can use it competently, the level of the leader's obligation is no longer relevant.[5] Some have tried to extend this argument further by noting that *siddurim* with translations enable even those who do not know Hebrew to pray and thus render them legally "able to pray independently" and thus unable to rely on the *Sha"tz* to fulfill their obligations.[6] That would mean that, in any community with abundant *siddurim* in translation, the *Sha"tz* in no way vicariously fulfills others obligations in prayer.[7] Questions of obligation would thus be irrelevant for determining who may or may not serve as a *Sha"tz* for the *Amidah*.[8] The public recitation of the *Amidah* would continue merely in order to fulfill the Sages' decree to require a repetition without engaging the composition of each individual community[9] and in order to enable the *Kedushah* and Priestly Blessing to be said.[10]

---

5. R. Uzziel's final conclusion is that allowing minors to lead is inappropriate, not because of concerns about obligation, but on account of *kevod tzibbur*. We will address that issue at length below, n81–112.

6. A straightforward reading of Mishnah Sotah 7:1 yields permission to pray in all languages. The ensuing discussion on Bavli Sotah 33a limits this permission to the case of בצבור and there are at least three interpretive positions that emerge. The Shulḥan Arukh sums it up in OḤ 101:4: יכול להתפלל בכל לשון שירצה, וה"מ בצבור, אבל ביחיד לא יתפלל אלא בלשון הקודש; וי"א דה"מ כששואל צרכיו, כגון שהתפלל על חולה או על שום צער שיש לו בביתו, אבל תפלה הקבועה לצבור, אפילו יחיד יכול לאומרה בכל לשון; וי"א דאף יחיד כששואל צרכיו יכול לשאול בכל לשון שירצה, חוץ מלשון ארמי – "One may pray in any language one wants, that is, in a community, but when alone, one must pray only in Hebrew. But some say that this [restriction to Hebrew] is only when asking for personal needs, such as praying for a sick person or on some other domestic sorrow, but the prayer that is fixed for the community – even an individual may say it in any language. And some say that even an individual asking for personal needs may ask in any language desired, other than Aramaic." The stringent first position here (derived from R. Yonah's reading of the Rif) would only permit prayer in other languges as part of the public *Amidah*. Following this more stringent reading would obviously cripple this argument.

7. R. Mayer Rabinowitz made this point in his responsum advocating the ordination of women as rabbis in the Conservative movement: "Today when all of our congregations have prayerbooks with translations for those who cannot read Hebrew, and often with explanatory notes, we are in the category of competent woshippers (*bekiim*), and our obligations cannot be fulfilled by a *sheliaḥ tzibbur*," "An Advocate's Halakhic Responses on the Ordination of Women," in *The Ordination of Women as Rabbis: Studies and Responsa*, ed. Simon Greenberg, JTSA, New York, 1988, p. 117. The responsum is also available online: http://www.rabbinicalassembly.org/teshuvot/docs/19861990/ordinationofwomen1.pdf.

8. Obligation would still be a relevant consideration for leading any part of the tefillah where one person clearly recites or performs something for others. See n7 in the Introduction. Even with respect to the *Amidah*, there might, of course, be any number of other restrictions around who can lead; Magen Avraham clearly would not have permitted Gentiles to lead the *Amidah*. But other considerations would relate to propriety or definitions of basic membership in the covenantal community, topics we will address below, as opposed to concerns regarding obligation.

9. Shulḥan Arukh OḤ 124:3: "קהל שהתפללו וכולם בקיאים בתפלה, אעפ"כ ירד ש"צ וחוזר להתפלל, כדי לקיים תקנת חכמים" – "If a community already prayed and all of them know the *Amidah*, nevertheless, a *Sha"tz* should repeat the *Amidah*, in order to fulfill the decree of the Sages."

10. See, for example, the Arokh Hashulḥan (124:3): "ודע דהטור כתב עוד טעם על חזרת הש"ץ משום קדושה ע"ש ונראה שהיה יכול לומר גם משום ברכת כהנים" – "Know that the Tur wrote another reason for the *Sha"tz*'s repetition, namely, on account of the *Kedushah*, see there. And it seems that he could have also added on account of the Priestly Blessing." The Priestly Blessing is said every

While this line of reasoning can muster some strong support,[11] a number of factors make it a less-than-ideal basis for a gender-blind *tefillah*.

1) Situations frequently arise in which there are no prayer books available, or none in translation in a place where some attendants cannot read Hebrew, or where the congregation includes a person who can read neither Hebrew nor the language into which the book is translated.
2) Being able to pray in another language might not render someone legally competent in prayer to the point of forbidding them to rely on a public prayer offered in Hebrew. In other words, in communities with many who cannot pray in Hebrew, members might still appropriately choose to have the *Sha"tz* fulfill their obligations in Hebrew.
3) Despite R. Uzziel's clear position stating that concerns about obligation would not prevent a minor or a woman to lead a community where everyone prays individually, it is possible that Magen Avraham himself would have objected to having a leader *incapable* of fulfilling the obligations of those present, even if there was no need to in the present case. If reciting the public *Amidah* fulfills the Sages' decree to say it, it might well be necessary to have a person meeting the normal requirements for a *Sha"tz*, even when all can pray independently.

Therefore, we will elucidate the question of a *Sha"tz* fulfilling others' obligations in prayer, and how gender figures into that equation. We have already seen that the core principle is that only one obligated in a particular *mitzvah* is fit to fulfill other people's obligations in it. There are two perspectives in the *Rishonim* as to the nature of the obligation of prayer; though there has been some misunderstanding regarding the less dominant of these positions, we

---

morning by the *kohanim* in the repetition of the *Shaḥarit Amidah* in most communities in the Land of Israel and most Sephardic communities even in the diaspora. The dominant Ashkenazi diaspora custom has been for it to be said by the *kohanim* only in the repetition of the *Amidah* for *Musaf* on Yom Tov and on Yom Kippur. However, even where the *kohanim* do not say the Priestly Blessing, the *Sha"tz* says a modified form of it. We should note here that it is historically likely that the "repetition" of the *Amidah* was an original, independent form of public prayer that functions as a model of communal worship. The private *Amidah* is likely a separate phenomenon, intended to structure the individual's prayer using the communal template. An analysis of this issue is beyond the scope of this discussion but would provide a very different lens through which to view the ongoing importance of the public *Amidah*, even in a community of literate and competent individuals. See Kaf Haḥayyim OḤ 124:2 for an analysis in keeping with this approach. See also G. Blidstein, "Sheliaḥ Zibbur: Historical and Phenomenological Considerations," *Tradition* 12 (1971): 69–77. Sensitivity to these origins is part of what motivates us not to rely solely on a sweeping disqualification of any concern for the public *Amidah*.

11. The position of R. Uzziel as minimally applied to a community fully competent in Hebrew prayer is particularly strong in this regard.

will see that according to both views, men and women are equally obligated in prayer, and are therefore, from the perspective of obligation in the *Amidah*, equally fit to serve as *Sha"tz*.

B. The Argument from Equality of Obligation

The **Mishnah Berakhot 3:3** establishes explicitly that men and women are equally obligated in the *Amidah* prayer:[12]

משנה ברכות ג:ג
נשים ועבדים וקטנים פטורין מקריאת שמע ומן התפילין **וחייבין בתפלה** ובמזוזה ובברכת המזון.

Mishnah Berakhot 3:3
Women, slaves, and minors are exempt from the reading of *Shema* and from *tefillin* and **are obligated in prayer** and in *mezuzah* and in grace after meals.

This statement effectively summarizes the issue of gender and obligation in *tefillah* and it is the starting point to which all later interpreters must return: The Mishnah, without dissension, makes clear that men and women share an equal obligation in prayer. But in order to understand the complexities of later discussions, more background is needed.

Mishnah Kiddushin 1:7 offers a general rule that women are exempt from positive *mitzvot* caused by time:

משנה קידושין א:ז
וכל מצות עשה שהזמן גרמה אנשים חייבין ונשים פטורות.

Mishnah Kiddushin 1:7
With respect to any positive commandment caused by time, men are obligated and women are exempt.

"Caused by time" classically means that a *mitzvah* comes into force by dint of a certain day or moment coming to pass. For instance, the obligation to sit in a *sukkah* kicks in with the arrival of the 15th of Tishrei. It is also classically a gendered *mitzvah*, incumbent only upon men and thus aligned with the rule articulated in Mishnah Kiddushin. In keeping with this rule, **Talmud Bavli Berakhot 20b** asserts that *tefillah* is **not** such a *mitzvah*, placing it instead

12. Throughout the Mishnah, the word "תפילה" often refers specifically to the *Amidah*, and that is its clear context here. For a few examples, see Berakhot 4:1, 5:4, Ta'anit 2:2, and Shabbat 1:2.

in the category of positive *mitzvot* **not** caused by time, thus explaining why women are likewise obligated.[13]

Two core positions exist in the *Rishonim* to explain women's obligation in prayer: The view of Rambam, and the view of Rashi, Ramban, and many others.

1. The Rambam's View: Biblical and Rabbinic Prayer

The first view is that of Rambam (Spain/North Africa/Egypt, 12th-13th c.), who maintains that prayer is a positive *mitzvah* **not** caused by time, because, on a Biblical level, the *mitzvah* to pray is inchoate: Neither the frequency, nor the time, nor the content of prayers is legislated by the Torah. That is, a daily utterance of some sort of personal prayer suffices on the level of Biblical law, so long as it includes the three main elements of praise, request, and thanks. Here are the relevant words of Rambam:

ספר המצוות לרמב"ם מצות עשה

(ה) והמצוה החמישית היא שצונו לעבדו יתעלה וכבר נכפל צווי זה פעמים, אמר "וַעֲבַדְתֶּם אֵת ה' אֱ-לֹהֵיכֶם" (שמות כג:כה), ואמר "וְאֹתוֹ תַעֲבֹדוּ" (דברים יג:ה), ואמר "וְאֹתוֹ תַעֲבֹד" (שם, ו:יג), ואמר "וּלְעָבְדוֹ" (שם, יא:יג) . . . ולשון ספרי, "'ולעבדו', זו תפילה" (דברים מ"א) . . .

(י) . . . ולשון התוספתא "כשם שנתנה תורה קבע לקריאת שמע כך נתנו חכמים זמן לתפלה" (ברכות ג:א). כלומר, שזמני התפלה אינם מן התורה. אמנם חובת התפלה עצמה היא מן התורה כמו שבארנו (ע' ה) והחכמים סדרו לה זמנים. וזהו ענין אמרם "תפלות כנגד תמידין תקנום" (בבלי ברכות כו:). כלומר, סדרו זמניה בזמני ההקרבה.

Rambam, *Sefer Hamitzvot*, Positive Commandments

(5) The fifth commandment is that we are commanded to worship the Elevated One; this commandment has been repeated several times: It says, "And you shall serve the Lord your God" (Shemot 23:25), and it says, "Him you shall serve" (Devarim 13:5), and it says, "Him you shall serve" (*ibid.*, 6:13), and it says, "and serve Him" (*ibid.*, 11:13) . . . In the words of the Sifrei: "'Serve Him' – this is prayer" (Sifrei Devarim 41).

(10) . . . The Tosefta says: "Just as the Torah fixed times for the reading of Shema, so the Sages gave a time for prayer" (Tosefta Berakhot 3:1), meaning, the times of prayer are not Biblical. Indeed, the obligation of prayer itself

13. There are two main versions of the text of the Talmud here, one which asserts this point outright, and one which implies it by entertaining a contrary possibility and rejecting it. This split was already noted by numerous *Rishonim*, including Rashba and R. Yehudah Heḥasid. See also Ma'adanei Yom Tov letter *tzadi* on Rosh Berakhot 3:13, and Dikdukei Soferim on Berakhot 20b. The latter version of the Talmud in turn gets emended by Rashi. For a full discussion of the textual history here, see Appendix A and the notes there.

is Biblical, as we explained (#5) [the previous paragraph], and the Sages assigned it times. This is the sense of the statement, "They established the prayers parallel to the *Tamid* sacrifices" (Talmud Bavli Berakhot 26b), that is, they established its schedule parallel to the sacrificial schedule.

רמב"ם הל' תפילה א:א–ב

(א) מצות עשה להתפלל בכל יום, שנאמר, "וַעֲבַדְתֶּם אֵת ה' אֱ-לֹהֵיכֶם": מפי השמועה למדו שעבודה זו היא תפלה, שנאמר, ולעבדו בכל לבבכם אמרו חכמים "אי זו היא עבודה שבלב זו תפלה", ואין מנין התפלות מן התורה, ואין משנה התפלה הזאת מן התורה, ואין לתפלה זמן קבוע מן התורה.
(ב) ולפיכך נשים ועבדים חייבין בתפלה, לפי שהיא מצות עשה שלא הזמן גרמא אלא חיוב מצוה זו כך הוא: שיהא אדם מתחנן ומתפלל בכל יום ומגיד שבחו של הקדוש ברוך הוא ואחר כך שואל צרכיו שהוא צריך להם בבקשה ובתחנה ואחר כך נותן שבח והודיה לה' על הטובה שהשפיע לו כל אחד לפי כחו.

Rambam, Laws of Prayer 1:1–2

(1) It is a positive commandment to pray every day, as it is written: "You shall serve the Lord your God." By tradition, they learned that this service is prayer, as it says, "and to worship God with all of your heart." The Sages said, "What is service of the heart? This is prayer." The number of prayers is not Biblical, the form of prayer is not Biblical, and prayer has no Biblically fixed time.
(2) Therefore, women and slaves are obligated in prayer because it is a positive commandment not caused by time, but the obligation of this commandment is like this: A person should supplicate and pray every day and tell of the Holy One's praise, and afterwards ask for his/her needs as a request and a supplication, and afterwards give praise and thanks to God for the good that has been bestowed upon him/her, each person according to his/her ability.

This view understands Biblically mandated prayer to be largely unstructured. The structures of prayer as we know it – specific content at specific times – are rabbinically enacted parameters to formalize that commandment. The details of these requirements fill Rambam's Hilkhot Tefillah from shortly into chapter one (*halakhah* 4) all the way through the sixth chapter. At the conclusion of his elucidation of rabbinic prayer, Rambam explicitly maintains that these rabbinic requirements are incumbent on women:

רמב"ם הלכות תפילה ו:י

נשים ועבדים וקטנים חייבים בתפלה וכל איש שפטור מקריאת שמע פטור מן התפלה...

Rambam, Laws of Prayer 6:10

Women, slaves and minors are obligated in prayer, and any man who is exempt from *Shema* is exempt from prayer . . .

There has been confusion regarding Rambam's position, as some have argued that Rambam thinks that women are obligated only in general, unstructured Biblical prayer, but are exempt from the specific rabbinic requirements, which may constitute a positive (rabbinic) commandment caused by time. Such a position requires reading the *halakhah* just cited as departing from the local context of rabbinic prayer and returning to recapitulate the ruling stated in 1:1–2 about Biblical prayer. Such a reading is unsustainable for three reasons:[14]

1) Context: After 5½ chapters entirely about the details of rabbinic prayer, would Rambam suddenly return to a different, long-completed topic, without giving any indication about the change? If he were here returning to the earlier topic of Biblical prayer, he would have informed the reader of this.
2) Redundancy: The Rambam already recorded the law about women's and slaves' obligation in Biblical prayer, above in 1:1–2; why repeat it here?
3) Content: Above, in 1:1–2, when recording the law of Biblical prayer, Rambam mentioned that women and slaves are obligated. Here, in 6:10, he mentions women, slaves, *and minors* as being obligated. Minors are never obligated by the Torah in *mitzvot*.[15] They are obligated rabbinically only in that their parents are obligated to train them. To say, therefore, that the reference here to women refers only to Biblical prayer requires not only understanding Rambam to be switching topics unannounced and redundantly rerecording a law from chapter one, but it also requires understanding him to be talking about two different topics within one phrase, making it illogical.

Indeed, **R. Yosef Karo** explicitly explains Rambam here to be describing rabbinic prayer.[16] Perhaps most simply: One would never expect Rambam – or any other post-Talmudic commentator – to exempt women from the *Amidah*, given that no prior source does so!

---

14. **R. David Golinkin** (United States/Israel, 20th–21st c.) makes a similar argument in his responsum "נשים במניין וכשליחת ציבור", cited above, Introduction, n1.

15. We are aware of Y.D. Gilat's provocative article challenging this presumption, but it is not relevant for understanding Rambam's use of the term קטנים. For Gilat's argument, see י.ד. גילת, פרקים בהשתלשלות ההלכה, בר־אילן, תשנ"ב, 19–31. For Rambam's approach, see the contrast between Mishnah Sukkah 2:8 and Mishneh Torah Hilkhot Shofar Sukkah VeLulav 6:1.

16. In the Kesef Mishnah on the second half of this passage, he writes: וכל איש שפטור וכו'. רוב הפטורים מק"ש נאמר בהם שפטורים גם מן התפלה ואף באותן שלא נתפרש פטורים מק"ו דק"ש דאורייתא פטורים **תפלה דרבנן** לא כ"ש; "Most who are exempt from *Shema* are also exempt from *tefillah*, and even those that are not explicitly exempted obviously are: if they are exempted from the Biblical obligation in *Shema*, isn't it obvious that they are certainly exempted from *tefillah*, which is only a **rabbinic obligation**?"

Rather, the interesting question is not whether, but why: Why are women obligated in rabbinic prayer according to Rambam? Shouldn't rabbinic prayer be considered a positive commandment caused by time, from which women are exempt, according to the Mishnah in Kiddushin? The Rambam explains in his commentary on that Mishnah:

פירוש המשניות להרמב"ם קידושין א:ז

ומצות עשה שהזמן גרמה היא שחובת עשייתה בזמן מסויים, ושלא באותו הזמן אין חיובה חל כגון הסוכה והלולב והשופר והתפילין והציצית לפי שחובתן ביום ולא בלילה, וכל כיוצא באלו. ומצות עשה שלא הזמן גרמה הן המצות שחובתן חלה בכל הזמנים כגון המזוזה והמעקה והצדקה, וכבר ידעת שכלל הוא אצלינו אין למדים מן הכללות, ואָמְרוֹ "כל", רוצה לומר על הרוב, אבל מצות עשה שהנשים חייבות ומה שאינן חייבות בכל הקפן אין להן כלל אלא נמסרים על פה והם דברים מקובלים, הלא ידעת שאכילת מצה ליל פסח, ושמחה במועדים, והקהל, **ותפלה**, ומקרא מגילה, ונר חנוכה, ונר שבת, וקדוש היום, כל אלו **מצות עשה שהזמן גרמה וכל אחת מהן חיובה לנשים כחיובה לאנשים**.

Rambam, Commentary on Mishnah Kiddushin 1:7

And a positive commandment caused by time is obligatory at a set time; outside of this time, its obligation does not take effect, such as *sukkah*, *lulav*, *shofar*, and *tefillin* and *tzitzit*, because they are obligatory during the day but not at night . . . And positive commandments not caused by time are those commandments that are always obligatory, such as *mezuzah*, building a railing, and *tzedakah*. You already know that we have a principle that one does not learn from [heuristic] rules,[17] and when [the Mishnah] says "all," it actually means "most." But [the lists of] the positive commandments in which women are obligated or are not fully obligated obey no general rule, rather, they are passed on by tradition. Is it not the case that eating *matzah* on the first night of *Pesaḥ*, rejoicing on the festivals, the public reading of the Torah every seven years, **prayer**, reading of the *megillah*, *Ḥanukkah* candles, Shabbat candles, and reciting *kiddush* are all **positive commandments caused by time, yet for each of them a woman's obligation is the same as a man's obligation**.

The Rambam here discusses Biblical laws, such as eating *matzah* on the first night of *Pesaḥ* and reciting *kiddush*, together with rabbinic laws, such as reading *megillah* and lighting *Ḥanukkah* candles. The "prayer" he refers to here is clearly rabbinic prayer, since he describes it as caused by time (i.e. happening at fixed times during the day); we have already seen that Biblical prayer, for Rambam, has no fixed times at which it must happen during the day. None-

17. Talmud Bavli Eruvin 27a, Kiddushin 34a.

theless, Rambam explains – accounting for Mishnah Berakhot – that women and men are equally obligated. His larger point is that one should take the Mishnah's rule about women's exemption from *mitzvot* caused by time not as an absolute, but as a non-exhaustive general indicator that describes a number of cases. As we noted, some have argued that Rambam thinks women are exempt from rabbinic prayer. If such a view is exceedingly difficult given his ruling in Mishneh Torah Hilkhot Tefillah 6:10, as we explored above, it is impossible in light of this comment in Rambam's commentary on the Mishnah.[18] Rambam uses different language in these different texts, but the data all point to a coherent position: There is only one kind of prayer, one that is Biblical but whose parameters are rabbinically articulated. Though we have been speaking of "Biblical" and "rabbinic" prayer, Rambam has no notion of a separate entity of inchoate, Biblical prayer that survives beyond the rabbinic structuring of prayer. Moreover, "Biblical" and "rabbinic" prayer, for Rambam, are *not* two conceptually distinct universes. Recall that, for Rambam, Biblical prayer is not *totally* inchoate. Rather, one must sequentially praise, request, and thank. As is well known, these are in fact the three main sections of the *Amidah* as formulated by the Sages.[19] Thus, when one engages in the rabbinically composed *Amidah*, one is simply using the Sages' model for fulfilling one's Biblical commandment. The Biblical *mitzvah* was not gendered, nor was the historical trigger for its rabbinic expansion as described by Rambam;[20] therefore, the

18. **R. Ovadiah Yosef** (Israel, 20th–21st c.), in Responsa Yabia Omer OḤ 6:17, opines that Rambam must have changed his mind between writing his commentary to the Mishnah and writing the Mishneh Torah, which was written later. One could theoretically argue that, in the commentary on the Mishnah, Rambam had not yet developed his theory of a more amorphous, less scheduled Biblical level of prayer and was therefore forced to posit that women are obligated in thrice-daily prayer. Once Rambam formulated his more robust theory of *tefillah* in the Mishneh Torah, his final word on the matter was that women are only obligated to pray once a day. While discrepancies between the commentary on the Mishnah and the Mishneh Torah are not uncommon, they are mainly useful when a true contradiction exists. Here, as we argued, there is nothing in the Mishneh Torah indicating any exemption for women, rather two explicit statements affirming their obligation in both the Biblical and rabbinic speheres. R. Ovadiah does not engage Hilkhot Tefillah 6:10 and its relevance to our discussion. R. Ovadiah may be drawn to his explanation of Rambam in order to implicitly justify the practice of women in his community not to pray multiple times a day. See below, n28–41, for our analysis of Magen Avraham.

19. See Talmud Bavli Berakhot 34a.

20. See Rambam Hilkhot Tefillah 1:4: כיון שגלו ישראל בימי נבוכדנצר הרשע נתערבו בפרס ויון ושאר האומות ונולדו להם בנים בארצות הגוים ואותן הבנים נתבלבלו שפתם והיתה שפת כל אחד ואחד מעורבת מלשונות הרבה וכיון שהיה מדבר אינו יכול לדבר כל צורכו בלשון אחת אלא בשיבוש ... ואינם מכירים לדבר יהודית ... ומפני זה כשהיה אחד מהן מתפלל תקצר לשונו לשאול חפציו או להגיד שבח הקדוש ברוך הוא בלשון הקדש עד שיערבו עמה לשונות אחרות, וכיון שראה עזרא ובית דינו כך עמדו ותקנו להם שמנה עשרה ברכות על הסדר ... כדי שיהיו ערוכות בפי הכל וילמדו אותן ותהיה תפלת אלו העלגים תפלה שלימה כתפלת בעלי הלשון הצחה ... When Israel was exiled in the days of Nebuchadnezzar the Wicked, they assimilated into Persia, Greece, and other nations and children were born to them in Gentile lands, and those children's speech was confused – each one's speech mixed up many languages, and one who would speak was unable to express oneself fully in one language, but only in a confused mix ... and they did not know

rabbinic parameters of prayer are non-gendered as well. His model explains how the gemara could refer to prayer as not caused by time (its Biblical core possesses this quality), even as it is an obligatory practice multiple times a day, at set times (the rabbinic extension of the Biblical core). Women would thus be obligated in the time-bound extension because of their obligation in the non-time-bound core.[21] The Rambam's model of prayer, though two-tiered, explicitly maintains the Mishnah's ruling that women and men are equally obligated in fixed prayer multiple times a day.

2. Rashi and Ramban: Prayer is Rabbinic

Rashi (France, 11th–12th c.) reveals a different approach. He explicitly rejects the notion that prayer is commanded by the Torah and explains that the Mishnah's reason for ruling that women and men are equally obligated in prayer is because prayer is a request for mercy, which is necessary for everyone.[22]

רש"י ברכות כ:

"**וחייבין בתפלה**" - דתפלה רחמי היא, ומדרבנן היא, ותקנוה אף לנשים ולחנוך קטנים.

Rashi Berakhot 20b

"... **and they are obligated in prayer**" – because prayer is [a request for] mercy, and it is from the Rabbis, who established it even for women and for educating children.

---

how to speak Hebrew ... On account of this, when one of them would pray, they would come up short on Hebrew words for expressing requests and praise for God; other languages would get mixed in. When Ezra and his court saw this, they established a fixed order of 18 blessings ... which would be widely learned and known. Thus the prayer of these inarticulates could be as complete as those with a clear command of the Hebrew language."

21. For an excellent formulation of this point, see Sefer Hamenuḥah on Hilkhot Tefillah 1:2: כלומר כיון שאין לתפלה זמן קבוע מן התורה אבל היא מצוה תמידית שחובה על האדם לעשותה תמיד נראה שהיא מצוה חביבה עד מאד ומפני זה לא רצו חכמים להפקיע נשים ועבדים ממנה. וכן אתה אומר לכל מצות עשה שאין הזמן גרמ'.

22. Rashi draws this notion of prayer being a request for mercy from two other passages in the Talmud Bavli. After Mishnah Sotah 7:1 lists prayer among the ritual speech acts which may be said in any language, the anonymous voice of the gemara on Sotah 33a explains that "prayer is a request for mercy, so however one needs to, one should pray" – "תפלה' - רחמי היא, כל היכי' דבעי מצלי". The second place is Pesaḥim 117b: After Rava rules that the blessing praising God for redeeming Israel is said in the past tense in *Shema* and *Hallel*, but in the present tense in prayer, the Talmud explains that the reason it is said in the present tense is because "prayer is a request for mercy": אמר רבא: קריאת שמע והלל - גאל ישראל, דצלותא - גואל ישראל. מאי טעמא – דרחמי נינהו. It is possible he was also influenced by Yerushalmi Berakhot 3:3, 6b, which comments on our mishnah: כדי שיהא כל אחד ואחד מבקש רחמים על עצמו. See Appendix A for the fuller textual background for and fallout from Rashi's position here.

Rashi is emphatic, here and elsewhere,[23] that regular *tefillah* has no Biblical core. In Rashi's formulation, regular *tefillah* only has one tier: The rabbinic requirement for fixed prayer multiple times a day.

Ramban (Spain, 13th c.) expands Rashi's approach, attacking Rambam and maintaining that there is no Biblical requirement of daily prayer; rather, the whole enterprise is a rabbinic enactment.

השגות הרמב"ן לספר המצוות, מצות עשה ה

כתב הרב המצוה החמשית שנצטוינו בעבודתו שנ' ועבדתם את י"י א-להיכם וגו' . . . ולשון ספרי ולעבדו זו תפלה . . . ואין הסכמה בזה. שכבר בארו החכמים בגמרא תפלה דרבנן . . . וכבר ראינו בהלכות תפלה (רפ"א) שאמר שחייב אדם מן התורה בתפלה בכל יום אלא שאין מנין התפלות ולא משנה התפלה מן התורה וכך כתב בזה המאמר במצו' עשירית שזמני התפלה אינם מן התורה אבל חובת התפלה עצמה היא מן התורה. וגם זה איננו נכון בעיני . . . וכבר אמרו (סוף ר"ה) ברב יהודה דמתלתין יומין לתלתין יומין הוה מצלי, לפי שהיה עוסק בתורה וסומך על מה שאמרו (שבת יא.) חברים שהיו עוסקין בתורה מפסיקין לק"ש ואין מפסיקין לתפלה, שהיא דרבנן לעולם. אלא ודאי כל ענין התפלה אינו חובה כלל אבל הוא ממדות חסד הבורא ית' עלינו ששומע ועונה בכל קראינו אליו . . . ומה שדרשו בספרי . . . אסמכתא היא או לומר שמכלל העבודה שנלמוד תורה ושנתפלל אליו בעת הצרות ותהיינה עינינו ולבנו אליו לבדו כעיני עבדים אל יד אדוניהם.

Ramban's challenges to Sefer HaMitzvot, Positive Commandment #5

The master [Rambam] taught that the fifth commandment is that we must worship God, as it is said, "And you shall worship the Lord your God" . . . and in the words of the Sifrei, "'Worship' – this is prayer" . . . This point is not agreed upon. The Sages already clarified in the gemara that prayer is only rabbinic . . . We also see that in Hilkhot Tefillah (chapter 1), he said that one is Biblically obligated to pray every day, but that neither the number of prayers nor the precise form of the prayers is Biblical. So, too, he wrote here in the context of the tenth commandment, where he said that prayer has no Biblically fixed time, despite the fact that the obligation to pray is itself Biblical. This also seems incorrect to me . . . It is reported that R. Yehudah would pray only every thirty days,[24] since he was constantly learning, and based himself on the view that scholars engaged in Torah must stop for *Shema* but not for prayer,[25] which is always only rabbinic in authority. Rather, prayer is not obligatory at all [on the Biblical plane] and it is merely one of the Creator's traits of kindness that the Blessed One listens to us and

23. Rashi Berakhot 20b s.v. *hakhi garsinan*: דהא לאו דאורייתא היא. See Appendix A for a fuller explication of this passage in Rashi.
24. Talmud Bavli Rosh Hashanah 35a.
25. Talmud Bavli Shabbat 11a.

> answers us whenever we call . . . and the exegesis in the Sifre . . . is merely a support [for a rabbinic practice] or means that part of our service to God must be study and prayer in times of need and that our eyes and hearts always be turned to him like those of servants to their masters.

For Rashi, Ramban, and all others who assume *tefillah* is rabbinic, the conceptual structure of women's obligation in prayer is even simpler. There is only one level of *tefillah,* and when rabbinic texts speak of women's obligation in prayer, they are obviously speaking about the regular and repeated obligation of daily prayer that is *tefillah.*[26]

To summarize, Rambam rules that prayer is commanded in a general way by the Torah, and applies equally to men and women, as it is not caused by time. When the Sages structured that general commandment into specific prayers at specific times, its equal application to women and men remained. Rashi and Ramban rule that there is no such thing as Biblically-commanded prayer. Prayer – as we know it, thrice daily and with a particular structure – was instituted by the Sages and applied equally to men and women. Either approach is an effort to explain the same fact, explicitly laid out in the Mishnah, namely, that women and men are equally obligated in prayer.

The **Shulḥan Arukh** (R. Yosef Karo, Turkey/Eretz Yisrael, 16th c.), in

---

26. How did Rashi, Ramban and others in this school address the fact that the gemara seems to refer to prayer as not being caused by time? A few approaches were taken: 1) Some argued that even rabbinic prayer is not caused by time, in the sense that there is no time at which prayer is inappropriate: Consider R. Yonah on Rif Berakhot 11a, who says: ואע"פ שהתפלה יש לה זמן קבוע אפ"ה כיון שאמרו הלואי שיתפלל אדם כל היום כולו כמצוה שאין הזמן גרמא דיינינן לה ולפיכך נשים חייבות. "Despite the fact that prayer has fixed times, nonetheless, since they said, 'Would that people would pray all day long,' it is treated like a commandment that is not caused by time. Therefore, women are obligated in it." The Talmudic passage quoted here can be found in various forms at Yerushalmi Berakhot 1:1/2b, 4:4/8b, Shabbat 1:2/3a; Bavli Berakhot 21a, Pesaḥim 54b. R. Yonah thus explains how we might regard *tefillah* as not caused by time without embracing Rambam's model of Biblical *tefillah.* The ideal of prayer as constant and unlimited is never lost via the Sages' establishment of fixed times, which should be seen merely as the minimum expression of prayer. Unlike eating *matzah* in the month of Tishrei, which is a religiously meaningless act, prayer at any time is meaningful and valued. This approach resonates with the phenomenon of *tefillat nedavah* that was endorsed by many authorities throughout the generations. See Shulḥan Arukh OḤ 107. Speaking less formally, even those opposed to *tefillat nedavah* might concede that prescribed prayers "wallpaper" the daily schedule, such that no time is bereft of such an obligation. See Levush OḤ 106:2. (Even the half hour after noon that is ineligible for either *Shaḥarit* or *Minḥah* is traditionally understood as a precaution to avoid confusion.) Something like this basic approach seems to be behind the analysis of Tosafot Berakhot 20b s.v. *peshita.* 2) Others seized on Rashi's erasure of the passage in the gemara that speaks about time-boundedness and *tefillah.* See Appendix A for a fuller analysis of Rashi's textual emendation. If the phrase is absent, one can then maintain that *despite* the fact that *tefillah* is indeed caused by time, *nonetheless* women are obligated in it because of its essence as a personal request for mercy. R. Yonah reports this possibility as well, when he continues in the above passage: אי נמי מפני שהיא רחמים.

None of these conceptual and literary debates affect the shared, practical consensus: Women are fully obligated in *tefillah.*

codifying this universally agreed upon point, follows a modified version of Rambam's language in the Mishneh Torah, stating that women are obligated in prayer because it is a positive *mitzvah* not caused by time:[27]

שולחן ערוך או"ח קו:א

ונשים ועבדים, שאע"פ שפטורים מק"ש חייבים בתפלה, מפני שהיא מ"ע שלא הזמן גרמא

Shulḥan Arukh OḤ 106:1

And women and slaves, even though they are exempt from the obligation of reciting the *Shema*, are obligated in prayer, because it is a positive commandment not caused by time.

3. The Problem of Women Who Do Not Pray: The Magen Avraham's Defense

Women's and men's equal obligation in prayer remained uncontroversial in halakhic literature until the 17th century. No authority anywhere before that time ever says anything that suggests that women are exempt from any part of the obligation in the *Amidah*.[28] Commenting on the Shulḥan Arukh's formulation that women are obligated in prayer since it is a positive *mitzvah* not caused by time, **Magen Avraham** writes the following:

מגן אברהם קו:ב

מצות עשה - כ"כ הרמב"ם דס"ל דתפלה מ"ע דאורייתא היא דכתיב ולעבדו בכל לבבכם וכו' אך מדאורייתא די בפעם אחד ביום ובכל נוסח שירצה ולכן נהגו רוב נשים שאין מתפללות בתמידות משום דאומרי' מיד בבוקר סמוך לנטילה איזה בקשה ומדאורייתא די בזה ואפשר שגם חכמים לא חייבום יותר והרמב"ן סובר תפלה דרבנן וכן דעת רוב הפוסקים.

Magen Avraham 106:2

"A positive commandment": So wrote Rambam, who thinks that prayer is a

27. From the Shulḥan Arukh's use of Rambam's formulation, one might conclude that he also endorses Rambam's framework of a Biblical requirement to pray daily. However, we saw above, in n26, R. Yonah's approach that it is possible to consider thrice-daily, rabbinic *tefillah* to be the only *tefillah* that there is and nonetheless to describe it as מצות עשה שלא הזמן גרמא. Indeed, R. Yosef Karo cites only Rashi's explanation of the gender-blind nature of the Mishnah (דרחמי נינהו) in Beit Yosef 106, and Taz OḤ 106:2 took for granted that the Shulḥan Arukh thought *tefillah* was rabbinic without any Biblical core. See also Perishah OḤ 106:4, who seems to equate the Shulḥan Arukh's usage of מצות עשה here with the usage of Tosafot Berakhot 20b s.v. *peshita*, which is predicated on *tefillah* being entirely rabbinic.

28. A way of corroborating this point is to search an electronic database for any conjunction of the words אשה (woman), תפילה (prayer), and פטורה (exemption) in all digitized Jewish literature dating prior to the 17th century. Such a search turns up nothing that suggests exemption for women in prayer on any level.

> positive Biblical commandment, as it is written, "and to serve God with all of your heart . . ." But Biblically, it is sufficient to recite one prayer a day, in any formulation that one wishes. Therefore, most women have the practice of not praying regularly, because immediately after washing their hands in the morning they say some request, and this is Biblically sufficient,[29] and it is possible that the Sages did not extend their obligation any further. But the Ramban thinks that prayer is rabbinic, and this is the opinion of most authorities.

Some authors have referred to Magen Avraham as a source for arguing that women are not obligated in prayer, and therefore, to restrict their eligibility to serve as *Sha"tz*. But Magen Avraham does not in fact argue that women are exempt; he confronts a reality in which otherwise pious women are not praying three times a day and attempts to justify this practice as having some basis, even if it is not normative.[30] In so doing, those women can be seen as not sinful, even if their practice is not what one would expect in light of the halakhic sources. This sort of argument, traditionally known as a *limmud zekhut*, aims to stretch the boundaries of legal analysis in order to justify already established religious practices.

We should note a few points in order to maintain a precise understanding of this text:

1) The Magen Avraham does *not* say that Rambam thinks women are exempt from regular, fixed prayer. As we saw, Rambam explicitly obligates them such prayer in Hilkhot Tefillah 6:10 and in his commentary to the Mishnah. Rather, Magen Avraham notes that according to Rambam, there is a Biblical core of prayer, which women in his cultural context do fulfill in their personal morning petitions, and suggests that maybe the Sages obligated them no further, even though we have no record of such a position: ". . . immediately after washing their hands in the morning they say some request, and this is Biblically sufficient, and *it is possible* that the Sages did not extend their obligation any further." He uses the

29. The equation of the practice described here by Magen Avraham with Rambam's Biblical prayer is somewhat imprecise, since Rambam thinks that the Biblical core requires sequential prayers of praise, request, and thanks.

30. We should not err in assuming that just because apparently Jewish women in mid-17th century Poland did not regularly pray the *Amidah*, therefore Jewish women never prayed the *Amidah* regularly and that their obligation has always been a dead letter. See R. Golinkin's responsum, "נשים במנין וכשליחות ציבור", cited in Introduction, n1, pp. 63–67 for a nice collection of evidence showing that women did pray regularly in many time periods and places. For one example, see R. Yonah on Rif Berakhot 7a, s.v. *gemara*.

conceptual model of two-tiered *tefillah* advanced by Rambam as a way of introducing a new way of reading earlier texts to justify contemporary practice.[31] Since this is incompatible with the clear equality of obligation assumed in all earlier sources, many later authorities considered this defense to be unsatisfactory, as we will see shortly.

2) Though Magen Avraham roots his defense of contemporary women in Rambam, he emphasizes that most authorities reject Rambam's whole approach and think that prayer is entirely rabbinic, as we saw above in the positions of Rashi and the Ramban. According to this view, there is no multi-tiered structure of *tefillah* that could be marshaled to support a gender gap in prayer obligation. The Magen Avraham's concluding words here suggest that he follows Ramban, ruling that prayer is entirely rabbinic, since he asserts that the majority of authorities rule that way.

Indeed, commenting on the topic of the proper way to end Shabbat before resuming work, Magen Avraham assumes that women are obligated in the regular *Amidah* multiple times a day. After the Shulḥan Arukh records the *halakhot* stipulating that one should not work before verbally confirming the ending of Shabbat and that the conventional place to do this is in the *Amidah* of Saturday night *Arvit*, the Rema (R. Moshe Iserless, Poland, 16th c.) comments regarding the proper way for women to end Shabbat, since they tended in his context not to pray *Arvit* on Saturday nights:

רמ"א על שו"ע או"ח רצט:י

וכן נשים שאינן מבדילין בתפלה יש ללמדן שיאמרו המבדיל בין קודש לחול קודם שיעשו מלאכה...

Rema on Shulḥan Arukh OḤ 299:10

... And one should also teach women who do not make *havdalah* in the *Amidah* to say "[Blessed is the One] Who separates holy from mundane," before they do any [forbidden] labor ...

On this ruling, Magen Avraham comments the following:

מגן אברהם רצט:טו

שאין מבדילין - **ואע"ג דחייבות בתפלה** כמ"ש סי' ק"ו מ"מ רובן לא נהגו להתפלל במ"ש ואפשר לומר כיון דתפלת ערבית רשות אלא דקבלו עלייהו כחובה והנשים לא קבלוהו עלייהו במ"ש:

31. Note that Magen Avraham would have to say that the Mishnah's ruling only applies to Biblical prayer in order for this reading to cohere, which is an exceedingly difficult claim to make. Though the other *mitzvot* mentioned in Mishnah Berakhot 3:3 (*tefillin*, *Shema*, *mezuzah*, and *birkat hamazon*) are all Biblical in nature, the term תפילה in Mishnah Berakhot refers to the *Amidah* when speaking about matters of obligation. See above, n12.

Magen Avraham 299:16

"Who do not make *havdalah*" – **Even though they are obligated in the *Amidah*, as is written in Siman 106**, nonetheless, most do not have the practice of praying at the end of Shabbat. Perhaps this is because the evening prayer is optional, save the fact that Jews accepted it upon themselves as obligatory, and women never obligated themselves to pray at the end of Shabbat.

Here, Magen Avraham explicitly notes that women are obligated in prayer, that this is reflected in Siman 106, and that any reality of women generally not praying was in tension with the law. His comment here demonstrates that his comment back in 106 was meant as an attempt to defend a non-ideal practice, and not a principled expression of the law. In both places, confronted with a clash between adjudicated law and popular practice of otherwise pious people, he, like many rabbis throughout history, suggests a conceptual framework in which the legal establishment need not think of those people as transgressive. Regarding Saturday night *Arvit* in particular, his defense is more modest than his more sweeping attempt in Siman 106: Since *Arvit* was originally not obligatory and became obligatory only through the power of custom, it is more reasonable to suggest that if the masses of women are not praying, maybe they never participated in the custom that transformed *Arvit* into a requirement, at least on Saturday nights.[32] This then strongly demonstrates that Magen Avraham did not truly endorse his suggestion (*limmud zekhut*) in Siman 106 – in part because it would have been impossible for anyone who thinks regular *tefillah* is entirely rabbinic to get behind it – and that in fact his starting assumption is one of gender equality vis-à-vis obligation in prayer.[33]

Nonetheless, a number of *Aḥaronim* have maintained Magen Avraham's defense without challenging the strength of its legal and textual foundations. For example, **Peri Megadim**,[34] after citing Rambam Hilkhot Tefillah 1:1–2 and

---

32. Note that Magen Avraham's language here only seeks to justify women who don't pray on Saturday nights, but the conceptual approach opens the door to letting them off the hook for evening prayer in general. This broader justification gained a number of adherents, including Shulḥan Arukh HaRav OḤ 106:2 and Mishnah Berurah 106:3. Of course, the status of women's obligation in *Arvit* has no bearing on the question of their fitness to serve as *Sha"tz*, since the whole question of obligation is relevant only for the matter of the *Sha"tz* fulfilling others' prayer obligation via the repetition of the *Amidah*. There is no repetition of the *Amidah* in *Arvit*.

33. See also Magen Avraham 70:1, where he cites R. Yonah's language explaining why women are obligated in *tefillah* as a *time-caused commandment*. Even more tellingly, he then proceeds to argue that though women are exempt, in his view, from the blessings surrounding *Shema*, they are obligated to say אמת ויציב, the *berakhah* of גאל ישראל immediately prior to the *Amidah*, because they should fulfill the obligation to juxtapose the theme of redemption to the *Amidah*. This is only coherent if he thinks women are obligated to say the *Amidah*. These points further reveal Magen Avraham's acceptance of the fact that women are obligated in thrice-daily recitation of the *Amidah*.

34. Eshel Avraham on OḤ 106:2. Peri Megadim was written by R. Yosef b. Meir Teomim,

Magen Avraham, says: ולפי זה יצא קולא בנשים די להם בפעם אחד במעת לעת – "According to this, a leniency emerged among women to suffice with once a day." Some late *Aḥaronim*, such as **Arokh Hashulḥan**[35] and, in our own time, **R. Ovadiah Yosef**,[36] have tried to strengthen Magen Avraham's defense of women who do not pray thrice daily by explaining that it was actually the position of Rambam that women are not obligated in rabbinic, time-oriented, specific prayer. This should be seen as a further attempt to justify ongoing practice, rather than as a principled reading. This is especially true of Arokh Hashulḥan, who also creatively attempts to justify women's non-regular prayer habits even according to Rashi and Ramban and concludes by openly acknowledging that he is driven to find a generous defense of popular practice:

ערוך השולחן קו:ז

... ולפ"ז בדוחק יש ליישב מה שנשים שלנו אינן זהירות בכל הג' תפלות לשיטת רש"י ותוס' ולהרי"ף והרמב"ם א"ש ודו"ק:

Arokh Hashulḥan 106:7

... and according to this, with great difficulty one may sustain the fact that our women are not meticulous in all three prayers, according to the position of Rashi and Tosafot, though according to the Rif and Rambam it makes sense.

As we saw above, any suggestion that Rambam thought that women were exempt from rabbinic prayer contradicts the evidence of chapter 6 of the Mishneh Torah. The Magen Avraham himself never claimed that Rambam held this view. Accordingly, a number of *Aḥaronim* called out this unwarranted expansion and rejected any use of Rambam to defend women who were not praying regularly. For one example, here are the comments of **R. Ben-Tzion Lichtman** (Russia/Beirut/Israel, 20th c.), on this passage of Magen Avraham:

בני ציון או"ח קו:א

... ויותר מזה קשה, דהרמב"ם כתב בסוף פ"ו נשים ועבדים וקטנים חייבים בתפילה. ובודאי מיירי בכל התפילות, ולא רק על... פ"א ביום באיזה נוסח שהוא, אלא בסתם תפילה מיירי בכל הפרק, ועוד דומיא דקטנים שחייבין בכל התפילות, והרי נראה ברור שגם הרמב"ם מחייב נשים בכל התפילות ודלא כמ"ש המ"א והפ"ם.

וזה עולה באמת לפי גרסתו בגמרא, "תפילה פשיטא מ"ד הואיל וכתיב... הו"ל מ"ע שהז"ג וכל

Ukraine/Germany, 18th c.

35. OḤ 106:7. Arokh Hashulḥan was written by R. Yeḥiel Michel Epstein, Lithuania, 19th–20th c.

36. Responsa Yabia Omer VI OḤ #6.

מ"ע שהז"ג נש' פטורות קמ"ל." ... וזהו כל החידוש שאף בהן נשים חייבות אע"פ שהחיוב דרבנן תלוי בזמן, והטעם הוא דכיון שעיקר חיוב התפלה מדאורייתא אינו תלוי בזמן ונשים חייבות בו אף חכמים לא הוציאו אותן מהחיוב שלהם אע"פ שקבעו לו זמן ...

Benei Tziyyon OḤ 106:1

... And a further difficulty is that Rambam wrote in the sixth chapter, "Women, slaves, and minors are obligated in prayer." And surely he is dealing there with all of the prayers, and not simply with the prayer of once a day in any form that one wants, but rather with the standard prayer that is the topic of that entire chapter; and furthermore, a comparison is made to minors who are obligated in all of the prayers, and it thus is seen clearly that also Rambam obligated women in all of the prayers, and it is not as was written by Magen Avraham[37] and the Peri Megadim.

And this emerges clearly from [Rambam's] version of the gemara: "Prayer – that is obvious! What would you have thought? Since it is written ... [you might have thought that] it is a positive commandment caused by time, and from all positive commandments caused by time women are exempt; therefore, it comes to teach us otherwise." ... And this is itself the whole innovation [of the gemara here], that women are even obligated in [the fixed times for prayer], even though the rabbinic obligation is dependent on time, and the reasoning is that since the core of the obligation for prayer from the Torah is not dependent on time and women are obligated in it, even the Sages did not exclude them from their obligation, even though they fixed a time for it ...

Indeed, other *Aḥaronim*, such as **Maharam ibn Habib** (Eretz Yisrael, 17th c.),[38] **R. Yitzḥak Taib** (Tunisia, 18th–19th c.),[39] and **R. Shmuel Ehrenfeld** (Austria, 19th c.),[40] insist that Rambam mandates that women pray three times daily. **R. Yisrael Meir HaKohen** (Lithuania/Poland, 19th–20th c.) does not relate to whether Magen Avraham's passage reflected the correct reading of Rambam; nevertheless, he expressly states that *halakhah* accords with the Ramban, that prayer is an entirely rabbinic commandment and unquestionably equal for men and women, and that women should therefore be urged to pray regularly:

---

37. Note that R. Lichtman cites Magen Avraham as ascribing to Rambam the view that women are only obligated to pray once a day. We argued above that Magen Avraham never claimed this, but this text is a good indicator of how powerful a meme it had become to justify women's lack of regular prayer by appealing to Magen Avraham's use of Rambam.

38. Kapot Temarim, Sukkah 38a.

39. Erekh Hashulḥan OḤ 106:1. See also Ben Yedid, the commentary of R. Yedidiah Shmuel Tarica (Rhodes, 18th c.), on Rambam Hilkhot Tefillah 1:2.

40. Ḥatan Sofer, Tefillah 3:102b.

משנה ברורה קו:ד

...אבל דעת הרמב"ן... חייבו אותן בתפילת שחרית ומנחה כמו אנשים הואיל ותפלה היא בקשת רחמים. וכן עיקר כי כן דעת רוב הפוסקים... ע"כ יש להזהיר לנשים שיתפללו י"ח...

Mishnah Berurah 106:4

... but Ramban's view ... [is that the Sages] obligated them in *Shaharit* and *Minhah* just like men since prayer is a request for mercy. This is the essence of the matter, since it is the view of most authorities ... Therefore, one must impress upon women that they pray the *Amidah* ...[41]

4. Other Defenses of Pious Women Not Praying

Other 20th century *Aharonim* have gone to lengths to emphasize that women are obligated in prayer according to everyone, including Rambam, yet have offered alternative frameworks for defending contemporary women who do not pray regularly. These defenses have pointed to lifestyle conflicts making it difficult for women in their particular contexts to pray with proper focus. **R. Ben-Tziyyon Lichtman** wrote as follows:

בני ציון קו:א

ולי נראה ללמד זכות על רוב הנשים שאין מתפללות בתמידות דרוב הנשים מוטל עליהן להתעסק בכל צרכי הבית ובטיפול ילדים והכנת צרכיהם, שמטריד הלב ומבלבל הכונה, ובמצב זה אין להתפלל כמו שכתב הרמב"ם בפ"ד מצא דעתו משובשת ולבו טרוד אסור לו להתפלל עד שתתישב דעתו... ואע"ג שעכשיו אין אנו נזהרי' בזה מפני שאין אנו מכונים כ"כ בתפלה, לגבי טרדות הנשי' שאני... **אבל אלו הנשי' שנמצאות במצב שיכולות להתפלל ודאי צריכות להתפלל כל הג' תפלות, כי מדינא נשים חייבות בכל התפלה אליבא דכו"ע.**

Benei Tziyyon OH 106:1

And it seems to me that the way to justify the practice of those women who do not pray with regularity is that most women are encumbered with dealing with the needs of the house and the care of children and preparation of their needs, which distracts the mind and disorients proper focus, and in such a state one should not pray, as Rambam wrote in chapter 4: "If one's mind is disoriented and one's heart distracted, it is forbidden to pray until the mind gets settled" ... And even though nowadays we are not concerned with this, since we are not so focused in our prayer [anyway], regarding the distraction of women [i.e. the raising of children] it is different ... **But those women**

---

41. In fact, the author of the Mishnah Berurah only took up this cause regarding *Shaharit* and *Minhah*, having adopted Magen Avraham's defense of women who do not pray *Arvit*, a defense we described above.

who find themselves in a situation where they can pray certainly must pray all three prayers, because on the basis of the law they are obligated in all of the prayers according to all authorities.

In our own day, **R. Yehuda Herzl Henkin** (Israel, 20th–21st c.) follows the Benei Tziyyon.[42]

Another *Aḥaron*, **R. Yekutiel Yehudah Halberstam** (Romania/Israel, 20th c.), followed a similar route in explaining that even according to Rambam, women are obligated in prayer, and that Magen Avraham himself understood this. He offered a similar, alternative defense of women who don't pray:

שו"ת דברי יציב או"ח סימן קכא

אך עדיין יש לי להצדיק המנהג שהזכיר המג"א, כיון דבש"ס עירובין ס"ה ע"א יכולני לפטור מדין תפלה שנאמר שכורת ולא מיין עיי"ש . . . ועכ"פ יש סמך גדול לנשים בזמה"ז שאינן בגדר ימוד את עצמו שיכול לכוון . . . וק"ו לנשים דטרידי טובא ורשות בעליהם עליהם והטף תלויים בהם, לזה נהגו רוב נשים שאין מתפללות בתמידות, ורק כשימודו בעצמן שיכולים לכוון עכ"פ לפי האפשרות, ולפענ"ד זה אמת . . . שכיון שבאמת מעיקר התקנתא היו חייבות בתפלה . . .

Responsa Divrei Yatziv OḤ #121

But I can still justify the practice described by Magen Avraham, since in the Talmud Eruvin 65a [it is said that] I can exempt from the law of prayer, [one about whom] it is written, "drunk, but not from wine," see there . . . and there is in any event certainly a sound basis for women today, who are not in the class of those who can assure that they are sufficiently focused . . . [given that] women are extremely burdened, subject to their husbands' authority and responsible for children. Therefore most women do not pray regularly, and only when they judge themselves to have sufficient focus do they pray, when it is possible. This, in my humble opinion, is correct . . . since they are in truth included [like men] in the original obligation of prayer . . .[43]

42. Responsa Benei Banim, II:6.

43. This passage in Divrei Yatziv is significant for two reasons. First, like Benei Tziyyon, it rejects Magen Avraham's suggestion that women are essentially any less obligated than men in daily prayer. Second, and more significant, it actively endorses women's full essential obligation in *tefillah* even in cases where a *berakhah levatalah* is at stake. The responsum here is dealing with the question of whether a woman who lit Shabbat candles may then pray *Minḥah* – even if she did not explicitly condition her lighting with this in mind. R. Halberstam rules that she may, because her obligation in *tefillah* is identical to men and is thus a standing responsibility that her lighting of the candles and early acceptance of Shabbat cannot eliminate.

Summary

In summary, throughout the classical and medieval halakhic literature, the full and equal obligation of women and men in prayer was maintained without controversy. In the period of the *Aḥaronim*, some authorities, beginning with Magen Avraham, attempted to defend the religious integrity of pious women who nonetheless did not pray regularly. The Magen Avraham's defense was far-reaching, but never claimed to be the ideal law. In any event, it met with resistance even as a defense by other authorities and even Magen Avraham himself seems to have abandoned it. A more solid defense argued that the proposed exemption is properly understood as an exemption for women engaged in childcare, *while engaged in childcare,*[44] a defense which is dependent on activity conflicts, not on gender, as it would just as reasonably be invoked to defend men who, on account of the pressures of childcare, become less meticulous about prayer than rabbinic law would have them be.[45] The essential equality between men and women regarding prayer thus remains, even as those in caretaker roles may find themselves with a contextual exemption in certain situations. None of this affects a person's ability to discharge others' obligations in prayer by serving as *Sha"tz*, since, as was already clear in the Mishnah, men and women are equally obligated in prayer.

Women's supposed exemption from prayer cannot serve as a justification for excluding them from serving as *Sha"tz*. There is no solid basis for any claim that women are, by dint of the fact that they are women, any less obligated than men in prayer. This is obviously true according to the dominant view of the Ramban (without any controversy) and is also true according to Rambam's two-tiered approach to *tefillah*. At most, some of the later uses of Rambam to generate a justification of women who do not pray are at most just that, a justification of a non-ideal situation. They have no place in any discussion surrounding an ideal approach to gender and prayer, nor in the context of a

---

44. Rabbi Menaḥem Nissel cites R. Yisrael Meir HaKohen, in Siḥot Ḥafetz Ḥayyim I:27, as also holding the view that women burdened with childrearing may be exempt from *tefillah* on account of these burdens. See Menaḥem Nissel, *Rigshei Lev: Women and* Tefillah*: Perspectives, Laws, and Customs*, Targum/Feldheim, 2001, p. 82–87, along with the notes there. R. Nissel also cites evidence that this was the position of 20th century luminaries such as **R. Shlomo Zalman Auerbach** (via oral tradition), **R. Ya'akov Kaminetzki** in Emet le-Ya'akov OḤ 106:131, the **Ḥazon Ish**, as cited in Responsa Maḥazeh Eliyahu 19:5), **R. Ḥayyim Pinḥas Scheinberg** (personal communication with R. Nissel), and **R. Moshe Shternbuch** in Moadim U-Zemanim I:9 and Teshuvot Ve-Hanhagot I:74, III:OḤ 36. He also emphasizes that R. Scheinberg, **R. Eliyahu Greenblatt**, and **R. Yosef Shalom Elyashiv** stress that a woman who is not in a situation of familial burden is obligated to pray regularly, pp. 85–86, n14–15.

45. Indeed, such a basis for exempting men who are primary caregivers is advanced by **R. Ben-Tziyyon Abba Shaul** in Responsa Or Letziyyon II 7:24.

community that is pursuing a more egalitarian approach to *tefillah*. While it is not our place to judge women who rely on Magen Avraham to justify their own practice, it is important to avoid allowing the justification of pious women who do not pray the *Amidah* regularly to undermine their fundamental obligation in prayer across halakhic time and space. Other defenses in the past century focusing on lifestyle conflicts have proven themselves more legally sound. Gender should thus not play a central role when it comes to obligation in prayer.[46]

46. Two arguments appear in the *Aḥaronim* claiming that women are exempt from *Musaf*. 1) Women are exempt from *Musaf* because this prayer exists as a memory of the public sacrifices, and women were not obligated to contribute to the pool of funds set aside for this purpose. (See Mishnah Shekalim 1:3.) This argument first appears in R. Shaul Berlin's collection of responsa, Besamim Rosh. (R. Berlin edited this collection and claimed that it contained lost medieval responsa, including many of the Rosh, R. Asher b. Yeḥiel. Many contemporary rabbis and modern scholars considered the work to be a fraud composed by R. Berlin himself. His work has nonetheless been quoted occasionally by a range of later *poskim*.) **Besamim Rosh #89** makes the above claim and then goes on to make the interesting claim that women nonetheless have the practice to pray "everything, and have obligated themselves in all the *mitzvot*" (וחייבו את עצמן בכל המצות). A similar argument for exemption is cited in **Responsa R. Akiva Eiger I:9**. **R. Yitzḥak Elḥanan Spector** rejects this argument outright in Responsa Be'er Yitzḥak OḤ #20, given that it would imply that no one under 20 is obligated in *Musaf*. See also Torah Temimah on Shemot 30:22 for a similar critique. 2) *Musaf* is a time-caused commandment and therefore, following the rule of the Mishnah in Kiddushin, women are exempt from it. This logic is advanced in **R. Yeḥezkel Landau**'s Tziyyun LeNefesh Ḥayyah on Berakhot 26a s.v. *veshel musafin*. This claim, at first blush, overtly contradicts the gemara, which already seems to have accounted for the general tension between women's obligation in *tefillah* and the principle of exemption from time-caused commandments. But R. Landau develops his point by using Rashi's text of the gemara, which emphasizes that women are obligated in prayer because it is a "request for mercy" (רחמי נינהו). Given that several *Rishonim* argue that *Musaf* is not a request for mercy and therefore one cannot make up for a missed *Musaf Amidah* by repeating the next *tefillah* (תשלומין), it must be that the basis for women's obligation is not present and therefore we revert to the rule in Mishnah Kiddushin. This is a difficult argument on a few counts, not least of which is that it is a debate among commentators as to whether one can make up for a missed *Musaf Amidah* (see Meiri Berakhot 26a). Furthermore, once women are included in the *mitzvah* of prayer, there is no indication that they are then excluded from any part of it, and it is surprising to think that such a significant exclusion would not have been mentioned anywhere by the *poskim*. Most important, R. Landau's "argument" here is essentially a theoretical analysis of what seems to be an extraneous word in the Tosafot there, and it is unclear whether he ever intended it to have practical halakhic force. In any event, **R. Mordekhai Ze'ev Ettinger** and **R. Yosef Shaul Nathanson** (in Magen Gibborim, Elef Hamagen 106:4) both rejected R. Landau's argument here, claiming that in fact the *Musaf Amidah is* fundamentally a request for mercy and that the ancient practice in Eretz Yisrael of saying an eighteen-berakhah *Amidah* for *Rosh Ḥodesh Musaf* confirms this point. Therefore, women are equally obligated in *Musaf*. In their words, הדין ברור, the law is clear on this matter. R. Spector also challenges R. Landau here. For a review of the basic positions on this topic, see **Responsa Yabia Omer II OḤ 6:4–6**. One can certainly construct out of these dissenting *Aḥaronim* a justification of those women who do not regularly pray *Musaf*. There is not, however, enough to work with to claim that communities that assume women have the same obligation as men in *Musaf* are somehow playing on the legal margins. With respect to *Ne'ilah* on Yom Kippur, nothing suggests that it is any more gendered than *Shaḥarit* or *Minḥah*. Indeed, in **Responsa Yabia Omer II OḤ 6:7**, R. Ovadiah Yosef states that women are obligated in *Ne'ilah*, despite the fact that he holds that they are normally exempt from *Musaf*. We will leave the discussion here with the unambiguous bottom line of R. Spector from the above teshuvah: וכן מוכח מסתימת הפוסקים דנשים חייבות בתפלה ולא חלקו בין מוסף לשארי תפלות: women are obligated in all types of *tefillah* without any distinction.

Some recent authors[47] have tried to argue for women's continued exclusion from serving as *Sha"tz*, even while acknowledging that such an exclusion cannot be justified on grounds of their not being obligated in prayer. They have argued, instead, that while women are obligated fully in individual prayer, there is a separate "*mitzvah* of public prayer", which is incumbent upon men, but not upon women, and that this gap precludes women from serving as *Sha"tz*. In an appendix, we address those concerns, arguing that the nature and contours of public prayer do not generate gender-based distinctions with respect to who may function as its leader.

II. RECITING THE *DEVARIM SHEBIKDUSHAH*

The other main function of the *Sha"tz* is to say *devarim shebikdushah*, which are said only in a *minyan*. We will here investigate whether gender affects fitness for leadership of these uniquely public parts of the prayer service.

Mishnah Megillah 4:3 lists a number of prayers and rituals which are said only in the presence of ten, including public Torah reading, having a *Sha"tz* lead prayer, adding God's name to the invitation to Grace after Meals (*zimmun*) and various occasional rituals:

משנה מגילה ד:ג

אין פורסין את שמע, ואין עוברין לפני התבה, ואין נושאין את כפיהם, ואין קורין בתורה, ואין מפטירין בנביא, ואין עושין מעמד ומושב, ואין אומרים ברכת אבלים ותנחומי אבלים וברכת חתנים, ואין מזמנין בשם, פחות מעשרה. ובקרקעות, תשעה וכהן. ואדם, כיוצא בהן.

Mishnah Megillah 4:3

We do not responsively recite the *Shema*,[48] nor have a communal prayer leader, nor offer the priestly blessing, nor read Torah, nor read from the prophets, nor perform the standing/sitting [ritual for the dead], nor say the blessing of the mourners nor the formal comforting the mourners, nor recite the wedding blessings, nor say *zimmun* with the Name in a group of fewer than ten. And when redeeming land we require nine and a *kohen*. And so too with [redeeming] people.

On Megillah 23b, **R. Yoḥanan** bases this on a verse and describes (at least some of) the rituals in this Mishnah as *devarim shebikdushah*, or sacred rituals:

---

47. For example, see R. Broyde and R. Wolowelsky's article cited in Introduction, n1 above.

48. The exact meaning of *pores al Shema* has been hotly debated. Our translation here follows Tosefta Sotah 6:3 and the analysis of Ezra Fleischer in עזרא פליישר, "לליבון ענין הפורס על שמע", *תרביץ* מא (תשלב): 133–144. It seems likely that this already assumes some sort of recitation of *Barekhu* as part of the *Shema* and its attendant *berakhot*. See Mishnah Tamid 5:1.

תלמוד בבלי מגילה כג:
מנא הני מילי?
אמר רבי חייא בר אבא אמר רבי יוחנן: דאמר קרא "וְנִקְדַּשְׁתִּי בְּתוֹךְ בְּנֵי יִשְׂרָאֵל" (ויקרא כב:לב) – כל דבר שבקדושה לא יהא פחות מעשרה.

Talmud Bavli Megillah 23b
How do we know this?
Said R. Ḥiyya b. Abba said R. Yoḥanan: The verse says: "And I will be sanctified in the midst of the children of Israel" (Vayikra 22:32) – any *davar shebikdushah* shall not be said with fewer than ten.

On Berakhot 21b, **R. Ada b. Ahavah** explicitly includes the *Kedushah* in this category of prayers which may be said only in the presence of ten:

תלמוד בבלי ברכות כא:
וכן אמר רב אדא בר אהבה: מנין שאין היחיד אומר קדושה – שנאמר, "וְנִקְדַּשְׁתִּי בְּתוֹךְ בְּנֵי יִשְׂרָאֵל" (ויקרא כב:לב) – כל דבר שבקדושה לא יהא פחות מעשרה.

Talmud Bavli Berakhot 21b
So said R. Ada bar Ahava: From where do we know that an individual does not say the *Kedushah*? As it says, "And I will be sanctified in the midst of the children of Israel" (Vayikra 22:32) – any *davar shebikdushah* shall not be said with fewer than ten.

In the time of the *geonim*, we find explicit statements requiring ten for *Kaddish* as well:

תשובות הגאונים - גאוני מזרח ומערב סימן קכו
עשרה שמתפללין וכיון שהגיעו לאל הקדוש הלך אחד מהן יסיימו את כל הברכות עד שלום רב אבל יתגדל ויתקדש אי איפשר לומר לו אלא בעשרה.

Geonic Respona – Geonim of East and West #126
When ten are praying and, upon reaching *ha'el hakadosh* [the conclusion of the third blessing of the *Amidah*, which includes *Kedushah*], [if] one of them walks out, they should finish all the blessings until *shalom rav* [the final blessing of the *Amidah*]. But they cannot say *Kaddish* unless there are ten [present at that point].[49]

49. The ruling offered here was not wholly accepted in later times. See SA OḤ 55:3.

Barekhu is included (along with *Kaddish*) among the rituals requiring ten for the first time in **Massekhet Soferim 10:6:**[50]

מסכת סופרים י:ו

אין פורסין על שמע... ואין עוברין לפני התיבה... ואין נושאין את כפיהן, ואין קורין בתורה, ואין מפטירין בנביא, ואין עושין מעמד ומושב... **ואין אומרין קדיש וברכו** פחות מעשרה...

Massekhet Soferim 10:6

We do not responsively recite the *Shema* . . . nor have a communal prayer leader, nor offer the priestly blessing, nor read Torah, nor read from the prophets, nor perform the standing/sitting [ritual for the dead] . . . **nor say *Kaddish* or *Barekhu*** with fewer than ten . . .

The items mentioned in Mishnah Megillah above, along with other *devarim shebikdushah* such as the recitations of *Barekhu, Kaddish,* and *Kedushah,* thus all require a *minyan* of ten. This position is maintained throughout subsequent halakhic literature. One typical formulation is that given in **Tur OḤ 55:1:**

ואומר קדיש ואין אומרים אותו בפחות מעשרה דכל דבר שבקדושה כגון קדיש וברכו וקדושה אין אומרים אותו בפחות מעשרה.

And then [the leader] says *Kaddish.* And it is not said in the presence of fewer than ten, for any *davar shebikdushah,* such as *Kaddish* and *Barekhu* and *Kedushah,* is not said in the presence of fewer than ten.

We will discuss the criteria for this quorum of ten later, but assuming such an appropriate quorum has been assembled, what role, if any, does gender play in leading these rituals? Talmudic literature neither discusses the possibility of a woman serving as *Sha"tz,* nor her saying *devarim shebikdushah* in a general

---

50. Debra Reed Blank has argued that this passage in Massekhet Soferim, particularly the additions of *Kaddish* and *Barekhu* to the Mishnah's list, may in fact be a gloss that dates from no earlier than the 13th century. See Debra Reed Blank, "The Medieval French Practice of Repeating *Qaddish* and *Barekhu* for Latecomers to the Synagogue," *Liturgy and the Life of the Synagogue* (2005): 84–88. As we noted in n48, the practice of *Barkehu* is already attested in some form in Mishnah Tamid 5:1; it also appears as a ritual done specifically in the synagogue in Mishnah Berakhot 7:3, though it is unclear if this is in the context of the *Shema* or public Torah reading. Either way, the plural grammatical form, the location in the synagogue and its contextualization in a discussion about *zimmun* indicates an assumed quorum. *Kaddish* also has early origins; see Talmud Bavli Berakhot 3a, 57a, Shabbat 119b, Sukkah 39a and Sotah 49a. Berakhot 3a sets the *Kaddish* in public places, like synagogues and houses of study, implying some kind of quorum. Sotah 49a associates *Kaddish* with at least some form of *Kedushah.* But there is no text in the classical rabbinic corpus that explicitly attaches the requirement for ten to *Kaddish* and *Barekhu,* even if this may have been obvious and commonly assumed.

way,[51] but it does discuss her participation in one of those *devarim shebikdushah*: Torah reading. There is a long literature discussing the ins and outs of the issue of Torah reading in theory and practice.[52] We will only review the most basic outlines of that discussion here, as part of the broader question of leadership of parts of the service that require a *minyan.*

A. Gender and Torah Reading

Tosefta Megillah 3:11 and the parallel *baraita* on **Talmud Bavli Megillah 23a** are the core sources that drive this discussion:

תוספתא מגילה ג:יא

... והכל עולין למנין שבעה אפי' אשה אפי' קטן
אין מביאין את האשה לקרות לרבים

Tosefta Megillah 3:11

. . . And all count towards the quorum of seven, even a woman, even a minor.
We do not bring a woman to read for the public.

תלמוד בבלי מגילה כג.

תנו רבנן: הכל עולין למנין שבעה, ואפילו קטן ואפילו אשה.
אבל אמרו חכמים: אשה לא תקרא בתורה, מפני כבוד צבור.

Talmud Bavli Megillah 23a

Our rabbis taught: All may count towards the quorum of seven, even a minor, even a woman.
But the Sages said: A woman should not read from the Torah because of the honor of the community.

The "quorum of seven" spoken of here refers to the seven *aliyot* that are distributed on Shabbat. Today, it is common practice for the Torah reader and the person reciting the blessings over the reading to be two different people.

---

51. To be sure, Talmudic sources in several places discuss the idea of whether women can participate freely with men in various rituals, including the quorum of *zimmun*, the invitation to a joint *birkat hamazon* following a meal, and the special groups (*ḥavurot*) formed to eat the Pesaḥ offering. These discussions begin with Mishnah Berakhot 7:2 and Mishnah Pesaḥim 8:7. But these sources do not engage the question of leadership, which might or might not have any connection to one's ability to form a group with the people one is leading. That will become particularly clear as we presently examine the case of Torah reading.

52. In particular, R. Mendel Shapiro and R. Daniel Sperber have treated this subject at length. See Introduction, n1 above. What follows here is a summary of their main points concerning Torah reading combined with our own analysis and perspective.

During the time when these texts were composed, however, the person having the *aliyah* and the Torah reader were always one and the same.[53] These two texts each have an opening line that includes more marginal members of the community: Women and children.[54] And they both have a second line that scales back or qualifies that inclusion specifically for women. In the Tosefta, there is a simple statement that a woman may not read Torah for the public – *larabbim*. In the *baraita* in the Bavli, it is a more general statement that a woman should not read from the Torah, but with an explicit reason given: The honor of the community – *kevod tzibbur*.[55]

Scholars have argued over how to interpret the legal relationship between the first and second lines of these texts.

1) Some have argued that the first lines represent an earlier time in Jewish history when women *were* allowed to read Torah, whereas the second lines reflect a later historical development that restricted their participation partially or entirely.[56]
2) Others have read this source as stemming from a single point in time, but laying out a difference between theory and practice.[57] In theory, women may read, but in practice they do not, and the practical concern on the table is "bringing a woman to read for the public" or violating "the honor of the community."

Either way, an honest assessment of the text will acknowledge that neither of the texts reads הכל עולין למנין שבעה **חוץ מאשה**, "all count towards the quorum of seven **except for a woman**," which is the way Tannaitic sources would convey a blanket gender-based exclusion. One way or the other, these texts envision a

53. Until the medieval period, there was no appointed Torah reader: In all classical rabbinic texts, having an *aliyah* means that one is reading it as well. See Tosafot Megillah 21b.

54. The expected third member of this group, slaves, is added by R. Yirmiyah on Yerushalmi Megillah 4:3, 75a. It is not clear from that source whether R. Yirmiyah considers the slave to be the same as a woman, subject to the concerns of the *kevod tzibbur* (i.e., he is commenting on the first line of the Tosefta/*baraita*) or whether he is issuing a practical ruling that positions the slave similarly to a minor, who is not subject to such concerns.

55. It is unclear whether the *baraita*'s term כבוד צבור is a restatement of the Tosefta's concern in other language or if it represents a different perspective with different parameters. The term כבוד צבור seems to be Babylonian Amoraic, as it is frequently used by Babylonian *Amoraim* and never appears in the rabbinic literature of Eretz Yisrael. As such, its use in this *baraita* seems to be by way of Babylonian influence.

56. See Ma'aseh Rokeaḥ (R. Masoud Hai Rokeaḥ, Turkey/Eretz Yisrael/Libya, 18th c.) on Rambam Hilkhot Tefillah 12:17 and חנה ושמואל ספראי, "הכל עולין למניין שבעה", תרביץ סו (תשנ"ז): 401–395.

57. A number of medieval and modern sources to be cited below follow this approach.

world in which it is at least *theoretically* possible for women to receive *aliyot*. This forces us to address two questions:

1) What does that theoretical inclusion look like? This question will focus on the first lines of the Tosefta and the *baraita*.
2) What practical conditions on the ground would need to be in play to turn that theory into practice? This question will focus on the second lines of the Tosefta and the *baraita*.

1. The First Clauses of the Tosefta and the Baraita: How Gender-Blind is Torah Reading in Theory and Why?

We begin by focusing on a situation where "the honor of the community" does not apply or has been overridden by other concerns. Assuming for a moment that this is possible, does Torah reading then become truly gender-blind? For the remainder of this section we will only engage with the first lines of the core texts above. Imagine that *kevod hatzibbur* is inoperative such that a pure legal analysis of the inclusion of women in the first clause is possible.

A number of sources address this question, both as a matter of theory and by way of defining the role of minors in Torah reading. Minors, after all, are never excluded by the second clauses of the Tosefta and the *baraita*, and thus their status with respect to public Torah reading is governed by the first clauses alone. Understanding varying practical approaches to minors and Torah reading is thus also very helpful for understanding the role of gender in Torah reading in situations where *kevod tzibbur* has somehow been addressed. Two main models emerge for how to understand the theory and scope of the inclusion of minors and women in Torah reading in the first clauses of the Tosefta and the *baraita*. We will briefly engage each of them.

a. Identity is not relevant for Torah reading

The first approach holds that Torah reading is gender-blind in theory and age-blind in practice. The first lines of the Tosefta and *baraita* say simply: Women and children are no different from adult men when it comes to Torah reading. They can have any or all of the *aliyot* in a given reading. The most prominent proponent of this reading is **Rabbeinu Tam** (France, 12th c.):

דברי רבינו תם המובאים ברא"ש ברכות ז:כ

...והא דסלקי קטן ועבד ואשה, דליתנהו בתלמוד תורה, למנין שבעה, משום דס"ת לשמיעה קאי,

וברכה אינה לבטלה, דלא מברכים אשר קדשנו במצותיו וצונו על דברי תורה, אלא אשר בחר בנו ואשר נתן לנו . . .

Rabbeinu Tam, as quoted in Rosh Berakhot 7:20[58]

. . . And the reason that a minor and a slave and a woman count towards the quorum of seven, even though they are exempt from the study of Torah, is because the Torah scroll is for hearing. And the blessing is not in vain, because they do not say "who has sanctified and commanded us regarding words of Torah," but rather "who has chosen us . . . and who has given us."

R. Tam explains that minors, slaves and women are not considered obligated in the study of Torah by classical rabbinic sources.[59] Nonetheless, this in no way contradicts their standing as Torah readers. The *mitzvah* of reading Torah is that the Torah be read – "the Torah scroll is for hearing" – but the identity of the reader (or their obligation in Torah study) is not germane. In fact, Torah reading is not about Torah study at all, as the blessings recited over it refer to the Jewish people's national election through the reception of the Torah, not about any specific commandment to learn it.[60]

This point regarding obligation is stated even more directly by **R. Menaḥem HaMeiri** (Provençe, 13th–14th c.):

בית הבחירה להמאירי מגילה כד.

. . . זה ששנינו קטן קורא בתורה, הטעם לכך משום שאין הכוונה בקריאת התורה אלא להשמיע

58. A version of this passage is also cited in Tosafot Ri Sirleon on Berakhot 47b.

59. Minors are exempt because they are exempt from all *mitzvot*. Women's connection with the command to study Torah seems to have been more contentious. On the matter of *teaching* one's daughter Torah, Mishnah Sotah 3:4 features a debate between Ben Azzai (who thinks it is mandatory) and R. Eliezer (who thinks it is forbidden or minimally foolish and unnecessary). The idea that a woman *herself* is not expected to study Torah seems taken for granted throughout rabbinic literature (arguably even according to Ben Azzai, who seems only to forcefully advocate for fathers teaching their daughters). Sotah 21a just assumes this point as a matter of fact. There is no formal text that backs it up until an anonymous midrash in Kiddushin 29b (unparalleled elsewhere) states that the Biblical command to teach one's children only applies to sons because of the Torah's use of the (arguably) gendered use of *beneikhem*: ולימדתם אותם את בניכם – ולא בנותיכם. (Note that the rest of the sugya's logic there holds that those who need not be taught Torah are not expected to learn themselves and that those who must be taught Torah *are* expected to learn themselves. This would then read back into Ben Azzai an obligation for women to learn Torah on their own, something that was unlikely to have been his original perspective.) This seems clearly a *post facto* justification of a gendered approach to Torah study that was a background assumption of the entire culture. In any event, the view that women are exempt is dominant if not universal and not challenged as a general principle. Slaves are generally treated as exempt from all obligations from which women have been exempted.

60. This last point should clarify why R. Tam would not have accepted a Gentile Torah reader, or (more anachronistically) a recorded reading. The reader must be a member of the covenantal community that received the Torah who can truthfully articulate that in liturgical form.

לעם, ואין זו מצוה גמורה כדי שנאמר בה הכלל שאמרו כל שאינו מחוייב בדבר אינו מוציא את אחרים ידי חובתם . . .

Beit Habeḥirah Megillah 24a

. . . That which we have taught, "A minor reads from the Torah," the reason for this is that the purpose of Torah reading is that the people hear it, and it is not a *bona fide mitzvah* such that we would apply the rule, "Anyone who is not obligated in something cannot fulfill the obligations of others . . ."[61]

One can see how this approach could justify minors, in practice, and women, in cases where *kevod tzibbur* does not preclude it, serving as the sole readers with no *aliyah* being off limits to them. In an unusual case, **Maharam of Rothenburg** (Germany, 13th c.) spells out these practical implications in a case where he determined that *kevod tzibbur* was overwhelmed by other concerns:

שו"ת מהר"ם מרוטנבורג חלק ד סימן קח

ועיר שכולה כהנים ואין בה [אפי'] ישראל אחד נ"ל דכהן קורא פעמים ושוב יקראו נשים דהכל משלימי' למנין ז' אפי' עבד ושפחה וקטן (מגילה כג.) ופי' רבי' שמחה זצ"ל דלאו דוקא למנין ז' אלא אפי' לשלשה דתנן סתמא בפ"ג דמגילה (כד.) קטן קורא בתורה [ומתרגם] ונהי דמסיק עלה אבל אמרו חכמי' לא תקרא אשה בתורה מפני כבוד הצבור היכא דלא אפשר ידחה כבוד הצבור מפני פגם כהנים הקוראים שלא יאמרו בני גרושות הם.

Responsa Maharam of Rothenberg, IV:1108

And in a town whose residents are all *kohanim* and there is not even one *Yisrael*,[62] it seems to me that a *kohen* should read twice and then women should read the rest, for all complete the quorum of seven, even male and female slaves and minors. And R. Simḥah explained that this refers not only to the quorum of seven but also to the quorum of three [the three *aliyot* called up on Monday and Thursday mornings, as well as on Shabbat afternoons], for the Mishnah states simply: "A minor may read from the Torah." And even though the Talmud concludes that the Sages said that a woman should not read because of the honor of the community, in a case where there is no alternative, let the honor of the congregation yield to the

---

61. Meiri himself did not agree with R. Tam's understanding of the blessings being unrelated to obligation. See n117 below, towards the end, for a fuller understanding of his position on this point.

62. This case builds on the ruling of R. Simlai in Yerushalmi Gittin 5:9, who stated that in a city made up (almost) entirely of *kohanim*, a *Yisrael* should take the first aliyah. While Maharam is playing out a worthy question even if it was entirely theoretical in his time, it may have been more practical than one would think. Many of the small communities in Northern Europe in his time were made up of just one or two families. If the patriarchs of those two families were *kohanim*, it could then easily be the case that all male residents of the town would be *kohanim*, provided they were all descended from the original patriarchs.

> concern that we will defame the *kohanim*, so that people will not say they are the children of divorcees.

Maharam confronts a situation where allowing *kohanim* to take *aliyot* other than the first two will subject them to gossip regarding the legitimacy of their status. He preferred the affront to communal honor of women reading to the potential defamation of *kohanim*. For our purposes, not only does his ruling reveal the possibility of overriding the concern of "the honor of the community," but that, once this concern is overridden, he felt women were eligible for any of the *aliyot*.[63] Many others side with this conceptual approach and permit a minor to serve as the sole Torah reader.[64] According to this approach, the first lines of the Tosefta and the *baraita* are blanket statements of inclusion: If *kevod hatzibbur* is not an issue, then women and minors can read and receive all *aliyot*, because the identity of the Torah reader does not matter.[65]

b. Torah Reading must be anchored by principals, not adjuncts

A second approach thinks very differently about the first lines of the Tosefta in the *baraita*. Picking up on the language of עולין למנין שבעה – "count towards the quorum of seven," this school emphasizes the potentially more limited

---

63. The first two *aliyot* had to go to a *kohen* for reasons having to do with lineage, not gender.

64. For a brief, but thorough collection of such views, see Responsa Yeḥaveh Da'at 2:15 and Yeḥaveh Da'at 5:25, starting with the second paragraph. Note that Maharam's specific ruling in the case of the עיר שכולה כהנים was ultimately not accepted. This was not on account of a rejection of the theory of R. Tam that stands behind it, but because many preferred an alternate solution for addressing the honor of *kohanim* without needing to override the concern of *kevod tzibbur* as relates to female Torah readers. Specifically, Responsa Rashba I:13 and I:733 rules that in a community entirely made up of *kohanim*, consecutive *aliyot* for *kohanim* present no problem, since everyone understands the context. Other solutions to the problem are cited in Beit Yosef OḤ 135:12.

65. As we saw, Maharam of Rothenberg quotes R. Simḥah as saying that the language of **למנין שבעה** used in the Tosefta and the *baraita* is not intended to be specific, and he appeals to the unqualified inclusion of minors in the language of Mishnah Megillah 4:6. Perhaps he thought that the Tannaitic sources refer to the Shabbat morning Torah reading and its seven *aliyot* simply because this is the most prominent form of Torah reading and the most ready reference point. See also the conclusion of Piskei Rid Megillah 23a. R. Yitzḥak b. Moshe of Vienna (in Or Zarua I, Responsa #752) argues that the choice of למנין שבעה is in fact deliberate and intended to clarify just how broad the inclusion is:

> והא דת"ר הכל עולין למנין שבעה אפי' אשה אפי' קטן דסד"א הואיל וכבוד שבת חמירא ותו דאיכא כינופיא דהכל בטלים ממלאכתם ובאים לבית הכנסת משום כבוד שבת וכבוד ציבור דרבים הם לא יהא קטן עולה קמ"ל, אבל שעולה למנין ג' ל"צ ליה למתני.

"Our Sages [used the number seven when they] taught, 'All count towards the quorum of seven, even a woman, even a minor,' because I might have thought that since the honor of Shabbat is a serious matter, and moreover, since a large multitude is present because they do not work and come to the synagogue, the honor of Shabbat and the honor of the community, because so many are present, would preclude a minor from reading. This text teaches us otherwise. But that a minor counts towards the quorum of three, no one needed to teach."

scope of a) "counting *towards*" – women and minors can only have *some* of the *aliyot* – and b) "the quorum of *seven*" – as opposed to a more limited core of *aliyot*, such as the first three or other possible configurations. This school's varying opinions share an approach that sees minors and women as theoretically included in public Torah reading, but only as adjuncts, "a supporting cast" to the main anchors: free, adult men.

The earliest indication we have of such a view is cited by Rambam in his commentary to Mishnah Megillah 4:6:[66]

פירוש המשניות להרמב"ם מגילה ד:ו
קטן קורא בתורה, אמר אחד מן הגאונים האחרונים שזה אחר השלישי.

Rambam, Commentary on Mishnah Megillah 4:6
"A minor reads from the Torah." One of the later *Geonim* reported that this only applies to *aliyot* after the third one.

This **Geonic view** clearly sees the permission for minors (and, by extension, women) to apply only to "added" *aliyot* beyond the original three. Since no Torah reading has fewer than three *aliyot*, these represent the core of the reading. Once that core has been completed by adult, free men, other adjunct members may fill out the remaining readings.

Ran, (R. Nissim b. Reuven of Gerona, Spain, 14th c.), offers a different but similar view:

ר"ן על מגילה דף כג עמוד א ד"ה הכל (יג. בדפי הרי"ף)
הכל עולין למנין שבעה ואפילו אשה ואפי' קטן. פי' עולין **להשלים** קאמר ולא שיהו כולם קטנים ולא נשים דכיון דלאו בני חיובא נינהו לא מפקי לגמרי. ולפום עיקר דינא נמי שאינו מברך אלא הפותח והחותם אשה וקטן אין קורין ראשון ולא אחרון משום ברכה לפי שא"א לקורין האחרים שיצאו בברכתם ומיהו השתא דתקון רבנן שיברכו כולם אשה וקטן קורין אפי' ראשון ואחרון . . .

Ran Megillah 23a (13a in the Rif's pagination)
All count towards the quorum of seven, even a woman even a minor. This means: They count to **complete** [this number], but [the *aliyot*] may not all go to minors or women; since they are not obligated, they cannot entirely fulfill the obligations of others. According to the original rule, when only the first and last readers said blessings [over the Torah] a woman and a minor could read neither first nor last, on account of the blessing. The other readers

66. It seems clear that Rambam himself did not hold this way, at least in cases of need. See his unqualified language in Mishneh Torah Hilkhot Tefillah 12:16–17 and his direct ruling in Responsum #184. See also a survey of some later opinions about his views on the matter appearing in Responsa Yeḥaveh Da'at 2:15.

could not fulfill their own obligation through the blessings [of a woman or a minor]. But now that the Rabbis decreed that each reader makes blessings, a woman or minor can read even first or last . . .[67]

ר"ן על מגילה דף כד עמוד א ד"ה קטן קורא בתורה (טו. בדפי הרי"ף)

קטן קורא בתורה. **להשלים** למנין ז' ולא שיהיו כלם קטנים ולא רובם כמו שכתבתי למעלה אלא על ידי **צירוף** קאמר **דמצטרף** לשבעה.

Ran on Megillah 24a (15a in the Rif's pagination)

A minor reads from the Torah. To **complete** the quorum of seven, but they cannot all be minors, nor even the majority, as I have written above, rather by **joining** they can **join** the quorum of seven.

Ran's position makes very clear that the identity of the Torah reader matters a great deal. While he rules that, in the present time, there is no restriction on *which aliyot* women or minors can have,[68] they cannot be the exclusive readers. He offers two different formulations in the two passages above, one that insists that women and minors not form *the totality* of the readers[69] and one that insists that they not form *a majority* of the readers. But essentially, these two formulations boil down to the same point: Women and minors are adjuncts when it comes to Torah reading and they cannot be the main or sole anchors of its public performance.

Why are women and minors adjuncts in this way? What is the theory behind this more restrictive reading of the first lines of the Tosefta and the *baraita*? The Ran spells out his reasoning: לאו בני חיובא נינהו – they are not obligated, or perhaps better: They are not members of the obligated class. On account of this, לא מפקי לגמרי – they cannot be the exclusive agents for fulfilling obligation. This might mean a number of things:

1) Women and minors are not obligated to study Torah. Public Torah reading is connected to this obligation and those who listen to public

67. Ran is referring here to the gap between what is assumed in Mishnah Megillah 4:1–2 (the first reader says an opening blessing and the last reader says a closing blessing) and the practice reported and sanctioned on Talmud Bavli Megillah 21b (each reader says an opening and closing blessing). The latter practice remains in force until the present day.

68. Again, in the case of women, this assumes that the issue of *kevod hatzibbur* has been somehow addressed or overridden.

69. A ruling identical to this formulation but with a fuller (and perhaps different) explanation is cited by Meiri in Beit Habeḥirah Megillah 23a: יש מי שאומר שמ"מ צריך בכל קריאה קורא אחד גדול והואיל וקרא אחד כבר נשלמה תקנת משה רבינו ואין כאן עוד קריאה אלא מתקנת עזרא שלא היה מנין הקוראים מתקנת משה רבינו אלא גוף הקריאה לבד ויכול להשלים הקריאה על ידי אשה או קטן אבל לא שתעשה כל הקריאה ע"י אשה וקטן.

Torah reading fulfill their individual obligations in this regard. Exempt people cannot therefore anchor this ritual and at least one or most of the readers need to fulfill the basic obligation of the individuals gathered to study Torah. Ran would then be in direct conflict with R. Tam's approach to Torah reading outlined above.[70]

2) Women and minors are not obligated to study Torah. Though public Torah reading does not involve vicarious fulfillment of individual obligations, it does involve the fulfillment of a *communal* obligation to read Torah. Ran would then be saying that a *community* cannot fulfill its obligation to hold a public Torah reading through the exclusive or dominant use of people not obligated in Torah study. This approach could be consistent with R. Tam's theory of Torah reading above. R. Tam spoke about considerations relating to individual obligation, but Ran would be adding a concern regarding the corporate, communal obligation of public Torah reading.[71]

3) Women and minors are generally less obligated in *mitzvot* or obligated in fewer *mitvzot* than are adult men.[72] They can be viewed, in this sense, as adjuncts of the religious community, as opposed to principals.[73] It is thus inappropriate and ineffective for a community to rely on such adjuncts to fulfill its communal obligations. A community should not

70. For examples of this reading of the Ran, see Eliyah Rabbah OḤ 282:7 and Shulḥan Arukh HaRav OḤ 282:5. This also seems to have been the approach of R. Yaḥya b. Yosef Salah (Yemen, 18th c.) in Responsa Peulat Tzaddik III:194. We know that not everyone accepted R. Tam's view that Torah reading was not an individual obligation. One of the strongest support texts for R. Tam's approach is the Talmud's report on Berakhot 8a that R. Sheshet paid no attention to Torah reading and would learn other material at that time. This suggests no individual obligation to hear it, in keeping with R. Tam. But R. Yonah, on this passage, reports a view that R. Sheshet was exempt because he was blind, but that others are individually obligated and thus forbidden from behaving in this way.

71. This approach, which emphasizes public Torah reading as a communal obligation that, while not individualized, nonetheless has real teeth, can be found in Ramban Milḥamot Hashem on Rif 3a s.v. *ve'od*. This view is cited by Ran there as well and it clearly influenced him.

72. Again, minors are exempt from *mitzvot* until they come of age. Women are exempt from some positive *mitzvot* classified as time-caused by Mishnah Kiddushin 1:7.

73. The idea that lesser obligation in *mitzvot* impacts the person's standing more generally is found in other medieval sources. Rambam's commentary on Mishnah Horayot 3:7 explains why that text prioritizes saving a man over a woman when both of their lives are at equal risk: כבר ידעת שהמצוות כולן מחויבות לזכרים, ולנקיבות מקצתן, כמו שהתבאר בקידושין, והרי הוא מקודש ממנה, ולפיכך קודם להחיות – "You know that all the *mitzvot* are obligatory for men, whereas only some are obligatory for women, as we explained in Kiddushin. Therefore, he is holier than her and therefore saving him takes priority." With respect to why it might be inappropriate for women to lead rituals for men, even when they share an equal obligation, Tosafot Harosh Sukkah 38a s.v. *be'emet* offers the following striking formulation: אפילו מיחייבי דאורייתא לא חשיבי להוציא אנשים דחשיבי טפי שחייבים בכל המצות – "Even if women are Biblically obligated [in *birkat hamazon*] they are still not important enough to fulfill the obligations of men, who are more important on account of their obligation in all *mitzvot*."

and cannot fulfill its core obligations by fielding "backbenchers" who are not representative of maximal obligation and responsibility.[74] This interpretation would also be consistent with R. Tam's approach above.

However we read the Ran, it should be clear that, according to his approach, those lacking in key obligations (whether they be in Talmud Torah or more generally) cannot be the sole Torah readers. Other subsequent *poskim* took this approach as well,[75] including **Rema** in OḤ 282:3. Thus, even controlling for *kevod tzibbur*, this view allows for women and minors to read only *some* of the *aliyot* in a given Torah reading.

c. *Applying and balancing the two approaches: R. Tam and Ran*

These two approaches yield divergent consequences.

According to R. Tam's approach, the identity of the reader is irrelevant, paving the way for an essentially gender-blind Torah reading.[76] This is accomplished, of course, without distinguishing in any way between women and minors and would achieve gender-blindness by essentially erasing the identity of the readers, rather than by asserting gender equality.

According to the Ran's approach, those who lack certain core obligations, whether regarding Torah study or *mitzvot* more generally, can only func-

---

74. A number of commentators seem to read Ran this way. See Older Responsa Baḥ #158 as well as the slightly different formulation of Levush 282:3, who emphasizes that there is a dishonor to the Torah scroll to remove it for the sake of women and minors. This reading of Levush seems to assume the more minimal reading of Ran that one can suffice with at least one free, adult male reader. (See also Meiri Kiryat Sefer 5:1.) These last two readings of the Ran focus on the impact of exemption on the community's ability to discharge its obligations with integrity and dignity. Perhaps the best articulation of these approaches can be found in the responsa of R. Avraham b. Mordekhai HaLevi (Egypt, 17th–18th c.), Ginat Veradim OḤ 1:36: והטעם דבעינן דתיתעביד תקנתא דרבנן בבני אדם גדולים... דההקפדה אינה על הספר אלא על הצבור דגנאי הוא לצבור שיהיו כל העולים לחובת היום כולם קטנים המבלי אין גדולים בצבור שיעלו שבעה קטני' לס"ת אבל לגבי הס"ת עצמו אין בזה גנאי אם יקרא בו הקטן יחידי לבדו דהא תורה דיליה היא נמי ומפי עוללים ויונקים יסדת עוז דהוי הבל שאין בו חטא. According to these readings of the Ran, there is nothing intrinsically or technically problematic about a minor reading Torah, but relying *solely* on minors risks turning the ritual into a disrespectful spectacle.

75. Rivash (R. Yitzḥak b. Sheshet Perfet, Spain, 14th c.) followed Ran's approach and extended it to forbid a minor from reading the *maftir* when a second scroll was removed for this purpose. He felt that Ran's concern applied to the reading from any given scroll and giving the minor *maftir* would violate the principle that adjuncts should not anchor a reading entirely on their own. See Responsa Rivash 35, 321 and 326. In fact, R. Tam himself is cited as supporting a similar policy regarding minors and *maftir* in Sefer Hamanhig Hilkhot Shabbat p. 165 (ed. Mossad HaRav Kook). As we have seen, R. Tam could not have based this view on the same theory as was proferred by Rivash, since R. Tam's theory of Torah reading rendered the identity of the reader generally irrelevant. For an attempt to provide a resolution of these two potentially contradictory views, see Responsa Tzitz Eliezer VII:1:23–26.

76. As emphasized throughout this section, this assumes that the concern of *kevod tzibbur* has somehow been addressed or overridden.

tion as adjuncts in public Torah reading and cannot anchor it on their own. For this approach, a gender-blind Torah reading would only be possible by claiming that contemporary women are in fact obligated in Torah study and/or the full complement of *mitzvot*. This would be a bolder interpretive move, though it would more directly address the growing gender egalitarianism in the broader society that motivates these conversations. We will encounter a few more positions like the Ran's that would require this sort of paradigm shift in order to be aligned with gender-equal practice. But put simply: The Ran only allows בני חיובא – members of the obligated class – to anchor a public Torah reading, making Torah reading only *partially* accessible to women and minors. Full gender equality under such a system would require arguing that contemporary women are indeed considered בנות חיובא, equally obligated in *mitzvot* as adult men.[77]

But whose approach should be followed? There is a respectable body of thought that asserts the dominance of the idea that the identity of the Torah readers is irrelevant, or minimally that this approach can be relied on whenever the situation is pressing for one reason or another.[78] Those who base a gender-blind Torah reading on this approach surely have a leg to stand on, particularly if they sense that there is a concrete risk in denying women *aliyot* in an increasingly gender-egalitarian world.[79]

The Ran's approach, however, remains compelling and difficult to dismiss. First, it is risky to ignore the wisdom of an alternate position and to crush it through positivist legal force alone. True, it is perfectly respectable and legitimate to claim that R. Tam's approach has many prominent defenders and adherents and that, even though the Rema cites the Ran, R. Yosef Karo himself may not have accepted it.[80] But this in no way addresses the *substance* of the Ran's claim, which is reasonable: How can a community look itself in the mirror when it attempts to fulfill its public obligation relying on ritually marginal members? Second, in the present case, relying on R. Tam risks clouding the

77. See our discussion of this sort of argument below, Part Two, n77–83.

78. R. Yoel Sirkes (Poland, 16th c.) in Older Responsa Baḥ #158 seems to sideline the Ran; R. David Luria (Russia, 19th c.) Responsum #3 dismantles this position entirely and allows minors to read the entire Torah portion without any hesitation. Even R. Yisrael Meir HaKohen, who upholds the Rema's ruling like the Ran, says in Sha'ar HaTziyyun 282:16 about the view of the Ran and the Rivash, "אינו דין ברור", and rules in Mishnah Berurah 282:13 that one may follow R. Tam's position when there is no other available reader. R. Ovadiah Yosef rules similarly in Yeḥaveh Da'at 5:25, granting the Ran's position only the status of an *ab initio* ideal preference.

79. This sort of fear of the gap between general and ritual expectations and participation is partially what led to the revolution in learning opportunities for women in the 20th century. It was viewed by some as untenable that women would pursue university degrees and be closed off to learning Torah at high levels while maintaining respect for and fidelity to Torah in the process.

80. Though the Ran is cited in Beit Yosef OḤ 282, there is no trace of this restriction in the Shulḥan Arukh.

substance of the specific issue: Is the difficulty with excluding women from Torah reading in the contemporary world that it places too much emphasis on the identity of the reader, or is the difficulty that it excludes *women*? Put another way: R. Tam's position leaves no room for the quite sensible instinct that some might have in the contemporary world, which is that women should be treated as equals to men, but minors should retain the status of adjuncts who should not (at least ideally) anchor a public Torah reading!

We in no way mean to undermine the legitimacy of following R. Tam's model here as a basis for justifying a gender-equal Torah reading. But this is one of a number of points in our analysis where consciousness of halakhic choices and consequences is particularly important. We will reserve more general comments regarding this dynamic for later on.

2. The Second Clauses: *Kevod Tzibbur* – The Honor of the Community

a. *Defining kevod hatzibbur*

We turn now to the second lines of the Tosefta and the *baraita*. Using the *baraita*'s terminology of *kevod tzibbur*: What is "honor of the community" and why did this consideration lead the Sages to exclude women from going up to bless and read from the Torah? "Honor of the community" appears in four other contexts in the Talmud Bavli, always as a reason to avoid some mode of performing public ritual.[81] The four other unseemly practices are: Reading Torah from a scroll containing only one of its five books, rolling the Torah scroll in public, allowing a minor to read Torah naked or in tattered clothing, and uncovering the ark in front of the community.[82]

תלמוד בבלי גיטין ס.

רבה ורב יוסף דאמרי תרוייהו: אין קוראין בחומשין בבית הכנסת משום כבוד הצבור.

Talmud Bavli Gittin 60a

Rabbah and R. Yosef both said: We do not read from *ḥumashim* [Torah scrolls containing only one of the five books] in the synagogue because of the honor of the community.

תלמוד בבלי יומא ע.

ובעשור של חומש הפקודים קורא על פה. אמאי? נגלול וניקרי!

אמר רב הונא בריה דרב יהושע אמר רב ששת: לפי שאין גוללין ספר תורה בציבור, מפני כבוד ציבור.

81. All the Talmudic cases in one way or another also seem to connect with Torah reading.
82. Our rendition of this last source follows Rashi's interpretation.

Talmud Bavli Yoma 70a

And [the paragraph about Yom Kippur in Bemidbar] is read from memory [by the High Priest]. Why? Let him roll the scroll and read it from the text! Said R. Huna b. R. Yehoshua, said R. Sheshet: We do not roll the Torah scroll in public because of the honor of the community.

תלמוד בבלי מגילה כד:

פוחח פורס על שמע וכו'.
בעא מיניה עולא בר רב מאביי: קטן פוחח מהו שיקרא בתורה?
אמר ליה: ותיבעי לך ערום? ערום מאי טעמא לא משום כבוד צבור, הכא נמי משום כבוד צבור.

Talmud Bavli Megillah 24b

A person dressed in tattered clothing may lead the responsive *Shema* . . . Ulla b. R. asked Abaye: May a minor dressed in tatters read from the Torah?[83] He said to him: Would you be in doubt about a naked minor!? Why would a naked minor be forbidden? Because of the honor of the community; here too, because of the honor of the community.

תלמוד בבלי סוטה לט:

ואמר רבי תנחום אמר רבי יהושע בן לוי: אין שליח צבור רשאי להפשיט את התיבה בצבור, מפני כבוד צבור.

Talmud Bavli Sotah 39b

And said R. Tanḥum said R. Yehoshua b. Levi: The prayer leader should not uncover the ark in front of the community because of the honor of the community.

The phrase *kevod tzibbur* expresses that certain ritual actions are disrespectful in a communal context. Reading from an incomplete Torah scroll that only contains one of the five books lacks seriousness. Rolling a Torah scroll in public to get from one section to another is disrespectful of the community's time and creates an awkward pause in the service. Reading Torah while scantily clad is improper and degrading. Removing the adornments from the Ark in the pres-

83. Rashi explains that the questioner understands that an adult in tattered clothing may not, on account of the verse, "Let [God] not see in you any nakedness" (Devarim 23:15), but perhaps a minor's nakedness would not be of concern, since Torah prohibitions such as that verse do not apply to them: "'קטן פוחח מהו שיקרא בתורה' - גדול פוחח הוא דאסור משום "וְלֹא יִרְאֶה בְךָ עֶרְוַת דָּבָר" (דברים כג:טו), אבל קטן אינו מוזהר, או דלמא לא פליג מתניתין בין קטן לגדול." Alternatively, a minor's inappropriate exposure may be less disrespectful than that of an adult vis-à-vis the onlooking congregation. Ritva notes that some versions of the gemara lack the word קטן here, in which case the question is about whether anyone, adult or minor, may read Torah while wearing tattered clothing. This would seem to depend on having a different version of Mishnah Megillah 4:6. Our version of that text is explicit that an adult in tattered clothing cannot read from the Torah, such that there would be no place for further Talmudic discussion.

ence of the community denudes the sacred space of its grandeur and lessens the awe surrounding the communal ritual. Given the intuitive nature of the consideration, it is not surprising that subsequent authorities apply this term to additional practices. For example, Rashi gives "honor of the community" as a reason to prohibit a minor from performing *birkat kohanim*: It is demeaning for the community to receive the blessing from a minor. Rambam employs it to explain the preference for a bearded *Sh"atz* and for a standing reader of Megillat Esther, both of which convey proceedings with the proper gravity:

רש"י מסכת מגילה כד.

ואינו נושא את כפיו - אם כהן הוא, שאין כבוד של צבור להיות כפופין לברכתו.

Rashi, Megillah 24a

"[A minor] may not raise his hands" – if he is a *kohen*, for it is not honorable for the community to be subject to his blessing.

רמב"ם הלכות תפילה ח:יא

... ומי שלא נתמלא זקנו אע"פ שהוא חכם גדול לא יהא ש"ץ מפני כבוד ציבור ...

Rambam, Laws of Prayer 8:11

... One whose beard has not filled out, even if he is wise and great, should not be a *Sha"tz* because of the honor of the community ...

רמב"ם הלכות מגילה ב:ז

...קראה עומד או יושב יצא ואפילו בצבור, אבל לא יקרא בצבור יושב לכתחלה מפני כבוד הצבור ...

Rambam, Laws of Megillah 2:7

... Whether one read [Megillat Esther] standing or sitting, the obligation is fulfilled, and even in the community, but *ab initio*, one should not read in a community while seated, because of the honor of the community ...

Why has it been considered an affront to communal honor for women to read Torah publicly? Many *Rishonim* are silent on the issue, apparently taking for granted the reasonableness of the statement. At least two *Rishonim* connect *kevod tzibbur* to another concept: מאירה – a curse that devolves on those who engage in certain kinds of ritual behaviors with social and religious subordinates. The concept of מאירה/curse is used in the context of the recitation of *birkat hamazon* and *Hallel*. Let's begin with these background texts:

משנה סוכה ג:י

מי שהיה עבד או אשה או קטן מקרין אותו עונה אחריהן מה שהן אומרין ותהי לו מאירה אם היה גדול מקרא אותו עונה אחריו הללויה

Mishnah Sukkah 3:10

One [i.e., an adult, free man] being led [in *Hallel*] by a slave, a woman or a minor must repeat the words after them and he should be cursed. If it was an adult leading him, then he responds "*Halleluyah*."

A full interpretation of this text is beyond the scope of our purpose here. What is clear is that the Mishnah seems to convey two ideas:

1. *Hallel* is normally or often done in a responsive mode, with a מקרא/leader chanting the text and with respondents answering with refrains such as הללויה.[84] Adult, free men should not rely on a slave, woman or minor to say the words of *Hallel* for them in a responsive form. They should say all of the words themselves.[85]
2. Even if the first concern is addressed and the free adult says *Hallel* in its entirety, the free adult is worthy of a מאירה/curse. The function of the מאירה/curse here is clearly unconnected to any issue of obligation fulfillment; the adult free man has said all the words of *Hallel* himself. But the exact reason for the מאירה/curse is not made explicit.

The Talmud Yerushalmi connects this Mishnah to another matter:

תלמוד ירושלמי סוכה ג:ט

תני אבל אמרו אשה מברכת לבעלה ועבד לרבו וקטן לאביו.

ניחא, אשה מברכת לבעלה עבד לרבו. קטן לאביו? לא כן א"ר אחא בשם ר' יוסי בן נהוריי כל שאמרו בקטן כדי לחנכו?!

תיפתר בעונה אחריהן אמן[86] כהיא דתנינן תמן מי שהיה עבד או אשה או קטן מקרין אותו ועונה אחריהן מה שהן אומרין ותהא לו מאירה

ועוד אמרו תבוא מאירה לבן עשרים שהוא צריך לבן עשר:

84. This practice of having a leader and being led in a responsive mode is referred to in a host of Tannaitic texts. See Mishnah Rosh Hashanah 4:7; Mishnah Sotah 5:4, Tosefta Pesaḥim 10:7–8, Tosefta Sotah 6:2–3.

85. There is an analogous concern with respect to a father leading small children in *Hallel* at the Seder. He should not rely on their completion of his opening call. Tosefta Pesaḥim 10:7. Neither that text nor Mishnah Sukkah 3:10 is clear if this is related to matters of obligation (i.e., if a person violated protocol here, would they need to repeat *Hallel*).

86. The word אמן is also present in the parallel at Yerushalmi Rosh Hashanah 3:10, but absent from the parallel at Yerushalmi Berakhot 3:3. We translate here in accordance with the vast majority of interpreters who, whether or not they have this word in their text, understand it to refer to an adult who repeats all the words of the *birkat hamazon* after being cued by a child.

Talmud Yerushalmi Sukkah 3:9

It is taught [in a *baraita*]: "Indeed,[87] a woman may say *birkat hamazon* for her husband, a slave may say it for his master and a minor[88] for his father."

A woman for her husband and a slave for his master make sense, but a minor for his father? Did not R. Aḥa say in the name of R. Yose b. Nehorai that [any obligations] articulated with respect to a minor are [merely] in order to educate him?![89]

[The *baraita*] makes sense if you assume the father repeats the words his son says, just like it says [in Mishnah Sukkah 3:10]: "One being led [in *Hallel*] by a slave, a woman or a minor must respond by saying everything they say and he should be cursed."

Furthermore, they said that a twenty-year old who needs a ten-year old should be cursed.

This passage in the Yerushalmi begins by quoting a *baraita* that notes that certain figures normally thought of as subordinates are qualified to fulfill the obligations of their superiors in *birkat hamazon*. The Yerushalmi accepts this for women and slaves, who share equal obligations to free men in *birkat hamazon*, according to Mishnah Berakhot 3:3. But it assumes that children, even if they are obligated in *birkat hamazon*, cannot possibly share an equal obligation with adults, so how can the *baraita* allow a minor to say *birkat hamazon* for his father? The Yerushalmi proposes that in this case, the father must be repeating after his minor son, thereby fulfilling all of his obligations on his own. It cites Mishnah Sukkah 3:10 as precedent for this kind of behavior.[90] The Yerushalmi then adds a point to the *baraita* on *birkat hamazon*, evoking the curse described in Mishnah Sukkah 3:10: A curse should also devolve upon a twenty-year old who needs the services of a ten-year old. This seems to suggest that the minor is leading *birkat hamazon* for his father on account of the latter's ignorance. The Yerushalmi thus understands the מאירה/curse

87. The word אבל here seems to be used in this sense here, as opposed to its other sense of "but." The parallels to this *baraita* in Tosefta Berakhot 5:17, Talmud Bavli Berakhot 20b and Talmud Bavli Sukkah 38a all read באמת instead of אבל. For this sort of usage of אבל, see Talmud Bavli Niddah 3b for one example.

88. In the parallels in the Tosefta and the Talmud Bavli, the text reads בן לאביו, which might well refer to a son who is an adult. With that text, the problem raised here by the Yerushalmi need not arise.

89. The Yerushalmi's point here is that the minor's obligations are not "real," they are simply a form of required training for religious adulthood. How can we allow an adult to fulfill his own obligations through the recitation of a minor?

90. It is not clear if the Yerushalmi assumes that Mishnah Sukkah 3:10 is concerned about matters of obligation as well or if it is just appealing to the possibility that one might allow someone to lead a ritual for them without truly being liturgically dependent on them.

to be directed at adult males who have not properly learned something in which they are obligated such that they must rely on those who are not obligated. It seems that no curse is applied to the husband who allows his wife to lead *birkat hamazon* for him – she is equally obligated and he need not even repeat after her when she recites the text. How would the Yerushalmi understand the application of the מאירה/curse to the man who repeats *Hallel* after women and slaves as well as minors? It would likely assume that women and slaves, though obligated in *birkat hamazon*, are exempt from *Hallel* and are thus similar to the minor who leads *birkat hamazon*. An obligated free, adult male would thus be subject to the מאירה/curse if prompted to say *Hallel* by a woman, slave *or* minor.[91]

In the Talmud Bavli, the Yerushalmi's application of the concept of מאירה/curse to the case of *birkat hamazon* is integrated into the *baraita* itself:

תלמוד בבלי מסכת סוכה לח.

ת"ר: באמת אמרו: בן מברך לאביו, ועבד מברך לרבו, ואשה מברכת לבעלה. אבל אמרו חכמים תבא מאירה לאדם שאשתו ובניו מברכין לו.

Talmud Bavli Sukkah 38a

Our Sages taught [in a *baraita*]: Truly, they said: A son may say *birkat hamazon* for his father, a slave for his master and a woman for her husband. But the Sages said that a curse should come upon a person whose wife and children say *birkat hamazon* for him.

Here we have a striking difference from the Yerushalmi: The curse is applied to the case of the woman and her husband as well (and presumably the slave-master case also). Whereas in the Yerushalmi, the concern triggering the מאירה/curse seems to have centered around relying on a non-obligated person for prompting, in the Bavli, the problem may be one of social status. Even though a woman and a man share an equal obligation in *birkat hamazon*,[92] the Bavli's version of the *baraita* condemns a man who is either dependent on his wife

91. Alternatively, one could suggest that the final line in the Yerushalmi is not meant to be limited to minors, but merely gives a minor-adult interaction as an example of an inappropriate inversion of conventional hierarchies. The מאירה/curse would then not be the result of an obligation gap, but reflective of a gap in social standing. This would render the Yerushalmi's approach identical to that of the Bavli's. This reading seems more strained with the Yerushalmi's initial nonchalant acceptance of women and slaves leading *birkat hamazon* for free, adult men and would have to read the second part of the passage as backing away from this initial approach.

92. On Talmud Bavli Berakhot 20b, Ravina wonders whether men and women in fact share an equal obligation in *birkat hamazon*, but the Bavli itself assumes that the *baraita* we are discussing here would normally be understood as assuming that women are in fact Biblically obligated in *birkat hamazon* just like men.

to bless for him or perhaps allows someone of subordinate social status to perform this ritual for him. This, in turn, means that perhaps Mishnah Sukkah 3:10's application of the curse to those who have *Hallel* recited for them by a woman need not be understood as stemming from an obligation gap. The function of the מאירה/curse may be grounded in notions of social hierarchy alone.

Ritva[93] (Spain, 13th–14th c.) and **R. Avraham min HaHar** (Provençe, 13th–14th c.) equate the concern conveyed by the term *kevod tzibbur* with the notion of מאירה as understood in the Talmud Bavli. The latter's formulation is as follows:

ר' אברהם מן ההר, מגילה יט:

והכי איתא בהדיא בריש ערכין (ב.) הכל חייבין [במגילה], הכל לאתויי נשים, וכדר' יהושע וכו'. מיהו ודאי לכתחילא לא תוציא אחרים, כדאמרינן במי שמתו (ברכות כ:) - תבא מארה לאדם שאשתו ובניו מברכין לו. ואמרינן בפרק עומד ויושב (מגילה כג.) - הכל עולין למנין שבעה, אפילו אשה או קטן, אבל אמרו חכמים, אשה לא תקרא בצבור מפני כבוד הצבור, וכו'.

R. Avraham min HaHar, Megillah 19b

And so do we have it explicitly at the beginning of Arakhin (2a): "'Everyone is obligated [in the *megillah*] – 'everyone' to include women, following R. Yehoshua [b. Levi, who ruled that women are obligated in the reading of the *megillah*]." However, of course, *ab initio*, she should not discharge others of their obligation, as we said on Berakhot 20b: "May a curse come to a man whose wife or children bless [the grace after meals] for him." And we said on Megillah 23a, "Everyone counts toward the seven, but the Sages said that a woman should not read for the community because of the honor of the community . . ."

R. Avraham min HaHar asserts that women and men have an equal obligation in *megillah* reading, such that, in terms of obligation, women would be valid to read the *Megillah* for men. Nonetheless, he says that women should *not* read for men, invoking the concerns of *kevod tzibbur* and comparing it to the case of מאירה. This is precisely the notion of מאירה as used in the Talmud Bavli: Even when obligations are equal or irrelevant, there is something shameful about a man having his wife or his child lead him in a ritual. Whether this is because the man is presumed to be liturgically illiterate or simply because his wife and children are his social and educational inferiors, he is worthy of condemnation. R. Avraham min HaHar clearly sees this in play in the context of female Torah readers as well: A woman's reading would unsettle the social

93. See his comments on Talmud Bavli Megillah 4a.

order and suggest ignorance on the part of the male congregants.[94] According to this line of thought, women are not a part of the educated class and are not socially expected to be able to read Torah.

Contemporary *poskim* such as **R. Yehudah Herzl Henkin** follow this connection,[95] explaining that the curse refers to the embarrassment of being made to look as if one is illiterate or otherwise unable to fulfill one's own obligations:

שו"ת בני בנים ב:ב

אמנם, מהו באמת פרוש כבוד הצבור לענין עליות נשים, לע"ד כיון שהריטב"א ... וביותר בירור ברבנו אברהם מן ההר ... מבואר שהוא ענין של מאירה פי' שבזיון הוא לצבור שנראה כאילו אין די גברים היודעים לקרוא בתורה ולכן הביאו נשים וכן פרש בפתח הדביר סימן רפ"ב אות ט', ולא נמצא בראשונים מי שחולק על זה לכן בוודאי הכי נקטינן ...

Responsa Benei Banim 2:2

Indeed, what is truly the meaning of "honor of the community" vis-à-vis *aliyot* for women? In my humble opinion, [in] the Ritva . . . and even more clearly, in Rabbenu Avraham min HaHar . . . it is explained to be the matter of a curse, i.e. that it is insulting to the community for it to seem as though there are not enough men who know how to read Torah, and that is why they summoned women, and this is also how Petaḥ haDevir (282:9) interpreted it, and there is no *Rishon* who disputes this, therefore, of course, this is how we hold . . .

R. Henkin's words speak for themselves. Most attempts to redefine *kevod tzibbur* to refer to something other than concerns about social honor and shame depart from the plain sense of these words and how they are used in other contexts. The concern of *kevod tzibbur* does not relate to matters of obligation and exemption, nor is it even connected to gender *per sé*.[96] Like the other

---

94. Note that the man is condemned for allowing his son (in the Bavli, almost certainly even his adult son) from saying *birkat hamazon* for him, whereas minors do not pose a concern for *kevod tzibbur*. This is likely because *birkat hamazon* is an individualized obligation that every man was expected to be able to perform, whereas Torah reading was a more specialized skill performed by a select few in front of the whole congregation. This underscores even more why it would have been surprising and unusual for a woman to have the skill to read when not even all men were expected to have this skill.

95. See also *שפרבר, דרכה של הלכה*, 24–28.

96. Matters of obligation and exemption were already addressed in our analysis of the first clauses of the Tosefta and the *baraita*. See above, n58–80. Despite what we have argued here, Aryeh and Dov Frimer, "Partnership Minyanim" argue that *kevod tzibbur* is *entirely* about either an obligation gap or concerns relating to sexual impropriety. They construct two "schools" corresponding to these concerns. Their analysis of the "schools" they posit is problematic: (1) They correctly cite a number of medieval authorities as being concerned about appointing leaders for parts of the service in which they are not obligated. Tosafot Sukkah 38a s.v. *utehi* and Tosafot Harosh Sukkah 38a s.v. *tavo* both state that the מאירה in Mishnah Sukkah 3:10 is focused on the

areas where it is invoked, *kevod tzibbur* is a *halakhah* rooted in social realities and protocols. We will now turn to the question of whether these types of concerns are designed to protect people from others who would violate their honor against their will, or whether they come to prescriptively assign this honor even for those who might not be concerned with it.

---

fact that someone not obligated in *Hallel* is leading the man in that liturgy, even if he repeats after them. This is inspired by a Yerushalmi-type reading of the problem of מאירה. But those *Rishonim* never apply that concern to Torah reading, which does not follow the same rules as other rituals. This is both in light of the fact that a minor may read Torah despite presenting a problem of מאירה in the context of *Hallel*, and because the "obligation" involved in Torah reading is somewhere on the spectrum of non-existent to unique. We believe the Frimers' attempt to exclude women from Torah reading via an obligation-based *kevod tzibbur* while justifying the inclusion of minors based on an educational agenda (חינוך) is a dodge and unsupported by the sources. Again, see our analysis above, n58–80. In any event, there is no indication that any *Rishon* maps this understanding of מאירה back onto *kevod tzibbur*. The Frimers cite a number of *Aḥaronim* who take this position – though not all of them obviously say what is claimed. Even if one follows these *Aḥaronim* over the explicit positions of the *Rishonim* – precisely what R. Henkin argues against above – matters of obligation would only be relevant for those (a) following the Ran's model and (b) wishing to provide an occasional woman with a minority of the *aliyot*. Any fully egalitarian Torah reading claiming the support of the Ran would need to address questions of obligation raised by the first clause of the *baraita* independent of any ancillary ones that arise via *kevod tzibbur*. We will return to more plausible applications of concerns surrounding obligations below, when considering leadership of the service more broadly. See n153. (2) As for attempts to read sexuality into *kevod tzibbur*, the term itself militates against such a reading. Tannaitic sources know well how to speak about sexual impropriety and they would have said something like: אשה לא תקרא בתורה מפני הרגל עבירה. R. Henkin has been among the most vocal in denying this as a plausible reading. Indeed, a number of medieval and modern authorities explicitly reject this interpretation (which is in any event untenable when applied to the other instances of the term in Talmudic literature). Sefer Hameorot Berakhot 45a (R. Meir b. Shimon Hame'ili, Provençe, 13th c.): וליכא משום פריצות הגדול עם הנשים... ועוד ראיה מדאמרינן בעלמא אשה לא תקרא בצבור משום כבוד צבור, **טעמא משום כבוד צבור אבל פריצותא ליכא**/"There is no sexual impropriety when an adult male [ritually joins in a *zimmun*] with women . . . a further proof of this is from the general statement that a women may not read from the Torah in public because of the honor of the community; **the reason is because of the honor of the community, but not because of sexual impropriety**." Sefer Hamenuḥah on Hilkhot Berakhot 5:7 (R. Manoaḥ of Narbonne, Provençe, 13th-14th c.) has a similar formulation. Responsa Piskei Uzziel Bisheilot Hazman #44 (R. Ben-Tziyyon Meir Hai Uzziel, Israel, 20th c.): ופירוש כבוד הצבור הוא שלא יאמרו: שאין בין האנשים מי שיודע לקרא בתורה אבל לא אמרו משום פריצות. See also Responsa Benei Banim 2:10. The Frimers cite a host of *Aḥaronim* who prevent women from reading Torah on account of sexual impropriety. The vast majority of them are in fact clear that this is *an entirely separate concern* than *kevod tzibbur*. As such, it may be a real issue worthy of consideration, but one that applies to any sort of public leadership by women. This sort of concern might be addressed by telling men who experience female Torah reading as sexually improper to stay away from such services rather than by excluding women from Torah reading. In any event, this is the sort of general, overarching issue that we are not addressing here and already referred to above, Introduction, n8. (3) The Frimers are also overzealous in the prosecution of their cause to exclude women from Torah reading. They accuse R. Shapiro and R. Henkin of ignoring *Rishonim* and *Aḥaronim* that supposedly contradict their theses. As we noted, some of the *Rishonim* and *Aḥaronim* the Frimers cite do not say what they claim they say. But more to the point, the Frimers ignore the very *Rishonim* and *Aḥaronim* that contradict their own thesis! Sefer Habatim, R. Yaakov Emden and R. Ben-Tziyyon Abba Shaul all offer analyses that only make sense if one outright *rejects* the considerations the Frimers posit as central and embrace *kevod tzibbur* as being a *halakhah* rooted in sociology. See below, n106 and onward.

b. May a "community" waive its "honor"?

When a restriction motivated by *kevod tzibbur* is in place, how does it function? Specifically, what if a given community decides that it is willing to have its honor compromised in order to serve another need? Are the restrictions we saw above merely protections for the community, such that the community has the ability to waive its honor when it so chooses? Or are these restrictions more prescriptive and binding, such that communities are forbidden from electing to forgo their own honor? This core question has produced a rich literature.[97] We will only draw out the core dispute and its consequences.

(i) *Kevod tzibbur* is a protection for the community that can be waived

R. Yosef Karo, in a number of places in his Beit Yosef, cites rulings that involve *kevod tzibbur* and indicates that when this is the central concern, the community is indeed allowed to waive its honor and set aside the restriction.

We saw above the Talmud's objection to reading from a partial Torah scroll on the grounds of *kevod tzibbur*. As the world gradually shifted from the use of scrolls to codices, it became more common to have manuscripts of the five books of the Torah bound as a book. The question arose: In a situation where no valid Torah scroll is available, is it possible for the community to forgo their honor and read from a codex?

בית יוסף אורח חיים סימן קמג

וכן כתב רבינו ירוחם (נ"ב חג כ.) דספרים שלנו שאינם עשויים כתיקון ס"ת אסור לקרות בציבור
ולא שייך הכא טעמא דמפני כבוד הציבור שיוכלו למחול על כבודם
ומיהו משמע מדבריו שבחומשים העשויים כתיקון ס"ת אם מחלו הציבור על כבודם קורים בו

Beit Yosef OḤ 143

. . . And so wrote R. Yeroḥam, that we may not publicly read from our books, which are not made in the form of a Torah scroll [i.e. they are codices, not scrolls]. The reason of "the honor of the community" is not germane here, such that the community would be able to waive its honor.

But implied in [R. Yeroḥam's] words is the claim that in the case of a scroll of a single book of the Torah, if the community waived its honor, it would be allowed to read from it.[98]

---

97. Shapiro and Sperber, Introduction, n1, treat this question at greater length.
98. See also Mordekhai Menaḥot #968 for a similar approach.

R. Yosef Karo assumes in this passage that when the only issue on the table is *kevod tzibbur*, the community can elect to waive the concern.[99] A similar dynamic is at work when he cites Rambam's explanation of the Talmud's prohibition on not having a bearded *Sha"tz* as being on account of *kevod tzibbur*: ולפי זה אם רצו הצבור למחול על כבודם נראה שהרשות בידם – "According to this explanation [of the problem], if the community wishes to waive its honor, it seems that they are permitted to do so."[100]

Finally, in Beit Yosef OḤ 53, R. Karo struggles to defend a practice of allowing a minor to lead *Arvit* on Saturday nights[101] in the face of the explicit ruling of Mishnah Megillah 4:6 that a minor may not lead the community in prayer. He cites the view of Ra'avad, who holds that the sole reason for the Mishnah's ruling is because it would be dishonorable for the community to have a minor lead them.[102] On this, Beit Yosef comments: ולפי טעם זה יש מקום למנהג לומר שהצבור מוחלים על כבודם – "If this is the reason [for the exclusion], then we can justify the practice by saying that the community waives its honor." Again, when *kevod tzibbur* is the sole concern, a community can forgo its honor and proceed with the otherwise problematic practice.

According to the Beit Yosef, *kevod tzibbur* is invoked to restrict certain practices which do the community dishonor, but ultimately, the community may waive the concern for its honor and perform that practice. To this view, the thrust of the gemara's restrictions seem to be that a minority interest may not impose its will on everyone if the main body of the community would be offended. However, if everyone thinks that it is acceptable or justified to violate their honor in this way, then it is permitted. Alternatively, the point could be that a community may not waive its honor consistently and regularly,

---

99. On the practical matter of this case, Beit Yosef cites the view of the Ra'aviah and others who argue that there are other issues besides congregational dignity at stake, such as a desire to drive the community to invest in a complete Torah scroll.

100. Again, in this case, Beit Yosef proceeds to cite a conflicting view of the Rosh, who seems to have disagreed with Rambam that the issue at stake with a non-bearded *Sha"tz* was indeed *kevod hatzibbur* alone.

101. This practice was instituted to let minors who were in mourning recite the prayers at this time, as the end of Shabbat was commonly regarded as a time when the souls of the recently dead return to *gehenom*. If a child led the prayers, however, the soul of his deceased parent could be protected. This mourning practice (not with respect to minors in particular) is mentioned in Kol Bo #114: ויש שמתפללין כל מוצאי שבת תפלת ערבית לפי שבאותה שעה חוזרין לגיהנם הרשעים ששבתו בשבת ואפשר שתגן עליהם אותה תפלה.

102. Ra'avad, cited in Responsa Rashba I:239, reasons that minors are rabbinically obligated to pray (see Mishnah Berakhot 3:3) and as such are no different from adults, who also have a rabbinic obligation (in keeping with the non-Maimonidean views we saw earlier in our discussion of the nature of obligation in prayer). Therefore, obligation cannot be the basis for forbidding a minor from leading. We will return to this text below. Many others felt that the rabbinic obligation of minors was of a lesser level than the rabbinic obligation of adults and would not have accepted Ra'avad's logic here.

but for occasional needs, they may choose to do so. Either way, the priority of this honor is determined by the subjective decision of the community in whose name it is invoked.

The ramifications for gender and Torah reading should be clear. Following the Beit Yosef's position, a community that desired to forgo its honor and allow women to read Torah would be properly exercising their right to waive *kevod tzibbur*. This is then one strong basis for permitting a more gender equal Torah reading.[103]

(ii) *Kevod tzibbur* is an objective standard of dignity

Against this, the **Baḥ** (R. Yoel Sirkis, Poland, 16th c.) insists that the whole point of the *kevod tzibbur* restrictions is to prevent the community from undermining its dignity in the face of competing interests. He also cites Rambam's view that the prohibition on having a non-bearded *Sha"tz* is due to *kevod tzibbur* but strongly objects that this implies any kind of waiver:

ב"ח או"ח סימן נג

ולפע"ד נראה דאף להרמב"ם... לא מהני מחילת הצבור דאין פירוש מפני כבוד הצבור שהוא כנגד כבודם לפני בני אדם שתועיל בו מחילת הצבור אלא פירושו שאין זה כבוד הצבור שישלחו לפניו יתעלה מי שאין לו הדרת פנים להליץ על הצבור דאף לפני מלך בשר ודם אין שולחין להליץ על הצבור אפילו אם הוא חכם גדול אלא אם כן שהוא בעל צורה ויש לו הדרת פנים שנתמלא זקנו כל שכן לפני מלך מלכי המלכים הקדוש ברוך הוא דלפי זה אין מקום כלל לומר דמהני למנותו כשרצו הצבור למחול על כבודם... אלא הדבר פשוט כיון שכך תקנו חכמים דחששו לכבוד צבור אין ביד הצבור למחול. ותו דאם כן כל הני תקנות שתקנו חכמים מפני כבוד צבור שלא לגלול ספר תורה בצבור וכן אשה לא תקרא בצבור מפני כבוד הצבור ופוחח לא ישא כפיו... אם אתה אומר דרשאין למחול, א"כ לא הועילו בתקנתם כלום, דכל צבור יהיו מוחלים!

Baḥ OḤ 53

In my humble opinion, even according to Rambam ... the community cannot waive its honor, because the meaning of "on account of the honor of the community" is not because it is disrespectful to the people present such that they could waive the concern. Rather, it means that it is not fitting for the community that they should send before the Exalted One a person lacking an impressive countenance to intercede on behalf of the community. Even a very wise person does not intercede on behalf of the community before a human king unless he is of striking appearance and has an impres-

103. Addressing *kevod tzibbur* returns us to our discussion in the previous section. Whether women participate as equals or as adjuncts would be driven by the R. Tam/Ran divide we explored above.

> sive countenance with a full beard. All the more with the Supreme King of Kings! In keeping with this, there is no place whatsoever to say that the community could appoint [a young man as the (permanent) prayer leader] when the community wishes to waive its honor . . . Rather, the matter is simple: Once the Sages legislated because of their concern for the honor of the community, a community has no license to waive it. Further, if it were the case [that the community could waive it], all these enactments that the Sages legislated because of the honor of the community, such as not rolling the Torah scroll before the community or that a woman not read in public because of the honor of the community or that a person in tattered clothing may not offer the priestly blessing . . . if you say that the community may waive [its honor], then the legislation has accomplished nothing, because every community will then waive it!

Communities may wish to cut corners because of expedience (rolling the Torah in front of everyone rather than preparing ahead of time, coming to shul in tattered work clothes rather than changing), or for other reasons. Against this impulse, the Sages assert that Torah reading and public prayer are serious, communal acts that require the highest levels of dignity. According to the Baḥ, the *kevod tzibbur* restrictions were enacted precisely to *prevent* communities from waiving their dignity. Even when the community is not concerned for its own dignity, the Sages are.

For the Baḥ, the honor of the community is about the community taking itself seriously. *Kevod tzibbur* is not a prerogative to be exercised or waived; rather it is a charge to keep, an expectation that communities live up to the standards of dignity and seriousness that they know they are capable of. *Kevod tzibbur* indeed refers to the dignity of the congregation, but not as viewed subjectively from within. Instead, the Baḥ's *kevod tzibbur* is the objective assessment of communal action when viewed from afar: Is the act in question something you would do when presenting yourself to an earthly sovereign? Would it meet your standards for seriousness in other realms of life? If not, then it is inappropriate to settle for something less in a communal, ritual context. Drawing the Baḥ's support for a gender-equal Torah reading would require the bolder and more direct claim that, at least in some pockets of the contemporary world, the concerns of specific issues of *kevod tzibbur* no longer apply or are overridden by other factors. Short of such a claim, individual communities cannot, according to the Baḥ, circumvent the concerns of the Tosefta and the *baraita*.

(iii) Applying and balancing the two approaches

Poskim over the past few centuries have split in their rulings on whether to follow the Beit Yosef or the Baḥ.[104] Some argue that a greater number of prominent authorities accord with the Beit Yosef's ruling that *kevod hatzibbur* may be waived,[105] and therefore communities should be able to waive their honor and allow women to read Torah. However, let it be noted that Beit Yosef's approach of waiver implies that a real offense is occurring, but that the community is willing to allow it in the name of other priorities. In other words, even if one concedes that it is dishonorable to allow women to read Torah in public, one might be willing to suffer this indignity in order to give women a greater sense of inclusion and connection. This approach is similar to those who would advocate for allowing adolescents to regularly lead parts of the service. No one would deny that their gravitas is considerably less than other, older candidates. But it might be worth suffering their less impressive appearance and demeanor in order to more deeply entwine them with communal prayer.

The advantage of the Beit Yosef's approach is plain: It requires no radical reimagining of *kevod tzibbur* and need not attempt to translate the gender revolution taking place in society into halakhic language. It simply states that the potential dishonor involved in a gender-equal Torah reading is not that big a deal and can be addressed through an elective waiver of the community. Its disadvantage is also plain: It engages assumptions about honor and dignity around gender that are increasingly foreign to contemporary social experience and does not acknowledge that possible discomfort with only-male Torah reading is generally grounded in something deeper than just wanting to give women a few chances to approach a Torah scroll.

The road to gender-neutral Torah reading through the Baḥ is simultaneously bolder and more honest. Communities with egalitarian social norms are not claiming that women should be able to read Torah and lead *even though* it is undignified; they are claiming that there is no less dignity in a woman reading than in a man reading. Perhaps they are even claiming that all-male Torah readings in a socially egalitarian context are themselves degrading.

As above in our discussion of R. Tam versus the Ran, we in no way intend to undermine the legitimacy of relying on the Beit Yosef's approach to *kevod*

---

104. See Shapiro, "*Qeri'at Ha-Torah*", pp. 35–36 for citations to a number of these authorities.

105. Peri Ḥadash strongly rejects the Baḥ's approach in the former's comments on OḤ 53, 143 and 144. See also R. Ḥayyim Palache (Turkey, 19th c.) in Responsa Nishmat Kol Ḥai OḤ #9. This voice includes, in our own time, R. Ovadiah Yosef in Responsa *Yabia Omer* OḤ VI:23, as well as, probably, other strongly authoritative modern *poskim*, such as the Mishnah Berurah and Arokh Hashulḥan. See Shapiro, *ibid.*, notes 203–204.

tzibbur as a basis for communities adopting or maintaining an egalitarian practice around Torah reading. But we also don't want to lose the wisdom of the Baḥ: Maintaining high communal standards of dignity – even when the community wants to waive them – makes just as much sense today as it did in the 17th century. It is therefore also important to ask not just whether *kevod tzibbur* can be circumvented, but whether it has been sufficiently redefined in our world around gender so as to produce a different ruling in practice.[106]

This notion, that the concern of *kevod tzibbur* spelled out in the *baraita* might not apply in all times and places, is not new. We find prominent voices among generations of *poskim* suggesting that, if communal honor would not be violated or if the available alternatives are worse, it would be appropriate for women to read.

R. David bR. Shmuel Kokhavi (Provençe, 14th c.) recorded the following:

ספר הבתים, בית תפילה, שערי קריאת התורה, שער שני, סימן ו
יש מן הגדולים שכתב שהמתפללין בבתיהם בעשרה אשה קוראה שם בתורה, שלא נקרא ציבור אלא כשמתפללין בבית הכנסת.

Sefer Habatim, Beit Tefillah, Sha'arei Keriat Hatorah 2:6
There is one among the great ones who wrote that when people pray with ten in their homes, a woman may read from the Torah there, for it is not called a "community" unless they are praying in a synagogue.

Sefer Habatim recognized that the concern of *kevod tzibbur* was grounded in social context: The same Torah reading in a private home might not share the concerns of the highly public space of the synagogue.

Later, in a different context, **R. Yaakov Emden** (Germany, 18th c.) produced similar reasoning:

---

106. R. Shapiro articulates this basic line of reasoning. He writes: "[The Baḥ says that] just as a community should choose the imposing figure over the wise man to represent it before the Lord, so the congregation should not denigrate *keri'at haTorah* by performing it through women. This line of thought is out of tune with modern perceptions... Jewish women are widely represented in the professions, including those, such as law and public office, which demand that they act as representatives and advocates for others" (p. 27). R. Shapiro's conclusion blends giving prominence to the Beit Yosef over the Baḥ with a willingness to think differently about how the Baḥ may apply to contemporary settings: "To recapitulate, there appears to be sound halakhic basis for the argument that... in synagogues where there is a consensus that *a woman's Torah reading does not violate community standards of dignity* [emphasis ours], women may be permitted to read Torah (or at least portions of it) as well. The only serious objection to *keri'at ha-Torah* by women is the one raised by the *baraita*, namely that women's Torah reading violates *kevod hatzibbur*, and *kevod hatzibbur* should be regarded as a relative, waivable objection that is not universally applicable" (pp. 51–52).

מגדל עז, הלכות יולדת, שוקת ב, דף יב עמוד ג

ונראה דכשמתפללין וקורין עשרה בצמצום בבית היולדת ואין בעלה כאן, יש להעמיד הדבר על הדין שאשה עולה וקוראה בתורה כהאי גוונא. אע"ג שאמרו חכמים לא תקרא בציבור מפני הכבוד, לא אמרו אלא בקהל רב, ושלא לעשות תדיר, אבל בהאי גוונא דהויא מילתא דלא שכיחא ומשום תקנתא דידה, איכא למימר לא גזרו, עכ"פ הרי בפירוש אמרו שעולה למניין ז', ואם לא עכשיו אימתי אלה הדברים איפוא הם אמורים, ובודאי לא יפול שום דבר מדבריהם ארצה שלא יהא לו מקום, ובאופן זה כדיעבד דמי. כך דעתי נוטה אם יסכימו עמי חברי.

Migdal Oz, Hilkhot Yoledet, Shoket B, 12c

It seems that when ten pray and read Torah in a small group in the house of the new mother, and her husband is not there, one may restore the basic principle that a woman may go up and read Torah. Even though the Sages said that she should not read in the community because of honor, they said that only with reference to a large congregation, and not to do so regularly, but in this situation, which is an irregular occurrence, and it is for her sake, one can say that they did not decree. In any event, they explicitly said that she goes up among the seven, and if not for now [=this sort of case], for when were these words intended? Certainly, everything the Sages said must have some applicable context, and in this sort of case, it is similar to a *post facto* case. So inclines my opinion if my colleagues will agree with me.

In our own time, **R. Ben Tziyyon Abba Shaul** (Israel, 20th c.) reasoned similarly, though he expressed practical reservations:

אור לציון, שו"ת חלק ב, הלכות פסוקות, או"ח א, עמוד ח

ואגב יש להעיר במה שכתב מרן בשו"ע . . . הכל עולים למנין שבעה, אפילו אשה וקטן שיודע למי מברכין, אבל אמרו חכמים אשה לא תקרא בציבור מפני כבוד הציבור, וצריך עיון, שאם עכ"פ אין אשה עולה מפני כבוד הציבור, מאי נפק"מ שאשה עולה למנין שבעה, ולשם מה כתב מרן הלכה זו. *ולכן היה נראה לומר שנפק"מ במקום שאין חשש משום כבוד הציבור*, כגון במקום שהמתפללים הם בני משפחה אחת, והאשה היא ראש הבית וכל שאר המתפללים הם בניה ונכדיה, שאז אין *חסרון כבוד הציבור במה שתעלה לתורה, בכה"ג שפיר יכולה לעלות לתורה ולהצטרף למנין שבעה.* ולמעשה צ"ע.

Or Letziyyon, Responsa II, Halakhot Pesukot, OḤ I, p. 8

We should consider that which our master wrote in the Shulḥan Arukh . . . "All may count for the quorum of seven, even a woman or a minor who knows to whom we bless, but the Sages said that a woman should not read in public because of the honor of the community." This requires further thought. If a woman cannot go up because of the honor of the community, what difference does it make that she can [theoretically] count for the quorum of seven, and why did our master bother to write this halakhah?

> *Therefore, it seems that there is practical relevance in a case where there is no concern for the honor of the community*, such as in a place where all those praying are members of a single family and the woman is the head of household and all the others praying are her children and grandchildren. *In that case, there is no diminishment of the honor of the public by her going up to the Torah, in which case she would be able to go up to the Torah and count towards the quorum of seven.* But regarding practice, more investigation is required.

Note that none of these views claims that the honor of the community has been *waived*. Instead, they each reason that, in the case they are discussing, it does not *apply*.[107] Calculations of communal honor play out differently in different social arrangements. That might be because of the more private nature of the ritual, its ad hoc nature, or the social context in which the woman having the *aliyah* quite obviously possesses as much gravitas as anyone else in the room.[108] Or Letziyyon's analysis is perhaps most helpful here: In many pockets of the contemporary world, society in its entirety has become like his small laboratory of gender equality. Just as the matriarch in his thought experiment poses no clear affront to the dignity of those in the room, it is now broadly true in many settings that women are not taken less seriously than men just because they are women, nor is their knowledge of ritual matters experienced as a slight to men or to the community as a whole. Or Letziyyon's hesitancy regarding practice is understandable, as it should be in any case grappling with a new and still unfolding social dynamic. But the years that have passed since he penned these words have only moved society more forcefully in the direction of gender equality and make less hesitance in this regard not only justifiable but quite plausibly wise. When women are fully educated, hold public office and run corporations, female leadership in the synagogue is no longer disrespectful. Faithfulness to the concept of *kevod tzibbur* itself demands that it be reevaluated in light of women's relationship to the broader cultural context. In communities where men and women are educated equally in Torah and general studies, where women and men increasingly share the corridors of

107. For another intriguing example of this sort, see Ḥashukei Ḥemed Gittin 60a, where **R. Yitzḥak Silberstein** addresses a case of prisoners who only have 5 separate scrolls of the five parts of the Torah. He concludes that none of the reasons for demanding a complete Sefer Torah apply and therefore permits reading in this context.

108. One remarkable historical instance of this dynamic is provided by **R. Daniel Sperber** in שפרבר, דרכה של תורה, 32–33 הע' 37. In 1901, Flora Sassoon, the famed business woman and Torah scholar, visited Baghdad. The community, which was at that time under the religious leadership of R. Yosef Ḥayyim Al-Ḥakham (the Ben Ish Ḥai), honored her by calling her to read Torah in the synagogue.

power and enjoy electoral success, it can be claimed that no shame or dishonor would any longer follow from having women read in the presence of men.

Perhaps even more dramatic are the claims that *kevod tzibbur* is at times overridden by other concerns. We saw above the view of Maharam of Rothenberg, who countenanced the idea that the risk of a greater indignity – to the *kohanim* – can justify overriding the normal concern regarding indignity surrounding gender. Similarly, in his glosses on our passage in the Talmud, R. Emden concisely explained that the gemara's restriction on women reading is not absolute. If excluding women from reading will cancel the Torah reading altogether for lack of competent men, then women may read all of the *aliyot*:

ר' יעקב עמדין, הגהות וחדושים, מגילה כג.
"אבל אמרו חכמים אשה לא וכו'": נראה דהיינו היכא דאפשר ורישא מיירי בדליכא שבעה (בהני עשרה דמצטרפי לדבר שבקדושה) דבקיאי למקרי ואיכא אשה בקיאה דלא סגי בלא דידה.

R. Yaakov Emden, Glosses & Novellae, Megillah 23a
"But the Sages said that a woman should not . . .": It seems that this means where possible, but the beginning [of the text, which stated that in principle women may read] is referring to when there are not seven who know how to read, but there is a woman who knows how, such that they can't suffice without her.

Along these lines, **R. Daniel Sperber** (Israel, 20th–21st c.) has argued for another overriding factor: The human dignity of women (*kevod haberiot*), which can be deeply harmed in the contemporary world when women are excluded from rituals. He argues that just as Maharam's concern for *kohanim* led him to override *kevod tzibbur*, so too contemporary practice should grant the human dignity of women no less weight.[109]

We are less certain as to whether *kevod haberiot* is an appropriate legal concept on which to base egalitarian Torah reading. *Kevod haberiot*, while highly evocative, is generally invoked for ad hoc situations and not because of a critique as to how a given *mitzvah* or rabbinic expectation makes a person feel.[110] We would translate the instinct behind this legal move differently: As the Baḥ emphasized, the restrictions around *kevod tzibbur* may not just be reflecting reality, but supporting and creating a reality of greater dignity and seriousness. To the extent that adhering to the restriction in question begins

109. Sperber, "Congregational Dignity and Human Dignity", cited in Intoduction, n1.
110. The core Talmudic passage is on Talmud Bavli Berakhot 19b–20a.

to *undermine* that dignity and seriousness, it is not clear that the earlier prohibition could even possibly be in place.

Specifically, it might be that, in our world, *kevod tzibbur* itself is what leads many people to want to have gender-equal Torah reading! We live in a world in which there are almost no all-male institutions left that are taken seriously at all. Other than sports teams, locker rooms and gentlemen's clubs, all major institutions of Western society allow women access as equals, at least in theory. One might reasonably claim that maintaining the exclusion of women from Torah reading in fact *denigrates* its status as a serious activity in communities that expect gender equality in other areas of their lives.[111] Given that maximizing communal honor was the driving internal *halakhic* consideration for gendering Torah reading in the first place, it is particularly compelling – in the name of *halakhic* values themselves – to revisit a gendered regime to the extent it threatens communal honor and dignity. An argument of this sort for egalitarian Torah reading would fill out the tradition above that reassesses socio-halakhic factors like *kevod tzibbur* and fully engage the Baḥ's concern for robust and objective standards of communal dignity.[112]

Summary

As the first clauses of the Tosefta and the *baraita* indicate, Torah reading is at least theoretically inclusive of women. R. Tam's theory of Torah reading supports the idea that this equality was total, whereas Ran felt it was only permissible to include women as adjunct participants.

The second clauses of the Tosefta and the *baraita* point to a practical ban on letting women read Torah. In the *baraita*, this is formulated as *kevod tzibbur*, "the honor of the community." *Kevod tzibbur* can be engaged either through the prism of waiver or reassessment.

Torah readings only open to adult males are coherent on the grounds that *kevod tzibbur* remains an obstacle to female participation. In communities where women are not educated equally to men, or where women do not in

111. Vered Noam has reflected on this point: סילוק הנשים מן העשייה הדתית הציבורית מסלק את העשייה הזאת עצמה מן החיים אל המוזיאון. – "Removing women from public religious acts removes the act itself from life into the museum." See ו. נעם, "מעבר למחיצה הפנימית", *מקור ראשון* 11.1.2013.

112. We should also note the explicit statements of a number of *poskim* that the prohibition of calling women to read is only *lekhatḥila* (*ab initio*), but that *bediavad* (*post facto*), having read, the reading is valid, or even just having been called up, they may go ahead and read. This view is seen not only from those sages mentioned above, such as Maharam, who allowed women to read in certain circumstances, but also from a number of others who never specifically discussed allowing it, yet said that it is valid *bediavad*, including two commentators to Tosefta Megillah 3:11, **R. David Pardo** (Ḥasdei David), and **R. Meir Friedman** (Tekhelet Mordekhai).

general serve in public capacities, the injury done to communal honor by allowing women to read Torah may remain intact. Communities with similar gender roles to those of the ancient and medieval world ought to be expected to have similar concerns on this front.

A fully egalitarian Torah reading can justify itself without reevaluating assumptions and categories by simply endorsing the approach of R. Tam and the approach that allows communities to waive *kevod tzibbur*. A more robust formulation of the gender-specific motivations for equality would need to articulate a redefinition of *kevod tzibbur* as described above and not suffice with a waiver alone. Finally, any effort to bring the Ran on board with a fully egalitarian Torah reading would have to reevaluate notions of gender and obligation more broadly, with regard to Torah study and potentially all *mitzvot*. Communities for which that broader reevaluation is not on the table, but for whom the Ran's approach is compelling, might well include women as adjunct participants without having them be fully equal to men.

B. Are Other *Devarim Shebikdushah* the Same as Torah Reading?

Our investigation of Torah reading has also established another important, and more general, point: Controlling for *kevod tzibbur*, there is nothing about a ritual's status as a *davar shebikdushah* that genders its leadership requirements in the presence of a valid *minyan*.[113] This flows from a simple reading of Mishnah Megillah 4:3, cited here again:

משנה מגילה ד:ג

אין פורסין את שמע, ואין עוברין לפני התבה, ואין נושאין את כפיהם, ואין קורין בתורה, ואין מפטירין בנביא, ואין עושין מעמד ומושב, ואין אומרים ברכת אבלים ותנחומי אבלים וברכת חתנים, ואין מזמנין בשם, פחות מעשרה. ובקרקעות, תשעה וכהן. ואדם, כיוצא בהן:

Mishnah Megillah 4:3

We do not responsively recite the *Shema*, nor have a communal prayer leader, nor offer the priestly blessing, nor read from the Torah, nor read from the prophets, nor perform the standing/sitting [ritual for the dead], nor say the blessing of the mourners nor the formal comforting the mourners, nor recite the wedding blessings, nor say *zimmun* with the Name in a group

113. We will explore the criteria for *minyan* in greater depth below. Our conclusions here hold even if the reader assumes a minyan of 10 adult men.

of fewer than ten. And when redeeming land we require nine and a *kohen.* And so too with [redeeming] people.

The Mishnah lists Torah reading in the midst of a host of other rituals requiring a quorum of ten. As we saw above, the gemara then explains the Mishnah's requirement of ten with the statement that any *davar shebikdushah* requires ten. The straightforward conclusion is that Torah reading is itself among the *devarim shebikdushah* referred to by the Talmud.[114] This is implied by the structure of Rambam Hilkhot Tefillah 8:4–6, which groups the first five rituals in our Mishnah, *Kaddish* and *Kedushah* together and describes them all as *devarim shebikdushah*:

רמב"ם הלכות תפילה ח:ד–ו

וכיצד היא תפלת הציבור יהיה אחד מתפלל בקול רם והכל שומעים, ואין עושין כן בפחות מעשרה גדולים ובני חורין . . . וכן אין אומרים קדושה ולא קוראין בתורה ומברכין לפניה ולאחריה ולא מפטירין בנביאים אלא בעשרה. וכן לא יהיה אחד מברך ברכת שמע והכל שומעים ועונין אחריו אמן אלא בעשרה, וזה הוא הנקרא פורס על שמע, ואין אומרים קדיש אלא בעשרה, ואין הכהנים נושאים ידיהם אלא בעשרה והכהנים מן המנין, שכל עשרה מישראל הם הנקראים עדה. . . וכל דבר קדושה לא יהא אלא בתוך העדה מישראל שנאמר ונקדשתי בתוך בני ישראל . . .

Rambam Hilkhot Tefillah 8:4–6

What is public prayer? One person prays aloud and the others listen. We do not do that with fewer than ten free adults . . . We also do not say *Kedushah,* nor read from the Torah with blessings before and after, nor read a final portion from the prophets unless there are ten. One should also not say the blessing over the *Shema* while others listen and respond unless there are ten. [This is what is known as *pores al Shema.*][115] And we do not say *Kaddish* unless there are ten, and the priests do not offer the priestly blessing unless there are ten. The priests count towards this ten, for any ten Jews are called an *edah* . . . And any *davar kedushah* should not be done except in the presence of an *edah* of the Jewish people, as it says, "I shall be sanctified in the midst of the Jewish people" . . .

---

114. See also Gittin 59b, where the language of דבר שבקדושה is used in the context of *aliyot* to the Torah, among other rituals.

115. Note that Rambam's definition of this term is different from our translation above. This is one of a number of medieval interpretations of the phrase פורס על שמע. See above, n48. See also Introduction, n5 above, which discusses how many contemporary communities have abandoned even practicing Rambam's definition of פורס על שמע, rendering it practically irrelevant for our discussion.

Many later authorities and interpreters therefore assert that Torah reading is a *davar shebikdushah.* **R. Mordekhai Yaffe** (Prague, Posen, 16th-17th c.) states this directly in Levush 143:1: "קריאת התורה היא דבר שבקדושה, ואין דבר שבקדושה פחות מעשרה כדילפינן מונקדשתי וגו" – "Torah reading is a *davar shebikdushah* . . ." Other prominent authorities who explicitly articulate this view include **R. Ovadiah of Bartenura**, **R. Yisrael Lifshitz**, **R. Yisrael Meir Hakohen**, **R. Yehiel Mikhael Epstein**, **R. Barukh Halevi Epstein** and **R. Moshe Feinstein.**[116] This would seem to settle the matter: The fact that a ritual act is a *davar shebikdushah* reveals nothing about whether it is gendered. It would then stand to reason that, controlling for concerns of *kevod tzibbur*, the recitation of *Kedushah, Kaddish* and *Barekhu* would be similarly non-gendered.

However, matters are not so simple: First, not all authorities accepted the notion that Torah reading is a *davar shebikdushah.*[117] The views of this camp

---

116. R. Ovadiah of Bartenura and Tiferet Yisrael on Mishnah Megillah 4:3; Mishnah Berurah 143:1; Arokh Hashulḥan YD 334:7; Torah Temimah Vayikra 22:32, note 195; Iggerot Moshe OḤ I:23.

117. The most prominent source in this regard is Eliyah Rabbah 128:1, who cites the Ran as demurring from Levush's conclusion that the priestly blessing and Torah reading are considered *devarim shebikdushah.* Eliyah Rabbah is referring to the following passage in the Ran:

ר"ן על הרי"ף מגילה יג:

ואין נושאין את כפיהם פחות מי'. דכתיב וישא אהרן את ידיו אל העם ויברכם וכתיב כה תברכו את בני ישראל אמור להם ובני ישראל עשרה משמע כדילפינן בגמרא לענין דבר שבקדושה מדכתיב ונקדשתי בתוך בני ישראל . . . ומיהו הני מילי כולהו אסמכתא דרבנן נינהו דסדר תפלה גופא דרבנן.

ואין קורין בתורה ואין מפטירין בנביא בפחות מעשרה. דתקנתא דרבנן הוא ולא תקון אלא בצבור . . .

מנא הני מילי וכו'. וכל דבר שבקדושה לא יהיה פחות מעשרה . . . והאי טעמא סגי לאין פורסין על שמע ואין עוברין לפני התיבה משום קדושה דאית בהו, ולאין נושאין את כפיהם מטעמא דכתיבנא במתניתין . . .

Ran on Rif Megillah 13b

"And they may not offer the priestly blessing with fewer than 10" – for it is written, "Aharon raised up his hands towards the people and blessed them," and it is also written, "So you must bless *benei yisrael* (the children of Israel), say to them." And *benei yisrael* signifies 10, as we learn here in the Gemara with respect to a *davar shebikdushah,* deriving this from the verse: "And I will be sanctified in the midst of the children of Israel" . . . But these are all only rabbinic laws and the verses are here for symbolic support, because all the laws of prayer are themselves rabbinic.

"And they may not read from the Torah nor add from the prophets with fewer than 10" – because these are rabbinic enactments and they were only enacted to be done in public . . .

"Any *davar shebikdushah* shall not be said with fewer than 10" . . . This reasoning is sufficient to explain [why we require 10] for the blessings of *Shema* and to have a communal prayer leader, since both of those rituals contain *Kedushah,* but [the basis for requiring 10] for the priestly blessing is what I wrote in explaining the Mishnah . . .

Ran here clearly states that the priestly blessing (נשיאת כפים) does *not* require 10 because it is a *davar shebikdushah,* but rather because the term בני ישראל– already associated with 10 in the context of *devarim shebikdushah* – is used to describe the object of the blessing. (This point was already made by Rashba on Megillah 23b.) Whether he feels the same way about Torah reading is less clear, and depends on one's reading of two clauses in the above passage: 1) When Ran says that Torah and Haftarah reading require 10 because they are rabbinic ordinances that must be done in a communal setting, this gives the impression that he is distinguishing them from the first items in the list (אין פורסין על שמע and אין עוברין לפני התיבה), to which he explicitly applied the gemara's grounding of the quorum of 10 in their nature as a *davar shebikdushah.* One might thus read him as saying that Torah reading is *not* a *davar shebikdushah.* On the other hand, he might simply be explaining that Torah reading follows the rules of *devarim shebikdushah* because it was

may cut against the plain sense of the Mishnah and may be generally under-

---

given holiness by the Sages as a public ritual and given the same status as the other initial items in the Mishnah's list. 2) In the last clause above, Ran seems to say that the rationale of *devarim shebikdushah* only applies to the first two items on the list, excluding Torah reading. But the continuation of the sentence suggests that this formulation may only be intended to buttress his claim that the priestly blessing is not a *davar shebikdushah*, but conceding that Torah reading is indeed in this category.

In other words, Ran's precise position on the status of Torah reading as a *davar shebikdushah* like any other is unclear, and this lack of clarity is reflected in the interpretations of him in later *Aḥaronim*. While Eliyah Rabbah reads him in conflict with Levush on the question of Torah reading, others resisted this reading. See Mishpetei Uzziel III OḤ #14 for one such example. See also **R. Aryeh Leib Ginzburg**, in Turei Even on Megillah 23b, who takes issue with the view of Rashba – cited by the Ran – that the priestly blessing is not a *davar shebikdushah*. He asks: ולדידי ק"ל הא אין קורין בתורה דתנא אחריו וודאי טעמא דצריך י' משום דדבר שבקדושה הוי וה"ט דריש' דאין פורסין ועוברין לפני התיבה. ואם איתא דטעמא דאין נושאין לאו מש"ה הוא אלא מפני הזכרת השם אמאי נקט לה באמצע בין הני דטעמא משום דבר שבקדושה. Why would Mishnah Megillah 4:3 begin with *devarim shebikdushah*, take a detour to the priestly blessing (claimed by Rashba and Ran not to be a *davar shebikdushah*) and then return to other *devarim shebikdushah*, such as Torah reading? Turei Even clearly never imagined that anyone – including Rashba – might think that Torah reading was not a *davar shebikdushah*. He would clearly have read the Ran in the alternate ways suggested above. Note also that while Peri Megadim and Beur Halakhah cite the Ran's dissent on characterizing the priestly blessing as a *davar shebikdushah* in OḤ 128, they make no mention of such a position of his with regard to Torah reading.

One other view worth noting is that of the Meiri on Megillah 23b: שאין הכהנים נושאין את כפיהם אלא בעשרה אף זו דבר שבקדושה היא וכן בקריאת התורה שהרי צריך לומר ברכו – "Torah reading is a *davar shebikdushah* because it includes the recitation of *Barekhu*." The formulation here indicates that Meiri did not consider the reading of Torah *itself* to be a *davar shebikdushah*, but rather that Torah reading had this status on account of the *Barekhu* recited by each reader. In fact, a similar point was made explicitly by **R. Menaḥem Azariah of Fano** (Italy, 16th-17th c.) in Responsum #91, where he says that while it is possible to debate whether the reading of the Torah is a *davar shebikdushah*, it is obvious that the recitation of *Barekhu* as part of having an *aliyah* is considered a *davar shebikdushah*: מ"מ אפי' לפי דעת החולקים בזה יש לנו דברים ברורים ושל טעם הם יחוייב השומע ומבין להודות בהם: הנה לדברי הכל ברכו את ה' המבורך הוא דבר שבקדושה. This point is then cited in Magen Avraham 146:6.

One might think that this insight would conclusively show that *devarim shebikdushah* are in no way gendered, since, controlling for *kevod tzibbur*, women would have said the blessings over their *aliyot*. But one would still have to contend with the view, cited in Meiri Megillah 23a, which negates the idea that women could ever have said the blessings over the Torah: ויש מי שמפרש שלא נאמרו הדברים אלא בזמן שהיו קוראין אמצעיים בלא ברכה ואשה יכולה לקרות באמצע אבל עכשו שכלן מברכין אין אשה קוראה כלל וכן הדין נותן שהרי היאך תברך והיא פטורה. "Some explain that [the *baraita*'s permission, in principle, for women to read Torah] only applied at the time when the intermediate readers [of any given set of Torah readers] said no blessing, such that a woman could be an intermediate reader. But now that all say a blessing, a woman cannot read at all. And this makes sense; how can she say a blessing when she is exempt?" A similar ruling is cited by R. David b. Shmuel Kokhavi in Sefer Habatim, Sha'arei Keriat Hatorah 2:6. This view is far from unanimous or authoritative and invites many layers of analysis; the interested reader can see Shapiro, "*Qeri'at ha-Torah*", pp. 12–15. In addition to R. Tam's explicit rejection of this approach, see Ran on Rif Megillah 13a s.v. *hakol* for another clear disagreement. Accommodating the view cited in Meiri and Sefer Habatim would indeed mean that a woman could not have any *aliyot* even if one controlled for *kevod tzibbur*, though perhaps she could read Torah in contexts where the reader and *oleh* are separate functions. Addressing this view would require engaging the analysis we offered regarding justifying a gender-equal Torah reading under the Ran's rubric of בני חיובא. For our purposes here, this view cited in the Meiri merely demonstrates further that there are important voices that would not consider female participation in Torah reading to be useful data for a more general conclusion regarding their ability to lead *devarim shebikdushah* such as *Kedushah, Kaddish* and *Barekhu*.

represented among later *poskim*, but any argument should take their approach into account as well.[118] If Torah reading is not a *davar shebikdushah*, it can no longer function as evidence for a gender-blind approach to such rituals. Even if there is no particular reason to think that rituals such as *Kedushah, Kaddish* and *Barekhu* are gendered,[119] satisfying this camp of interpreters demands grounding that claim in sources unrelated to Torah reading.

Second, and more important: Even if *devarim shebikdushah* are not ipso facto gendered (whether or not Torah reading is appropriate evidence for this), they might be gendered due to other concerns, such as a gender gap in obligation. In fact, Mishnah Megillah 4:5– 6 makes abundantly clear that one cannot extrapolate from one type of *davar shebikdushah* to another:

משנה מגילה ד:ה–ו

המפטיר בנביא הוא פורס על שמע והוא עובר לפני התיבה והוא נושא את כפיו ואם היה קטן אביו או רבו עוברין על ידו:

קטן קורא בתורה ומתרגם אבל אינו פורס על שמע ואינו עובר לפני התיבה ואינו נושא את כפיו.

פוחח פורס את שמע ומתרגם אבל אינו קורא בתורה ואינו עובר לפני התיבה ואינו נושא את כפיו.

Mishnah Megillah 4:5–6

The one who says the *haftarah* leads the responsive reading of the Shema and publicly recites the *Amidah* and says the priestly blessing. If [the one who said the *haftarah*] was a minor, then his father or teacher goes in his place.

A minor reads from the Torah and translates but does not lead the responsive reading of the *Shema*, nor publicly recites the *Amidah* nor says the priestly blessing. A person dressed in tattered clothing does lead the responsive reading of the *Shema* and translates, but does not read Torah, nor publicly recites the *Amidah* nor says the priestly blessing.

---

118. In the words of R. Uzziel in Mishpetei Uzziel III OḤ #14: לפום ריהטא דסוגיא משמע דפורסין על שמע וקורין בתורה ומפטירין בנביא חד טעמא וחד דינא הוא.

119. Indeed, R. Mendel Shapiro explicitly says that he knows of no objection to women saying *devarim shebikdushah* in general: "I have heard the argument put forward that women may not say *birkhot haTorah* of *keri'at ha-Torah* because they are *davar shebikdushah* . . . which women may not recite, but I have found no evidence to support this conclusion. *Devarim shebikdushah* require an appropriate *minyan*. Absent such a *minyan*, they may not be said by men or women. **Where there is such a *minyan*, there is no reason to suppose that women may not say *devarim shebikdushah*** [emphasis ours]. I have also heard it argued that women are precluded from saying the *Barekhu* that precedes the *birkhot haTorah* said by those called to the Torah. I have found no basis for this position and can only speculate that its origin may be in the perception of *Barekhu* as a *devar shebikdushah* that women may not say. Again, there is no reason to believe that women may not say *devarim shebikdushah* in the presence of a *minyan* of ten men . . ." Shapiro, "*Qeri'at ha-Torah*", n90.

This Mishnah shows that a person can be included in Torah reading and still be excluded from other rituals. Whatever the reason for the minor's exclusion from leading the rituals of *pores al Shema* and the public *Amidah,*[120] it is clear that these exclusions coexist with his inclusion in Torah reading. There are strong reasons to assume that Torah reading would indeed function the same as *Kedushah, Kaddish* and *Barekhu*. After all, having an *aliyah* to the Torah involves the recitation of *Barekhu*! Nonetheless, we have seen that extrapolating from one category to another can be unsound. Specifically, perhaps one who leads *devarim shebikdushah* is fulfilling the individual obligations of others in these parts of the liturgy and perhaps women are exempt from these requirements and thus unable to lead. Therefore, we must turn to a more piecemeal examination of *Kedushah, Kaddish* and *Barekhu* to see if the requirements for leading them are gendered in any way.

C. Other *Devarim Shebikdushah: Kedushah, Kaddish* and *Barekhu*

In this section, we will explore three central questions:

1) Are individuals obligated in *devarim shebikdushah*? If not, then the ability for a given person to lead them should in no way depend on the level of their obligation.
2) If there is some sort of individual obligation in *devarim shebikdushah,* is this obligation fulfilled vicariously through the prayer leader? If, instead, the obligation is fulfilled by congregants on their own, then level of obligation would similarly be irrelevant when choosing a leader.
3) If the obligation is fulfilled vicariously through the leader, is the obligation in *devarim shebikdushah* gendered?

Only if the answer to all three questions is yes would there be any sense to gendering leadership of *devarim shebikdushah* based on concerns surrounding obligation. If the answer to any of the questions is no, we would expect the conversation to return to considerations of *kevod tzibbur,* already highlighted and discussed in our treatment of Torah reading above.

---

120. Rashi thinks the issue with *pores al Shema* relates entirely to obligation. See Rashi Megillah 24a s.v. *katan* and s.v. *pores et Shema*. He thought that the issue with the priestly blessing was the indignity done to the congregation by having a minor bless them. See s.v. *ve'eino nosei et kapav*. With regard to his inability to recite the public *Amidah*, Ran on Rif Megillah 15a thinks this is an issue of obligation gap as well. By contrast, Ra'avad, cited in Responsa Rashba I:239, felt the issue was one of congregational indignity – גנאי לציבור.

1. Individual Obligation in *Kedushah, Kaddish* and *Barekhu*?

As was the case with public Torah reading, we would not naturally expect there to be an individual obligation with regard to *devarim shebikdushah*, given that these liturgical elements can *only* be said in a communal context. Not surprisingly, there is a strong strand of the tradition that denies that an individual obligation exists at all. With respect to *Kedushah*, **Rashi** is a good exemplar of this view:

מחזור ויטרי סימן מד

ועל עשרה שהתפללו כולו ושמעו קדוש' וברכו וסדר תפילה, שיכולין להימנות להמניין אחר בשביל אחד שלא התפלל... ואפילו אחד מאותן שהתפללו כבר יכול לחזור ולהתפלל להוציא את החייב, וסומך ר' ומראה פנים. מן הציבור שמתפללין י"ח כל אחד לעצמו. וחוזר וכופלו השליח ציבור בשביל קדושה. נמצא שהמתפללין נימנין לסדר המניין על הקדושה לבדה. נענה מאן דהו וא'. שמא בשביל הקדושה שלא אמרו כל אחד לעצמו הן נימנין. נמצאו עדיין מחוייבין בדבר. והשיב ר'. **לא מצינו בכל התלמוד חיוב קדושה אלא חביבה היא לנו ואינה בפחות מעשרה.**

Maḥzor Vitry 44[121]

Regarding ten people who have prayed everything and have heard *Kedushah* and *Barekhu* and the full order of prayer: They can count towards another quorum for one who has not yet prayed . . . and even one of those who has prayed already can repeat the *Amidah* to fulfill the obligation of the one still obligated. And my master [i.e., Rashi] provides support for this ruling from the fact that though the community prays the *Amidah* individually, the leader repeats it in order to say *Kedushah*. We see, therefore, that those who already prayed count towards the quorum on account of the *Kedushah* alone. Someone challenged this and said: Perhaps, in your example, they are counted towards the quorum only because they have not yet heard *Kedushah*? They are therefore still obligated and can therefore count in the *minyan*! My master responded: **We do not find anywhere in the Talmud an obligation to hear *Kedushah*; rather, it is dear to us and it cannot be said in a group of fewer than ten.**

Rashi argues that our deep attachment to *Kedushah* is essentially performative and emotional. Categorizing *Kedushah* as an obligation to be fulfilled misses the point. The same logic (and the same absence of Talmudic evidence to the contrary) would seem to extend to *Kaddish* and *Barekhu* as well.[122] A

121. For parallels to this text, see Responsa Rashi #92, Sefer HaOrah II:1129, Siddur Rashi #59 and Issur veHeter LeRashi #124. In the responsum, the argument is explicitly connected to the Massekhet Soferim text we analyzed above, n50.

122. The notion that these parts of the service are "dear" and not to be missed is reflected in

clear practical corollary to this approach is assumed by the **Mordekhai** (R. Mordekhai b. Hillel, Germany, 13th c.). He comments on Yerushalmi Megillah 4:4, which condemns those who leave a *minyan* of exactly ten people that has begun one of the rituals that requires a *minyan*. He includes an important additional clause:

מרדכי מגילה רמז תתי

ועל היוצאים **שאין מניחין שם י'** נאמר ועוזבי ה' יכלו:

Mordekhai Megillah #810

And regarding those who leave **and do not leave behind ten**, it is said: "Those who abandon the Lord shall be consumed."

Mordekhai goes out of his way to clarify that no opprobrium is attached to one who leaves a *minyan* as long as the *minyan* remains intact. **Rema OḤ 55:2** later clarifies the implications of this approach: אבל אם נשארו י' מותר לצאת/"If 10 remain, it is permitted to leave." This is true even though the rituals to which this discussion applies include *Kedushah, Kaddish* and *Barekhu*.[123] This is essentially a claim that the only obligation here is on the community as a whole, but it does not devolve on specific individuals in any way.

The practical corollary of this approach to *devarim shebikdushah* is that questions of obligation are beside the point when thinking about who is qualified to lead these parts of the service. This notion achieves clear expression in **R. Yosef Karo**'s treatment of the question of a minor leading *Arvit*, which we briefly explored above. Many communities had the practice of allowing boys under the age of 13 to lead the evening prayer on Saturday night.[124] R. Karo, in the Beit Yosef, grapples with the validity of this common practice in

---

a range of practices designed to enable latecomers who missed these parts to find a way to get a second chance to hear/say them. The earliest source of this sort is Seder Rav Amram Gaon, Siyum Hatefillah (near the end of that section), which allows for saying *Barekhu* at the end of the service for those who come late to *Shaḥarit* and even allows interrupting between the final blessing after *Shema* before the *Arvit Amidah* to do the same! This later develops into an even more robust set of practices of this sort, sometimes used to accommodate even a single straggler. For a fuller history, see Reed Blank, "The Medieval French Practice", cited above at n50.

123. Beur Halakhah 55 s.v. *aval* argues that neither Mordekhai nor Rema allow for walking out in the middle of *Kedushah* and that their discussion is not meant to refer to that ritual. But his concern relates to the impropriety of walking out in the middle of this particularly focused ritual and is not addressing the question of walking out in advance of its recitation, which Mordekhai would clearly permit.

124. As noted above, these boys were mourners, and their prayers were understood to be particularly effective for protecting the souls of the deceased. See above, n101.

the face of sources, starting with Mishnah Megillah 4:6, that unambiguously forbid a minor from serving as a *Sha"tz*.[125] Here is his analysis:

בית יוסף אורח חיים סימן נג

ומדברי רבינו ודברי המפרשים שכתבתי משמע בהדיא שקטן אינו רשאי לירד לפני התיבה אפילו באקראי בעלמא ויש לתמוה על מה שנהגו שקטן יורד לפני התיבה במוצאי שבתות להתפלל תפלת ערבית

ואפשר לומר דלא הקפידו חכמים אלא בתפלת שחרית שיש בברכת יוצר ובתפלה קדושה וגם שצריך שליח ציבור לחזור התפלה להוציא הרבים ידי חובתן וקטן כיון דלאו בר חיובא הוא אינו מוציאם כדתנן כל שאינו מחוייב בדבר אינו מוציא את הרבים ידי חובתן

ושמעתי שהרב ה"ר יוסף אבודרהם קרא תגר על מנהג זה שנהגו הקטנים לירד לפני התיבה במוצאי שבתות והסכים על ידו הרב הגדול מה"ר יצחק די ליאון ז"ל לבטל המנהג

ומצאתי להרשב"א שכתב בתשובה (ח"א סי' רלט) בשם הראב"ד דטעמא דתנן דקטן אינו פורס על שמע ואינו עובר לפני התיבה דכיון דברכות ותפלות דרבנן נינהו וקטן שהגיע לחינוך דרבנן הוי אמינא אתי דרבנן ומפיק דרבנן קמ"ל דמשום כבוד הצבור לא עבדינן גנאי הוא לצבור שהקטן מוציאן עכ"ל. ולפי טעם זה יש מקום למנהג לומר שהצבור מוחלים על כבודם ואפילו למאי דפירש רש"י דטעמא דמתניתין משום דכל שאינו מחוייב בדבר אינו מוציא את הרבים ידי חובתן איכא למימר דתפלת ערבית שאני דרשות היא.

Beit Yosef Oraḥ Ḥayyim 53

From the words of our master [the Tur] and the words of the commentators that I have recorded, it seems blatantly clear that a minor cannot lead the community in prayer, even on a happenstance basis. Therefore, the practice of having a minor lead the community in prayer at the end of Shabbat by leading the evening prayer is surprising.

But it is possible to argue that the Sages were only particular [about banning a minor from leading] regarding *Shaḥarit*, which has *Kedushah* in the first blessing before the Shema and in the *Amidah*, and during which the leader must also repeat the *Amidah* to fulfill the obligations of others. Since a minor is not obligated, he would be unable to fulfill their obligations, as it is taught, "One who is not obligated in something cannot fulfill the obligations of others" . . .

I have heard that R. Yosef Abudraham attacked this practice of allowing minors to lead the evening prayers on Saturday night and our teacher R. Yitzḥak de Leon agreed with him that the practice should be stopped.

But I found that the Rashba wrote in a responsum in the name of Ra'avad that the reason that a minor cannot lead the responsive reading of the *Shema*

---

125. The various sources that prohibit someone whose beard has not filled in from serving as *Sha"tz* only make the assumption that a minor is invalid all the more obvious. See Tosefta Ḥagigah 1:3 and Talmud Bavli Ḥullin 24b.

nor lead the community in prayer is because it would be disgraceful for the community to have a minor fulfill their obligations. Given that all blessings and prayers are only rabbinic in status and a minor who is capable of praying is also rabbinically obligated, I might have thought that one rabbinically obligated person [the minor] can fulfill the obligations of another rabbinically obligated person [an adult member of the congregation]. The Mishnah comes to teach us that we do not do this on account of *kevod tzibbur*. According to [Ra'avad's] reason, we can justify the practice by saying that the community waives its honor. And even according to Rashi, who explained the Mishnah as being based in an obligation gap, one can say that *Arvit* is different, because it is optional [and therefore no obligations need to be fulfilled].

The Beit Yosef's argument here has a number of steps. He notes the apparent problematic nature of the practice and cites several contemporary authorities who try to stop it. He nonetheless attempts to justify it in the following two ways:

1) Perhaps the Mishnah's statement of קטן ... אינו יורד לפני התיבה only applies to *Shaḥarit*,[126] where *Kedushah* is said, and where the *Amidah* is said aloud and the one saying it must be able to fulfill the obligations of others. This resolution rests on the assumption that a minor is not obligated in *tefillah* at the same level as an adult. In this justification, the Mishnah is primarily concerned about this obligation gap in the *Amidah* (Rashi is quoted to this effect at the end of the passage),[127] and some other concern about *Kedushah* (הקפידו חכמים), which does *not* have to do with obligation, but seems to be a matter of dignity or gravitas that makes it inappropriate for a minor to say *Kedushah* for the community. The concerns would then not apply to *Arvit*, where there is neither *Kedushah* nor a public *Amidah* recitation, and the communities' practice makes sense.
2) Perhaps the Mishnah's statement of קטן ... אינו יורד לפני התיבה has nothing to do with obligations. In principle, Ra'avad argued that a minor who

126. The concerns here would apply to *Minḥah* as well, but Beit Yosef is simply contrasting *Arvit* with the most problematic alternative, which is *Shaḥarit*, with its double appearance of *Kedushah*.

127. It is worth noting that in our version of Rashi, he explicitly invokes the obligation gap only as the reason why a minor cannot be פורס על שמע. Beit Yosef understood this to be the reason for both ואינו פורס על שמע and the following phrase: אין עוברין לפני התיבה. Support for this reading can be found in Ran on Rif Megillah 15a, who explicitly applies the concern about obligation to both clauses.

> knows enough is just as obligated in all the blessings and prayers as any adult, since the common source of their obligations is rabbinic authority. Therefore, Ra'avad argued that the Mishnah's concern – with respect to the leading of all services, not just *Arvit* – is one of congregational dignity. In keeping with this analysis, Beit Yosef suggested that a community might waive its dignity, which these communities elected to do for Saturday night *Arvit*.

Beit Yosef does not seem to side wholly with Ra'avad's analysis at the end, but a combination of Rashi and Ra'avad's frames can justify the specific practice he is trying to defend.[128] Two points are salient for our conversation: First, in his initial line of defense, Beit Yosef does *not* use the language of obligation to describe the obstacle to a minor leading *Kedushah*. Second, Beit Yosef never imagines that leading *Barekhu* and *Kaddish* present any concern grounded in obligation. Indeed, in his quest to justify the practice of a minor leading *Arvit*, Beit Yosef is *only* concerned about obligations relating to the *Amidah* and issues of propriety surrounding having a minor in a leadership position. For him, there is nothing to address with respect to *Barekhu* and *Kaddish*, because no individual obligation is being fulfilled. There is no individual obligation in *devarim shebikdushah*; rather, the community performs these rituals as part of public prayer and must do so in the presence of a valid *minyan*.

In the Shulḥan Arukh, R. Karo delivers his verdict:

שו"ע או"ח נג:י

יש ללמוד זכות על מקומות שנוהגים שהקטנים יורדין לפני התיבה להתפלל תפלת ערבית במוצאי שבתות.

Shulḥan Arukh OḤ 53:10

There is room to justify those places where the custom is for minors to lead *Arvit* at the end of Shabbat.

Magen Avraham (53:12) clarifies what lies behind this ruling, when he says, דהא אינו מוציא הרבים ידי חובתן דהא אין מחזירין התפלה רק שאומר קדיש וברכו – "For the minor does not fulfill the obligations of the congregants, because the *Amidah* is not recited publicly; he only says *Kaddish* and *Barekhu*."[129]

---

128. See R. Ovadiah Yosef in Responsa Yabia Omer IX OḤ #100, 4 who criticizes someone for trying to claim Beit Yosef is justifying communities where minors lead *Shaharit*, based on his use of the Ra'avad. R. Ovadiah argues that Beit Yosef only accepted Ra'avad as a supplemental justification that could coexist with Rashi and thus would only apply to *Arvit*, where no public *Amidah* is recited.

129. Note also the carefully chosen language of the Meiri on Beit Habeḥirah 23b to describe

The ramifications of this view for leadership of *devarim shebikdushah* are clear: Questions of obligation are irrelevant, since the leader does not fulfill any obligations for others when leading them in rituals like *Kaddish* and *Barekhu*. The only potential concerns are those that relate to issues of dignity, gravitas and seriousness. Following this approach would essentially return us to the discussion of *kevod tzibbur* that we explored above in the context of Torah reading. Determining whether a person could lead *devarim shebikdushah* would be no different from analyzing their effect on communal honor as a Torah reader and the practical conclusions would be the same.

However, not all authorities seem to have thought about *devarim shebikdushah* in this way. Specifically, some voices have a more nuanced approach to the question of individual obligation and *devarim shebikdushah*. Consider the following passage from **Ramban**, who argues that *devarim shebikdushah* are *communal* obligations, rather than individual ones:[130]

מלחמות ה' על רי"ף מגילה ג.

השנויים במשנתינו כולם חובות הצבור הן ואינן אלא במחויבים בדבר אבל מגילה כשם שהצבור חייב כך כל יחיד ויחיד חייב . . .

Milḥamot Hashem on Rif Megillah 3a

Those things mentioned in our Mishnah [Megillah 4:3] are all communal obligations, and they apply only to groups obligated in them,[131] but *megillah*, just as the community is obligated, so too each and every individual is obligated . . .

Ramban here is responding to a claim made by R. Zeraḥiah HaLevi, who suggested that the exclusion of the reading of the *megillah* from Mishnah Megillah 4:3, proved that it did not require a *minyan*. Ramban disagrees, arguing that the reason that act is left out of this list is not because it does not require a *minyan*, but because of the nature of its obligation. Acts such as Torah reading and the leading of communal prayer (which includes the saying of the *devarim shebikdushah*, i.e., *Barekhu*, *Kaddish*, and *Kedushah*) are not obligatory on individuals, as opposed to the reading of the *megillah*, which, even though it

the nature of *Kaddish* and *Kedushah*: כעין חובה. Meiri, in that passage, is invested in giving some obligatory status to *devarim shebikdushah* such that they will be immune from restrictions surrounding תפילת נדבה – strictly voluntary prayers. Nonetheless, he does not/will not make the case that a *bona fide* obligation is at stake when reciting them, suggesting his agreement with the approach that individualized obligation is not in play here.

130. The Ran on the Rif here cites the view of the Ramban approvingly as well.

131. This follows the reading of Ran, who interprets the phrase מחוייבים בדבר to mean a group of people who have not yet performed the ritual in question, such as *Kaddish* or *Kedushah*.

should be read with a *minyan*, remains obligatory on each individual in that community. This seems to accord well with the approach we saw in the Beit Yosef, which leaves no room for individual obligation in *devarim shebikdushah*.

But Ramban also uses the phrase מחוייבים בדבר, which suggests that those gathered *do* have some sort of obligation in *devarim shebikdushah*. The phrase clearly cannot refer to individuals being obligated in this particular act from the moment they wake up in the morning, since Ramban's entire point in this passage is to deny that such an individual obligation exists with respect to the rituals being discussed here in the Mishnah.[132] And Ramban may here mean nothing more than an obligated *community*, in the sense of a *minyan* of people who have "not yet heard" these things said, who have not yet gone through the paces of these rituals. Perhaps the language of חייב does not indicate an obligation that must be checked off, but rather a sense that the person has not yet done the action in question.[133]

Also possible, however, is that we are dealing with the sort of obligation that devolves upon the individual *when in an appropriate group*.[134] Consider the paradigm of *zimmun*: No individual is obligated to search out a group of three with which to eat a meal.[135] But once a group of three has formed, each individual possesses an obligation to participate in the communal invitation and blessing.[136] Ramban may be imagining that *devarim shebikdushah* work the same way: There is no individual obligation to participate in them – unlike the reading of the *megillah*, for example – but once in a group of ten that has not yet performed these rituals, the individuals in the group all become obligated.

Whatever the Ramban's plain meaning, there is clearly a strand running through halakhic literature that speaks about some sort of obligation in *devarim shebikdushah*.[137] Here are a few examples:

---

132. Ramban here seems to be paraphrasing an earlier formulation of this idea expressed by R. Meshullam b. Moshe in Sefer Hahashlamah on Megillah 5a in the following clear language: דכל הני דקתני במתניתין אין פורסין על שמע ליכא חיובא כלל בציר מעשרה אבל במגילה איכא ביחיד.

133. In a similar fashion, R. Hayyim Yosef David Azulai and Arokh Hashulḥan both interpret Massekhet Soferim's statement that women are "חייבות בקריאת ספר" as merely indicating that it is appropriate for them to hear the reading (Kisei Haraḥamim on Soferim 18:4; Arokh Hashulḥan YD 282:11). R. Shlomo Riskin cites these sources in his article, "Torah *Aliyot* For Women," *Meorot* (Fall 2008): 2–19, to claim that women lack an individual obligation in Torah reading. Nonetheless, he problematically and inconsistently insists that Ramban's similar language here *does* signal an individual obligation.

134. We are grateful to R. Yossi Slotnik for suggesting this line of analysis.

135. Indeed, in the case of the last meal before *Tisha B'Av*, SA OḤ 552:8 counsels against sitting in a group of three so as to avoid the creation of this *zimmun* obligation.

136. Mishnah Berakhot 7:1.

137. This strand might plausibly have drawn support from Talmud Bavli Berakhot 21b, where the Talmud entertains (and rejects) a view that even individuals might say *Kedushah*, and cites (and rejects) a view that explicitly allows for interrupting the *Amidah* in order to respond to

רש"י מגילה כד.
הוא עובר לפני התיבה - **להוציא את הצבור בקדושה** שבתפלה.

Rashi Megillah 24a
[The one who recites the *haftarah* should also be the one] who recites the public *Amidah* – **In order to fulfill the obligations of the community in *Kedushah*** in the *Amidah*.

רש"י ברכות מז:
מצוה דרבים – **להוציא רבים ידי חובתם בקדושה**.

Rashi Berakhot 47b
A *mitzvah* for multiple people/a community – **To fulfill the obligations of multiple people/a community in *Kedushah*.**

תוספות מגילה כד.
אבל אינו פורס על שמע - ואפילו לרבי יהודה דמכשיר ליה במגילה לעיל (דף יט:) הכא מודה **שלא יוציא אחרים ידי חובתן בדבר** שבקדושה

Tosafot Megillah 24a
[A minor] may not be *pores al Shema*[138] – Even R. Yehudah, who validates a minor for the reading of the *megillah* would concede here that **he should not discharge the obligations of others in a *davar shebikdushah* . . .**

חידושי הרשב"א מגילה כד.
אבל אין פורס על שמע. דכיון דאיכא דבר שבקדושה אינו בדין **שיוציא בו את הרבים ידי חובתן** . . .

Rashba Megillah 24a
[A minor] may not be *pores al Shema* – Given that there is a *davar shebikdushah*, it is not right for him **to fulfill the obligations of others** . . .

Kaddish. While none of this requires positing an individual obligation, it certainly underscores the power of these rituals and makes their later interpretation as obligations even more intelligible.

138. Above, we translated this term as "responsively reading the *Shema*," in keeping with what seems like the best interpretation of rabbinic sources. For Rashi and Tosafot, however, this term already referred to something different. When latecomers arrived at the synagogue towards the end of the service, one person would get up and say *Kaddish*, *Barekhu* and the first blessing prior to the *Shema* (which included its own form of *Kedushah*). See Rashi Megillah 23b s.v. *ein porsin*. Rashi Megillah 24a s.v. *katan* states that a minor cannot be *pores al Shema* because he is exempt and cannot fulfill the obligations of the assembled congregants. This almost certainly refers to his lack of obligation in *Shema*, as opposed to obligations in *Kaddish* and *Barekhu*; see Rashi s.v. *poheah*, where Rashi justifies a person in tattered clothing as *pores al Shema* because he is מחויב **בברכה**, indicating that the concern regarding obligation is focused on the blessing before *Shema*, not on *Kaddish* or *Barekhu*.

The plain sense of these sources is not entirely clear. In particular, Rashi here uses the language of obligation to speak about *Kedushah*, whereas the citation of him in Maḥzor Vitry was adamant that no such obligation exists. One might resolve this apparent contradiction by saying that Rashi here is using להוציא imprecisely, as we suggested with Ramban above. One might make the same claim for Tosafot and Rashba as well.[139] However one deals with the precise interpretation here, we see that minimally the *language* of obligation has begun to surface for *devarim shebikdushah* and therefore the concept, even if not fully developed here, would not be far behind.[140] Indeed, one can even see how

139. Tosafot's language might not be referring to *devarim shebikdushah* as a class of things obligatory for individuals *on account of their being devarim shebikdushah*. Rather, it might merely be using the phrase to refer to some of the specific items in this list – i.e., *Shema* and the *Amidah* – which present a problem for the minor because he is not obligated *in those specific practices*. Indeed, note the language of Meiri in Beit Habeḥirah 24a, which might even be a paraphrase of Tosafot: ואם הוא קטן ואינו ראוי להוציא את הרבים בפריסת שמע ותפלה. No mention is made of a separate problem regarding fulfilling obligations in *devarim shebikdushah* on account of them having that status. For a reading of the Tosafot in this way, see Responsa Mishpetei Uzziel III OḤ #14. Rashba's language here and in the following part of the passage sounds as if it is about the *impropriety* of allowing a minor to fulfill the obligations of others in *something else* (like the blessings of *Shema*) when a *davar shebikdushah* is involved (seemingly the *Kedushah* embedded within the first blessing of the *Shema*). This would then be opposed to a statement that it is *impossible* for a minor to fulfill another's obligation *in a davar shebikdushah*. Note also that R. Yosef Karo, despite his clear stance above that there are no issues of obligation with regard to *Barekhu* does not hesitate to use the language of להוציא in the context of *Barekhu* in OḤ 236:2. This might also be evidence for the notion that the language of להוציא could be read as "giving others the opportunity to respond" such that they can, *through their response*, fulfill the *mitzvah* of sanctifying God's name publicly. See our analysis of a passage from Shibbolei Haleket below, p. 64. Another interesting text comes from R. Eliezer b. Natan (Germany, 12th c.) in Ra'avan #73:

שו"ת ראב"ן עג

שאלני אחי ר' חזקיה הקורא בתורה למה אומר לציבור ברכו את ה' המבורך, יברך ברכת התורה ודיו. והשבתי לו לפי שעזרא תיקן לישראל שיהו קורין בתורה בב' וה' ובשבת והקורא בתורה מוציא את הציבור ידי חובתן מקריאה, לפיכך הרי הוא אומר לציבור אתם צריכין לברך ולקרות כמוני תסכימו לקריאתי ולברכתי ותברכו עמי והם עונין ומברכין. וכן ש"ץ אומר ביוצר ומעריב, **לפי שהוא מוציא את הציבור ידי חובתן ואומר להם תסכימו לקריאתי ולברכתי ותברכוהו עמי והם עונין ומברכין ויוצאין ידי חובתן** . . .

Ra'avan here discusses the function of *Barekhu* and *zimmun* as setting up the conditions for one person to fulfill the obligations of others in a ritual that is no more the leader's responsibility than it is the congregants' responsibility. In Torah reading, the designated reader is essentially an emissary for all members of the community and thus they must participate in part – by answering to *Barekhu* – in order to have their obligation fulfilled in the Torah reading itself. (This accords with the views we saw above that posit some kind of individual obligation in Torah reading.) The same is true, writes Ra'avan, for the *Barekhu* that introduces the blessings of *Shema*, where the leader – in a configuration most services no longer have today – is fulfilling the obligations of the group in those blessings. But note that the obligation spoken of here is not *Barekhu itself*, but rather some other obligation that follows. The call-and-response quality of the *devarim shebikdushah* themselves is not something described as being vicariously fulfilled. Rather, it requires participation in order to be realized. General caution is thus warranted in interpreting a phrase such as להוציא את הרבים בקדושה (or some similar variant). Such phrasing *might* refer to an individual obligation to hear *devarim shebikdushah*, it might refer to an obligation that devolves upon the individual once a group has been formed, or it might simply be language capturing the idea that the leader enables the community to fulfill its *corporate* obligation in *devarim shebikdushah*.

140. Massekhet Soferim 10:6 uses the language of individual obligation as well in the context of *Kaddish* and *Barekhu* – יצא ידי חובתו. We do not cite this text again here, however, since that

a strong desire to say *devarim shebikdushah* might have morphed – perhaps first anthropologically and later halakhically – into a more formal sense of individual obligation.

One can see this sort of thinking at work in later reinterpretations of some of the sources we looked at above. For instance, we cited above the Mordekhai's position that one may leave a *minyan* as long as ten are left behind, which seemingly indicates indifference to whether a given individual participates in *devarim shebikdushah*. This is glossed by **R. Ya'akov Lorberbaum** (Derekh HaḤayyim, Laws of Kaddish #9): יכולין הנשארים לצאת אם כבר שמעו קדושה וברכו והקדישין עד אחר עלינו – "The extras [above the quorum of ten] may leave *if they have already heard* Kedushah, Barekhu *and the* Kaddishes *up until* Aleinu."[141] This eviscerates much of the force of the Mordekhai's ruling, but gives a clear sense of the culmination of a discourse that thinks about *devarim shebikdushah* as liturgical pieces that are obligatory on the individual. This school of thought provides a contrast to the model of R. Yosef Karo that we saw above and sees an individual obligation to participate in *devarim shebikdushah*.

2. Sha"tz as agent for *Kedushah*, *Kaddish* and *Barekhu*?

Even according to this view, however, we must ask how the individual obligation is actually fulfilled. For instance, when a person hears a *berakhah* made by someone else, the individual listener has an individual obligation to respond *amen*, but in no sense is the one who makes the *berakhah* fulfilling the listener's obligation to answer *amen* just by saying the blessing. The individual obligation is fulfilled by *answering amen*, not vicariously by the person who said the blessing, nor by the *amen* of another congregant. Similarly, even if there is an individual obligation to sanctify God's name through *devarim shebikdushah*, this might well be accomplished by the individual's recitation of various phrases – such as יהא שמא רבה מברך or קדוש קדוש קדוש or ברוך ה' המבורך לעולם ועד – and not about having the *Sha"tz* perform these rituals on his or her behalf.

Indeed, consider the following passage:

שבלי הלקט ענין תפילה סימן כ

וכן מצאתי לרבינו ישעיה זצ"ל אע"ג דאמרינן שומע כעונה הני מילי בברכות אבל בקדוש ומודים

---

passage seems to be a later addition to Soferim based on the very traditions we see emerging here in Rashi and Tosafot. See Reed Blank above, n50.

141. The *Kaddishes* after *Aleinu* were generally treated as less serious and "optional."

ואמן יהא שמיה רבא שהן קלוסין חשובין לפני הקב"ה אינו יוצא ידי חובתו בשמיעה עד שמוציא בפיו עם הצבור . . .

Shibbolei Haleket Tefillah #20
And so too I found in the name of R. Yeshaya [of Trani]: Even though we normally say that one who listens [to the *berakhah* made by another] is considered as if he said it himself, that only applies to *berakhot*. But with regard to *Kedushah* . . . and *Kaddish*, which are lofty expressions of praise for God, one does not fulfill one's obligation just by listening; rather, one must actively voice the words along with the community.

This source uses the language of individual obligation to talk about *Kedushah* and *Kaddish*, but it denies that the leader can vicariously fulfill this obligation for anyone else. Indeed, this is the most straightforward way to understand the essence of the rituals of *Kedushah*, *Kaddish* and *Barekhu*. The function of the leader of these rituals is to prompt the community to sanctify God publicly together. The leader either calls on the community to bless God (in the case of *Barekhu* – ברכו את ה' המבורך) or to sanctify God (in the case of *Kedushah* and *Kaddish* – נקדש/נקדישך/יתגדל ויתקדש). The truly significant work of blessing and sanctification happens through the communal response (ברוך ה' המבורך/קדוש קדוש קדוש/יהא שמה רבה מברך), which is *not* delegated to the leader. Even if one chooses to see part of the obligation to sanctify God's name as playing out in an individual obligation in *devarim shebikdushah*, that obligation might well be about *participation* in those rituals, rather than simply being present for them while another leads, which is not the way they are structured. Among later authorities, this point was emphasized by **R. Yeḥiel Mikhael Epstein**. He engages with a ruling of the Rema that if a *Sha"tz* deliberately intends *not* to fulfill the obligations of someone in the community whom he hates, then no one's obligations are fulfilled. R. Epstein claims this law no longer applies in a community where everyone knows how to pray on their own, because the *Sha"tz* then no longer functions as an agent of individuals in the community.[142] He then addresses the objection that the *Sha"tz* would still be necessary as an agent for *devarim shebikdushah* such as *Kedushah*, *Kaddish*, and *Barekhu*:

ערוך השלחן או"ח תקפא:ה
ואי משום קדיש וקדושה וברכו אין זה יציאת חובה דכל עשרה מישראל עונין דבר שבקדושה ומי שיש בשעת מעשה עונה עמהם וכן בעניית אמן

142. This claim originates with Magen Avraham cited above, n3.

Arokh Hashulḥan OḤ 581:5

And if [you are concerned] on account of *Kaddish, Kedushah* and *Barekhu*, there is no fulfillment of obligation involved. Any group of ten Jews answers to a *davar shebikdushah*. Whoever is there answers with them. And so it is with answering *amen*.

This same line of thinking is advanced by **R. Uzziel**, who also notes its practical ramifications for our question. He noted that the very structure of *Kedushah* is such that questions of obligation play no role in determining who is fit to lead this *davar shebikdushah*. Accordingly, controlling for issues of *kevod tzibbur*, in principle a minor or woman can lead *Kedushah*, and serve as *Sha"tz* in general:

שו"ת משפטי עוזיאל כרך ג, מילואים ב

...במקום שהשומעים אומרים מלה במלה אחרי המברך והקורא אינו אלא מקריא לפניהם הדברים, הרי שהם יוצאים ידי חובתן בברכת עצמם והקורא אינו אלא מסדר הדברים פותח וחותם כל ברכה. **וכן בקדושת השם פותח דברי קדושה והקהל עונים אחריו שפיר יכול המקריא להיות קטן או אשה...**

Responsa Mishpetei Uzziel III, Miluim 2

... In a place where the listeners say each word after the one making the blessings, and the reader is only reading the words before them, they fulfill their obligations with their own blessings and the reader only sets the pace by reciting the beginning and end of each blessing. **So is it with the *Kedushah* – he opens the words of the *Kedushah* and the community answers after him – so the reader could properly be a minor or a woman ...**[143]

In a later section of this responsum, R. Uzziel objects to following through on this suggestion in practice, because he feels that letting a minor (and presumably a woman) lead would violate Baḥ's notion of *kevod tzibbur* and cannot be addressed through a simple communal waiver of that concern. That would once again return our conversation to the playing field of *kevod tzibbur* discussed in the context of Torah reading. According to the approach represented by R. Yeshaya of Trani and R. Uzziel, the individual obligation in *devarim shebikdushah* is fulfilled by each and every congregant, such that there is no need to ascertain that the leader is equally obligated. The only potentially relevant concerns are those related to congregational dignity and propriety.

Nonetheless, there are other voices that clearly advance the idea that individuals are obligated in *devarim shebikdushah* and see a critical role for

143. The logic he employs here applies equally to *Kaddish* and *Barekhu*, which have congregational responses that are structured similarly.

the *Sha"tz* in fulfilling this obligation. **R. Natan b. Yehudah** (France, 13th c.) writes that any *Kaddish* said by minors must not be an "obligatory" one, since otherwise, these children, not being "obligated," would not be able to fulfill the obligations of other individuals, based on the rule discussed above in Mishnah Rosh Hashanah 3:8:

ספר המחכים ד"ה הקורא
נר[אה] שכל אותם קדישים שאומרים קטנים לא נתקנו אלא לחנכן במצות דאי הוו חובה האיך מוציאין את הקהל, שכל שאינו מחוייב בדבר אינו מוציא אחר ידי חובתו.

Sefer Hamaḥkim s.v. *hakorei*
It seems that all the *Kaddishes* that minors say were only instituted in order to educate them in *mitzvot*. If they were obligatory, how could they fulfill the obligations of the community? Anyone who is not obligated in something cannot fulfill another person's obligation.

But these claims are rare in the *Rishonim*,[144] and the topic receives more attention from the *Aḥaronim*. For example, in the passage below, **R. Shneur Zalman of Liady** (Russia, 18th c.) expands on the discussion of the minor leading *Arvit* on Saturday night. The Shulḥan Arukh had justified this practice and Magen Avraham clarified that this justification was bound up with a theory of obligation being irrelevant for *Kaddish* and *Barekhu*. Rema, on Shulḥan Arukh OḤ 55:10, says that places that do not already have such a practice on Saturday nights should not take the initiative to institute it. This text, after quoting the Shulḥan Arukh with Magen Avraham's clarification, spells out one possible interpretation of this hesitation to fully embrace the practice:

שולחן ערוך הרב או"ח נג:יג
יש ללמד זכות על מקומות שנוהגין שהקטנים יורדים לפני התיבה להתפלל ערבית במוצאי שבתות לפי שאין מוציאין את הרבים ידי חובתן שהרי אינן מחזירין את התפלה רק שאומרים ברכו וקדיש ובמקומות שלא נהגו כן אין לקטן לעבור לפני התיבה אפילו בתפלת ערבית (משום ברכו שבה

144. Agur #334, quoting Maharil, is another example: נשאל גדול הדור מוהר"ר יעקב מולן. איך המנהג בקדיש יתום... ולמה הקטנים אומרים זה הקדיש הואיל והוא דבר שבקדושה. והשיב הרב... ונקרא זה הקדיש קדיש יתום בשביל שהקטנים שאינם יכולים להתפלל בצבור יכולים לומר קדיש זה כי נתקן בשביל המתים ולכן הקטנים יכולין לאומרו כי איננו חובה כשאר הקדישות של תפלה... One source sometimes inaccurately cited as evidence of an obligation in *devarim shebikdushah* is that of Meiri on Berakhot 45a. In discussing the difference between women's participation in *zimmun* and their participation in the reading of *megillah* and Torah, Meiri discusses a gender gap between men and women regarding obligation. However, he is discussing there the difference between men and women with regard to obligation in *zimmun* (cf. Rashi on Berakhot 45b, s.v. *de-afilu*), *not* with regard to any "obligation" in *devarim shebikdushah*. See Appendix C on *zimmun* for our full analysis of the passage in Sefer Hamikhtam on which this Meiri is based.

... ואין ברכו של תפלת שחרית וערבית דומה לברכו של קריאת התורה שקטן יכול לאמרה לפי שאינה חובה כל כך ... אבל אלו הן חובה על כל צבור לשמען שחרית וערבית) וקטן שאינו חייב אינו מוציאם ידי חובתן.

Shulḥan Arukh HaRav OḤ 53:13

There is room to justify those places where the custom is for minors to lead *Arvit* at the end of Shabbat, because they do not fulfill the obligations of others, seeing as they do not repeat the *Amidah* and merely say *Barekhu* and *Kaddish*. But in places that do not already have this practice, a minor should never lead, not even *Arvit* (because of *Barekhu* ... and the *Barekhu* of *Shaḥarit* and *Arvit* is different in this regard from the *Barekhu* of Torah reading, which a minor may say, for the latter is not really an obligation, whereas the entire community is obligated to hear the former), and a minor, not being obligated, cannot fulfill their obligations.[145]

The last part of this passage clearly approaches *devarim shebikdushah* as individual obligations that require an obligated individual to lead them on behalf of congregants. As we have noted throughout this section, this approach is hardly universal among later authorities. **R. Ovadiah Yosef** surveys the views of *Aḥaronim* who see an individual obligation in *devarim shebikdushah* but rejects them.[146] Nonetheless, for those following this line of reasoning, we would then need to ask: Do men and women have an obligation gap when it comes to *devarim shebikdushah*?

3. Are *Kedushah*, *Kaddish* and *Barekhu* gendered?

We have already seen several views that are concerned that minors do not have the appropriate level of obligation to fulfill the obligations of others (such as they are) in *devarim shebikdushah*. Does this concern related to age map on to gender as well? The simple answer is that there is no direct evidence

145. Note that Rema himself gives no reason for his desire to limit the practice, which in fact just seems to flow from R. Yosef Karo's own ambivalence, despite the fact that the latter ends up justifying it. Rema might simply be filling in what he felt was implicit in the Beit Yosef, might prefer a less convoluted reading of the Mishnah's seemingly comprehensive ban on allowing minors to lead, or he might be toeing the line on issues related to *kevod tzibbur*, cited in Beit Yosef as Ra'avad's reason why a minor cannot lead any of the *tefillot*. Shulḥan Arukh HaRav is the first to suggest that one would oppose the practice because of issues related to obligations grounded in *Kaddish* and *Barekhu*, though this is a plausible continuation of the discussion we saw in Sefer Hamaḥkim and, possibly, Massekhet Soferim, cited at n50, above. Note, however, that the distinction between different kinds of *Barekhu* posited here is explicitly rejected by Or Letziyyon II 5:14, who says that a minor may say *Barekhu* following the mourner's *Kaddish* based on the fact that he is already permitted to do so in the context of Torah reading.

146. Responsa Yabia Omer VIII OḤ 14:3–4.

suggesting that it does, even as there is no concrete record of a woman serving as a *Sha"tz* in any of the classical sources either. To the extent that *Kedushah, Kaddish,* and *Barekhu* do devolve as individual obligations, they would seem to be located under the rubric of the controlling *mitzvah* of *kiddush hashem* – the sanctification of God's name in public. Indeed, the verse ונקדשתי בתוך בני ישראל – I shall be sanctified in the midst of the Jewish people – is the scriptural anchor for these various parts of the liturgy. Rabbinic sources assume women are obligated to sanctify God's name in public in the same way that men are.[147] Minors might be unfit agents for this *mitzvah* because they are *generally* unfit as agents, because *they are minors*. There is no evidence that the blanket concern regarding obligation and maturity would translate to gender.[148]

In fact, **R. Yair Bacharach** (Germany, 17th c.) makes explicit that there is nothing gendered about *Kaddish,* arguing that the only obstacle to women saying it is custom: Women in theory can say *Kaddish,* he says, since there is universal agreement that they are obligated in martyrdom (*kiddush hashem*), which falls under the same controlling idea of sanctifying God's name as do *devarim shebikdushah* and is attached to the same set of verses:

שו"ת חות יאיר סימן רכב

שאלה דבר זר נעשה באמשטרדם ומפורסם שם. שאחד נעדר בלי בן וצוה לפני פטירתו שילמדו עשרה כל יום תוך י"ב חודש בביתו בשכרם ואחר הלימוד תאמר הבת קדיש... ולא מיחו בידה חכמי הקהילה והפרנסים. ואף כי אין ראיה לסתור הדבר כי גם אשה מצוות על קידוש השם, גם יש מנין זכרים מקרי בני ישראל... מ"מ יש לחוש שע"י כך יחלשו כח המנהגים של בני ישראל שגם כן תורה הם ויהיה כל אחד בונה במה לעצמו ע"פ סברתו... ולכן בנדון זה שיש אסיפה ופרסום יש למחות.

Responsa Ḥavvot Yair #222

Question: A strange thing happened in Amsterdam and was well publicized there. A man died without a son and he ordered before his death that ten men learn every day in his house for twelve months and after their learning his daughter should say *Kaddish*... and the sages and leaders of the community did not object. And even though there is no evidence to contradict them in this matter, for women are also commanded to sanctify the Name and there is also a quorum of males who are called "*B'nei Yisrael*"... nonetheless, we should worry that by such an act Jewish customs will be weakened... and everyone will build an altar of his own according to his own theories... therefore in this case, where the act is public we should protest.

---

147. More to the point: there is no reason one would ever have assumed that this sort of *mitzvah* was gendered. Talmud Bavli Sanhedrin 74b assumes that Esther was obligated in this *mitzvah.*

148. Put simply, no one prior to contemporary opponents of egalitarian *minyanim* suggests that women are "exempt" from *Kedushah, Kaddish* and *Barekhu.*

The logic here is clear: On the axis of obligation, there is no reason why gender should be a factor in determining who says *Kaddish*. Other factors, such as communal stability and religious propriety loomed large in Ḥavvot Yair's time, as they do today. But these factors should not be confused with matters of obligation and exemption.[149] This logic would seem to extend to all other *devarim shebikdushah* – such as *Barekhu* – which are also just manifestations of the same gender-blind command to sanctify the Divine Name in public.

The responsum of **R. Uzziel** cited earlier clarifies the non-gendered nature of *Kedushah*. Responding to a question about minors in a school leading a *minyan* that includes ten adults, R. Uzziel makes the point that the text of *Kedushah* is simply an expansion of the third *berakhah* of the *Amidah*, known as קדושת השם. Given that a woman is obligated in this *berakhah*, as she is in all other *berakhot* of the *Amidah*, how could it be that she is unable to fulfill the expanded version of this *berakhah* recited in public?

R. Uzziel argues that minors cannot so obviously fulfill the obligations of adult males in *Kedushah* (or any other part of the *Amidah*), but directly implies that women, since they are fully obligated in *tefillah*, may:

> ואל תשיבני מדתנן: נשים ועבדים וקטנים פטורין מק"ש ומן התפילין וחייבים בתפלה ומזוזה... הא למדת שקטנים חייבים בתפלה **ובכלל תפלה הוא גם קדושת ה'**, וכיון שכך מוציאים את הרבים ידי חובתם.
>
> ואין זו תשובה. שהרי פירש רש"י: דתפלה רחמי ומדרבנן היא, ותקנוה אף לנשים ולחנוך קטנים.

---

149. Some try to deflect the relevance of the Ḥavvot Yair here by suggesting that his entire discussion is about a "non-obligatory" *Kaddish* being said in a private home. (See our citation of Sefer Hamaḥkim above, p. 65, for one example of this distinction. Some later *poskim* make this distinction as well; see Responsa Beit Yehudah #22 for one example.) They read Ḥavvot Yair as if there is an introductory passage saying, "Given that this is not one of the obligatory *Kaddishes* said in the synagogue and no issues of obligation are at stake, women's obligation in *kiddush hashem* is sufficient to establish the theoretical legitimacy for them to say *Kaddish*." Suffice it to say that this is not what the Ḥavvot Yair says. In fact, it would have been much simpler for him to have made this claim, but he did not, recognizing that there is no real basis for positing a gendered obligation gap with respect to *Kaddish*. Indeed, the concern that there is no real gendered difference with regard to *Kaddish* has led some later authorities to prevent women from even saying the mourners' *Kaddish*, for fear that once this door is opened, there will be no real grounds for claiming that women cannot recite the other *Kaddishes* in the service as well. If one assumes that such an egalitarian approach to *Kaddish* is unwise and dangerous on the grounds of *kevod tzibbur* and general religious destabilization, then this is a reasonable fear. The most poignant and passionate articulation of this fear can be found in R. Ya'akov Emden's Mor Uketziah #55: ואין צריך לומר שאין הבת הקטנה מוציאה את הרבים בקדיש ואע"פ שאין צריך לצירופה מכל מקום פשיטא דאפילו גדולה לדברי הכל אינה מוציאה את הרבים ידי חובתן אף לדברי האומר שמצטרפת (ולא דמי לקטן מטעמים דאמרן וזה אין צריך לפנים. והרי גדולה מזו אמרו אפילו בברכת הזמון דחייבת בה התנו בפירוש ובלבד שלא יזמנו בשם... על אחת כמה וכמה שלא יעלה על הדעת שתעמוד בת קטנה (שאפילו בקטן דאתי לכלל מצות ושייך בה מכל מקום הדבר מפוקפק בידינו) בצבור להוציאן בדבר שבקדושה שאין למעלה ממנו מה שאפילו גדולה אינה רשאה לעשות בשום אופן ישתקע הדבר ומי שחידש מנהגים כאלו... עתיד לתן את הדין ואם לא תוגדר פרצה זו תמה אני אם לא תקרב אשה גדולה לעבור לפני התיבה גם להיות שליח צבור תבקש בכח גדול שהרי ודאי יפה כחה מקטנה (שהורע כחה בקה"ת ובזמון). See also Responsa Yaḥel Yisrael #84.

דוק ותשכח דחובת קטנים אינה אלא ממצות חנוך ואינה כחובת הנשים שחייבות כאנשים מתקנת רבנן.

> And don't respond to me from that which is taught in a Mishnah: "Women, slaves, and minors are exempt from the saying of *Shema* and from *tefillin*, but are obligated in the *Amidah* and *mezuzah* . . ." [and say based on this text:] You have learned that minors are obligated in the *Amidah* and **included in the *Amidah* is *Kedushah*.** And therefore, they may fulfill the obligations of others.
>
> For that is not a good response. After all, Rashi explained: "Prayer is a request for mercy, and it is rabbinic, and they declared it also for women and for the education of minors." You see from here that the obligation of minors is only a derivative of the general obligation in education, and it is not like the obligation of women, who are obligated like men according to the decree of the rabbis.

Though R. Uzziel in this passage rejects this proof for minors, he does not reject the assumption on which it is based, namely, that the *Kedushah* is subsumed as part of the general obligation of prayer.[150] Given that the obligation in the *Amidah* is gender-blind, so would be any obligation in the *Kedushah* that is simply an elaboration on its third blessing. The sources we have seen provide solid grounding for egalitarian practice in this area, *even if* we assume that the leader is vicariously fulfilling the individual obligations of the assembled congregants.

Again, there is no strong textual or conceptual background to any claim that tries to gender *devarim shebikdushah*. Is there any way to ground an insistence on non-egalitarian practice in this area in anything other than the concerns of dignity, propriety and religious stability that we have affirmed as relevant throughout?

We suppose it would be possible to make one of the following three claims:

---

150. A similar idea seems to lie behind the view of the Arokh Hashulḥan OḤ 69:14, cited in Yabia Omer 8:14 discussed above. The Arokh Hashulḥan argues that, while one may not read Torah unless there are ten individuals who have not yet heard it read, one may still say *Barekhu* and *Kedushah* so long as there are six present who have not yet participated in those rituals, because the latter are "ענייני תפילה שכל יחיד חייב בזה," issues related to prayer in which individuals have a distinct obligation – presumably resulting from their obligations in prayer more generally. R. Ovadiah contrasts the view of the Arokh Hashulḥan with that of the Ramban, showing that the latter clearly rejects the former's distinction between Torah reading on the one hand and *Barekhu* and *Kedushah* on the other. But in any event, the sense that *Kedushah*, at least, to the extent that it makes a claim on the individual, does so via its connection to prayer more generally, also supports the notion that, like *tefillah*, there is nothing essentially gendered about it.

1) In Ran's model of Torah reading, we explored one reading of his position that might claim that only members of the fully obligated class (free, adult men) should anchor the community's responsibility of Torah reading.[151] In the case of Torah reading, Ran saw the possibility of including women and children among the readers as dependent on their adjunct role in the proceedings. In the case of *devarim shebikdushah,* one could argue that each ritual item stands on its own, unlike the case of a subdivided, single Torah reading. One could then claim that having a female leader for any *davar shebikdushah* would put the community in the position of being represented by an adjunct member in an unacceptable way.[152] Gender equality would only follow upon making a broader claim of gender equality in *mitzvah* obligation in the contemporary world.[153]
2) Perhaps, like *zimmun,* the obligation in *devarim shebikdushah* indeed devolves upon individuals once they form a group. But perhaps this obligation only devolves upon those who are constitutive of the group in the first place. As such, if one assumes that women and minors do not count towards the *minyan,* perhaps this obligation never devolves upon them. If one couples this assumption with the idea that the *Sha"tz* then vicariously fulfills this obligation for the congregants – as opposed to prompting them to do it for themselves – one could construct a system whereby obligation plays some sort of role in barring women from leading *devarim shebikdushah.* Gender equality in this regard would then depend on the question of gender equality in the formation of a *minyan.*[154]

---

151. Note that the reading of Ran that sees the focus on the gender obligation gap in Torah study would not be relevant here, as women *are* obligated in *kiddush hashem.*

152. One could imagine an approach that would make a more modest claim and allow women to lead a minority (or at least not all) of the *devarim shebikdushah* in any given service, parallel to the distribution Ran allows in Torah reading.

153. In fact, as we noted above, n73, Tosafot Harosh Sukkah 38a s.v. *be'emet* argues that even when women share an equal obligation with men in a specific ritual, the fact that they are not maximally obligated in general makes them unfit, outside of the intimate circle of family, to serve as public communal emissaries: אפילו מיחייבי דאורייתא לא חשיבי להוציא אנשים דחשיבי טפי שחייבים בכל המצות – "Even if women are Biblically obligated [in *birkat hamazon*] they are still not important enough to fulfill the obligations of men, who are more important on account of their obligation in all *mitzvot.*" This approach essentially argues that the scope of one's religious obligation, not social standing, ultimately determines a person's capacity for communal, ritual leadership. (Whether it is tenable or coherent for there to be a gap between those two is a worthy question in its own right. See below, Part Two, n78–83.) One could easily imagine applying this concern to minors leading parts of the service, even if issues of obligation were addressed.

154. If one followed all the (uncertain) assumptions needed to get this sort of argument off the ground, one might draw further support from views on מאירה that we explored above in our discussion of Mishnah Sukkah 3:10 in n84–96 and in n96. Passages in various Tosafot reveal an understanding of מאירה that is focused on the indignity of an obligation gap even when the congregants are not relying on the leader to fulfill their obligations. If the person leading is not

3) One could take a piecemeal approach to *devarim shebikdushah* and claim that some are gender equal and some are not. Specifically, one could make the claim that *devarim shebikdushah* follow the status of the rituals in which they are embedded. *Kedushah* in the *Amidah*, which is itself gender equal, would be gender-blind. The *Barekhu* of Torah reading might be theoretically gender blind, but the *Barekhu* introducing the blessings of *Shema* – which are themselves gendered – might itself be gendered.[155] This position is somewhat awkward and requires dividing between things that seem very much the same.

We offer these thoughts not by way of undermining our arguments above, but in an effort to make sense of as wide a range of approaches as possible. In particular, there is some sense to the first possibility suggested here, which is that communities should only allow themselves to be publicly represented and led in holy matters by those who bear a maximal load of ritual responsibility. We confess to not finding the second and third suggestions here very convincing. Such theories are also not truly necessary. There is a very solid basis for maintaining non-egalitarian practice with respect to leadership of the parts of the service that require a *minyan* of ten: *kevod tzibbur*. While we discussed the solid ground for waiving or reassessing this concern in the contemporary world, it is surely intelligible (aside from whether it is plausible or objectionable) that a community would maintain that *kevod tzibbur* remains a live concern with gendered ramifications today. There is no need to run away from that conversation by forcing the creation of gender obligation gaps in *devarim shebikdushah* that are not clearly supported by traditional sources.

Summary

Devarim shebikdushah, such as Torah reading, *Barekhu*, *Kaddish*, and *Kedushah*, need to be said in a *minyan*. There is no explicit discussion in classic sources over who is fit to lead most of these rituals, such as *Barekhu*, *Kaddish*, and *Kedushah*. There *is* discussion over who is fit to perform one of the items on the Mishnah's list, namely, Torah reading. The Talmud states that in

religiously accountable for the ritual they are performing, the dignity of the proceedings suffers. Perhaps one could argue that this would extend to allowing someone to lead who is not able (and not responsible) to make up the *minyan*. That would hardly be a position commanding wide agreement; we saw many sources in our discussion that quite clearly rejected such a correlation between *minyan* membership and the ability to lead the *minyan*.

155. Such a position might make a bit more sense of Shulḥan Arukh HaRav's claim that one cannot extrapolate from the *Barekhu* of Torah reading to the *Barekhu* of *Shema*, though his language does not sound like he is advancing this sort of argument.

principle, women may do so, but adds that the Sages said that women should not read because of "the honor of the community," understood by several *Rishonim* to mean that men would be humiliated by the implication that they are incapable and must rely on a woman. Authorities split over whether individual communities may waive concern for their honor. There is solid basis for endorsing such a waiver. Even those who think such honor is objective and not subject to communal discretion might reassess whether it applies in contemporary society. If there is no longer any affront to communal honor via women's public performance of important communal duties, this concern may simply no longer be in play, such that the question of its potential waiver is no longer relevant.

We also explored the specific cases of *Kedushah, Kaddish* and *Barekhu*. We demonstrated the viability of a position that denies that obligation is relevant at all, as codified in the Shulḥan Arukh and Magen Avraham's explanation thereof. Even among those who spoke of individualized obligation, we demonstrated the strand of thought that sees this obligation as being fulfilled through the participation of each individual in these communal rituals. Finally, even working with a model of vicarious fulfillment, there is no reason to assume a gender gap with respect to these rituals: As Ḥavvot Yair and Mishpetei Uzziel make clear, these rituals are rooted in the obligations to sanctify God's name (*kiddush hashem*) and to pray (*tefillah*), in which women have equal obligation.

Nonetheless, the Ran's approach to Torah reading might provide useful insight into those who are firmly committed to non-egalitarian leadership of the service. One might claim that until there is broader equality between men and women in *mitzvot* more generally, having a gender-blind practice is no different than opening up the *bimah* to children in a way that might well be forbidden and inappropriate. As we have said repeatedly, we by no means see this as a *necessary* reading of the sources, and many great authorities (R. Tam, R. Yosef Karo) clearly do not accept it. But we respect this view, which does find some support in the *Rishonim*,[156] and will say more about how to address it later on.[157]

However we address the concerns of obligation (or lack thereof), the heart of our conversation will also always return to the issue of *kevod tzibbur*; just as communal honor limits the pool of appropriate Torah readers, so too it will shape who is fit to assume communal leadership of other prayers. We surveyed that question above and it has been dealt with at length elsewhere.[158]

---

156. See n153.
157. Below, Part Two, n78–83.
158. Even when the concerns are not described with the technical term of *kevod tzibbur*, issues of honor, dignity and propriety continue to surface in various forms. Another halakhic

Beyond that, the question is one of custom and stability: What seemed reasonable (or at least not worthy of controversy) to the rabbis of Amsterdam seemed radical and destabilizing to the Ḥavvot Yair. The same disputes abound today; many contemporary communities that address these questions worry that a greater degree of egalitarianism in the synagogue does and will correlate with general laxity with regard to *mitzvot*. Others argue precisely the opposite: Against a broader social backdrop of gender equality, any service that is *not* egalitarian will risk driving people away from committed Jewish practice. The real argument, therefore, is over the extent to which women assuming the role of *Sha"tz* destabilizes widespread custom. One must weigh the risks of such destabilization against the religious risks of excluding women living in a social environment that grants them access to even the highest corridors of power.

Precisely such an argument led **R. Ahron Soloveichik** (United States, 20th c.) to cite the Ḥavvot Yair as support for his ruling permitting (and requiring permission for) women to say *Kaddish* in the synagogue. While the threat in the time of the Ḥavvot Yair was, in his view, the dissolution of the unified Jewish community, R. Soloveichik felt the greater risk in his own day to be the temptations of heterodoxy, such that contemporary Orthodoxy's mission was to permit participation by women to the extent possible while retaining maximal allegiance to tradition among the Jewish population:

עוד ישראל יוסף בני חי סימן לב

ועיין בתשובות חוות יאיר ... שכתב שאם אין למת בן רק בת ... מצד עיקר הדין הבת יכולה לומר קדיש אלא שלא תעשה כן שעל ידי זה יתחלשו מנהגי ישראל וכיון דאיכא פרסום יש למחות. ונראה עכשיו שכמה אנשים ונשים מישראל לוחמים בעד שווי הנשים לעומת האנשים ביחס עם עליות בשביל הנשים א"כ אם הרבנים החרדים ימנעו אשה מלומר קדיש במקום שישנה אפשרות שע"י זה תתרבה ההשפעה של הרבנים השמרנים והריפורמים אז אסור למנוע בת מלומר קדיש.

Od Yisrael Yosef Beni Ḥai #32

See Responsa Ḥavvot Yair . . . where he wrote that if the deceased has no son, but only a daughter . . . according to the essence of the law, the daughter may say *Kaddish*. However, she should not do so because this will lead to

discussion of this sort is articulated in the terms of זילא מילתא, the notion that a certain protocol is beneath one's dignity. The language of זילא מילתא is used by Tosafot Sukkah 38a s.v. *be'emet* to describe Halakhot Gedolot's objection to women reading *megillah* for men in public. This concern functions independently of obligation; even when a woman is equally obligated to a man, such considerations can apply. For the application of such considerations to *Kiddush* on Shabbat, see Rahel Berkovits, "Women's Obligation in *Kiddush* of Shabbat", from *Ta Shma: The Halakhic Source Guide Series*, JOFA 2008 and the sources cited there. These issues, like *kevod tzibbur*, must be addressed based on the social context that they are designed to respond to. Cf. Ra'avad's discussion of the reasons why a minor cannot lead prayers for an adult even when they share an equal obligation. See above n102, n120 and n128.

the weakening of Jewish practice and since the case was public, one should object.

It seems that today, when there are many Jewish men and women fighting for gender equality with respect to *aliyot* for women, if Orthodox rabbis prevent a woman from saying *Kaddish* in a context where it is possible that this will lead to increased influence of Conservative and Reform rabbis, it is forbidden to prevent a daughter from saying *Kaddish*.[159]

In addition to these considerations of stability and custom, contemporary opposition to women's inclusion in communal prayer roles may reflect political concerns regarding broader social boundary issues. Indeed, in a 2004 responsum, R. Yehuda Herzl Henkin opined that nowadays the reason to restrict women from having *aliyot* to the Torah is not communal honor, but as a bulwark against assimilation:

שו"ת בני בנים ד:ג

... היום שרק הבעל־קורא קורא בתורה ואילו העולים לתורה מברכים אבל אינם קוראים אם כן בטל ענין כבוד הצבור ... וכתבתי כמה פעמים שלדעתי עיקר איסור עליות נשים היום אינו משום כבוד צבור אלא משום שהן פתח למתבוללים.

Responsa Benei Banim IV:3

... Today, when the reader reads Torah, whereas those with *aliyot* to the Torah say the blessings but do not read, the whole matter of communal honor is irrelevant ... I have written several times that in my opinion the essence of the prohibition on giving *aliyot* to women today is not on account of communal honor, but because they are an opening to assimilationists.

Similarly, in his response to R. Mendel Shapiro's aforementioned article, R. Henkin concludes his opposing argument as follows:[160]

Where does all this leave us? Regardless of the arguments that can be proffered to permit women's *aliyot* today – that *kevod hatzibbur* can be waived, that it does not apply today when everyone is literate, that it does not apply when the *olim* rely on the (male) *ba'al keriah* and do not themselves read – women's *aliyot* remain outside the consensus, and a congregation that

---

159. The denominational assumptions in this passage remain a matter of lively dispute today. We cite R. Soloveichik here not as an endorsement of his specific concern but for his sensitivity to the ways in which Ḥavvot Yair's concerns may play out very differently in different times and places.

160. See R. Henkin's comments in his responses to R. Shapiro's article, cited in Introduction, n1.

> institutes them is not Orthodox in name and will not long remain Orthodox in practice. In my judgment, this is an accurate statement now and for the foreseeable future, and I see no point in arguing about it.

In these two passages, R. Henkin is discussing only the issue of *aliyot* for women; nevertheless, similar considerations animate discussions of other issues of gender in synagogue life, even if they are not explicitly acknowledged. Of course, these assessments are subjective and often controversial: R. Henkin's concern with certain practices being outside of the Orthodox consensus is less of a concern for R. Daniel Sperber, who has emerged as a forceful advocate for women's *aliyot* in the context of Orthodox communities. Some communities may well evaluate that maintaining difference from non-Jews or from self-defined heterodox Jewish groups trumps many local, internal issues. In their estimation, blurring those boundaries may lead to other more serious problems than those caused by unnecessary exclusion of women. Our own sense is that, in many communities, the exclusion of women from public roles poses a great risk to the ongoing stability and vitality of Torah in an increasingly egalitarian world. We approach our own leanings on these questions of communal honor, dignity and stability with a sense of humility and hope others will have similar honesty and transparency to do the same.

PART TWO

Counting in a *Minyan*

I. BIBLICAL AND CLASSICAL RABBINIC SOURCES

The number ten has ancient significance as a figure signifying a quorum. For example, in **Rut 4:2**, ten elders are assembled for the legal procedure of enacting a kinsman's redemption or relinquishing an inheritance claim: וַיִּקַּח עֲשָׂרָה אֲנָשִׁים מִזִּקְנֵי הָעִיר וַיֹּאמֶר שְׁבוּ פֹה וַיֵּשֵׁבוּ – "And he took ten men from the elders of the city and said, 'Sit here,' and they sat." Non-rabbinic sources also prominently feature ten as the minimum needed for a quorum in various communal settings.[1] The Sages found ways to connect this number back to verses in the Torah itself. In **Mishnah Sanhedrin 1:6**, we see that the term עדה/community, which is used by the Torah to describe a judging body, is understood to be represented by a panel of ten:

משנה סנהדרין א:ו

ומנין לעדה שהיא עשרה, שנאמר: "עַד מָתַי לָעֵדָה הָרָעָה הַזֹּאת" (במדבר יד:כז), יצאו יהושע וכלב.

Mishnah Sanhedrin 1:6

How do we know that an *edah* [a term evoked in Bemidbar 35:24–25 as a judicial unit] is ten? As it says, "Until when will I have to bear this evil *edah* [referring to the spies, who were twelve in number], and Yehoshua and Kalev do not count [because they brought back a good report, leaving ten]...

1. For two examples, see the Damascus Document, col. X, and the Community Rule, col. VI. See S. Metso, "Whom Does the Term Yaḥad Identify?" in *Defining Identities: We, You, and the Other in the Dead Sea Scrolls*, F. Garcia Martinez and M. Popovic, eds., 2007.

This Mishnah identifies the traditional number of ten as the minimum number that could plausibly be called an עדה/community. It grounds this in the use of the term עדה to refer to the ten spies (of the twelve total) who brought back a negative report of the land of Israel to Moshe (as told in Bemidbar 13–14). This wicked group is (the smallest group) called an עדה in the Torah, thus establishing other uses of the term עדה – as in the context of the judging court mentioned in Bemidbar 35 – as referring to a minimum of ten people.

Mishnah Megillah 4:3, without any recourse to supporting verses or justification, requires ten for a variety of functions, including the repetition of the *Amidah* and Torah reading:[2]

משנה מגילה ד:ג

אין פורסין את שמע, ואין עוברין לפני התבה, ואין נושאין את כפיהם, ואין קורין בתורה, ואין מפטירין בנביא, ואין עושין מעמד ומושב, ואין אומרים ברכת אבלים ותנחומי אבלים וברכת חתנים, ואין מזמנין בשם, פחות מעשרה. ובקרקעות, תשעה וכהן. ואדם, כיוצא בהן:

Mishnah Megillah 4:3

We do not responsively recite the *Shema*, nor have a communal prayer leader, nor offer the priestly blessing, nor read Torah, nor read from the prophets, nor perform the standing/sitting [ritual for the dead], nor say the blessing of the mourners nor the formal comforting the mourners, nor recite the wedding blessings, nor say *zimmun* with the Name in a group of fewer than ten. And when redeeming land we require nine and a *kohen*. And so too with [redeeming] people.

Strikingly, this text does not specify who is eligible to count as one of the ten. All we can infer is that, except for the evaluation of land, there is no need for one of the ten to be a priest.[3] But what other limits are there on the constitution of this group? The Mishnah's silence on this point only reinforces the idea that we are dealing with a preexisting notion of a quorum that has certain assumed protocols that are not fully spelled out here.

Later texts attempt to ground the quorum of ten required for these rituals in verses, by trying to extract meaning from the verse ונקדשתי בתוך בני ישראל – "I shall be sanctified in the midst of the children of Israel." This verse from Vayikra 22:32 is understood to be the scriptural anchor for the sacred rituals requiring a *minyan* listed in Mishnah Megillah. The term *devarim shebikdushah*,

2. We explored this mishnah in greater depth above and saw how later sources clarify that *Kedushah*, *Kaddish* and *Barekhu* are also among the rituals that require a group of ten.

3. The requirement for a priest has echoes in non-rabbinic literature as well. See above, Introduction, n1.

applied to many of the rituals in this list, is understood to be a manifestation of the broader *mitzvah* to sanctify God's name in public. Texts in the Talmud Yerushalmi and the Talmud Bavli attempt to cross-reference the language of this verse with other verses in order to justify the necessity of a quorum of ten:

ירושלמי מגילה ד:א/דף עד עמוד ג

אמ' ר' סימון נאמר כאן "**תוך**" ונאמר להלן "וַיָּבֹאוּ בְּנֵי יִשְׂרָאֵל לִשְׁבֹּר **בְּתוֹךְ** הַבָּאִים" (בראשית מב:ה). מה "תוך" שנאמר להלן עשרה, אף כאן עשרה. אמר ליה רבי יוסה בי רבי בון, אם מ"תוך" את למד סגין אינון! אלא נאמר כאן "בני ישראל" ונאמר להלן "**בני ישראל**" מה להלן עשר' אף כאן עשרה.

Yerushalmi Megillah 4:1, 74c

Said R. Simon: It says here, "**in the midst**" (*tokh*) and it says there,[4] "And *benei yisrael* came to get grain **in the midst** (*tokh*) of those coming"; just as *tokh* there signifies ten, so here too it is ten. Said to him R. Yose b. R. Bun: If you derive it from *tokh*, there will be too many![5] Rather, it says here "*benei yisrael*" and it says there "*benei yisrael*"; just as there it refers to ten, so here too it refers to ten.

This passage in the Yerushalmi picks up on linguistic affinities between the verse in Vayikra and another verse in Bereishit which describes the descent of the *ten* children of Israel (the man, i.e., Jacob) to Egypt in the midst of all the others seeking food during the famine.[6] Whether through use of the common word תוך/"in the midst," or the use of בני ישראל/"The children of Israel" in a verse speaking about only ten people, these scriptural arguments aim to prove that the verse ונקדשתי בתוך בני ישראל applies to groups of at least ten.

The Talmud Bavli features a slightly different and more complex derivation:

תלמוד בבלי מגילה כג:

מנא הני מילי?

אמר רבי חייא בר אבא אמר רבי יוחנן: דאמר קרא "וְנִקְדַּשְׁתִּי בְּתוֹךְ בְּנֵי יִשְׂרָאֵל" (ויקרא כב:לב) – כל דבר שבקדושה לא יהא פחות מעשרה.

מאי משמע?

דתני רבי חייא: אתיא "תוך" – "תוך": כתיב הכא "וְנִקְדַּשְׁתִּי **בְּתוֹךְ** בְּנֵי יִשְׂרָאֵל", וכתיב התם, הִבָּדְלוּ **מִתּוֹךְ** הָעֵדָה (במדבר טז:כא), ואתיא "עדה" – "עדה", דכתיב התם, "עַד מָתַי לָעֵדָה הָרָעָה הַזֹּאת" (במדבר יד:כז), מה להלן עשרה – אף כאן עשרה.

4. Bereishit 42:5.

5. Meaning, "those coming" were many more than ten. A term more clearly referring to ten people is required.

6. Benjamin was left back in Canaan (Bereishit 42:4). Joseph, of course, was in Egypt.

Talmud Bavli Megillah 23b

How do we know this [that we need a quorum of ten]?

Said R. Ḥiyya b. Abba said R. Yoḥanan: The verse says: "And I will be sanctified in the midst of the children of Israel" (Vayikra 22:32) – any *davar shebikdushah* shall not be said with fewer than ten.

What suggests this?

R. Ḥiyya taught in a *baraita*: We derive it from the double usage of "midst": It says here, "And I will be sanctified **in the midst** of the children of Israel," and it says there, "separate yourselves out **from the midst** of this *congregation*" (Bemidbar 16:21); and then we derive it from the double usage of "congregation", it says there, "How long must I suffer this evil *congregation*" (Bemidbar 14:27): Just as there it refers to ten, so here too it refers to ten.

Here we have an unusual double association that produces the expected outcome. Like the Yerushalmi, this text begins with the double appearance of תוך/in the midst. But here, the association points us not to the Jacob/Joseph narratives, but to a verse taken from Bemidbar's telling of Koraḥ's rebellion. That verse on its own has no context of ten, but it features *both* the term תוך *and* the term עדה, allowing us to return to the text about the ten spies who return an evil report. Through these two steps, we once again have an anchor for the number ten being the minimum required to trigger the relevance of Vayikra 22:32.[7]

Neither text gives us much further insight into who qualifies to make up this group of ten. That discussion is anchored around Mishnah Berakhot 7:2, which more broadly also engages the question of *zimmun,* the invitation to a joint blessing after eating a meal. Mishnah Berakhot 7:2 states: נשים ועבדים וקטנים אין מזמנין עליהם – "One does not make a *zimun* with women, slaves and minors." The interpretation of this text has a complex history; we will not go into it here.[8] The quorum spoken of here is a quorum of three, with a likely

7. This sort of doubled *gezerah shavah* is so unusual that it seems plausible that something like the following happened: A tradition regarding the double usage of תוך came to Babylonia from Eretz Yisrael. Perhaps it arrived without specifying what other verse was referred to, perhaps it arrived with the challenge we see lodged against the use of תוך in the Yerushalmi itself, perhaps the Babylonian Sages who received it could not imagine grounding a ritual practice in a verse prior to the giving of *mitzvot* at Sinai. One way or the other, it is easy to imagine how a prior midrash involving תוך would inspire a search to connect it to the rock solid association of ten with עדה found in the Mishnah. With these two building blocks in place, the structure was completed by locating a verse containing both תוך and עדה to serve as the bridge. The doubled *gezerah shavah* may thus make more sense as connecting two prior traditions rather than as an original quest to wend such a complex path through the Torah's language.

8. For one summary and analysis, see: י. גרשון, "שלש דעות מזמנות: לשאילת צירופן של נשים לזימון בחוג המשפחה", *אקדמות* כו (תשע"א): 7–23. See also ד. קורן, "על שיטת ר' יהודה הכהן בעניין צירוף נשים לזימון עם גברים", *מילין חביבין* ה (תשעא): כו–נ. Koren argues there that this text only precludes a *zimmun* that

extension as well to the quorum of ten referred to in Mishnah Megillah 4:3 for the *zimmun* that incorporates God's name. This text is obviously situated in the context of a shared meal and may well present concerns that are not relevant to the context of prayer. Specifically, concerns regarding joint meals between men and women in general may well be behind the Mishnah's rule with respect to a mixed-gender *zimmun*.[9] In any event, this mishnah is the anchor for **Berakhot 47b–48a**'s broader discussion of various traditions that attempt to define our quorum of ten more precisely:

תלמוד בבלי ברכות מז:-מח.
אמר רבי יוסי: קטן המוטל בעריסה מזמנין עליו.
והא תנן: נשים ועבדים וקטנים אין מזמנין עליהם!
הוא דאמר כרבי יהושע בן לוי, דאמר רבי יהושע בן לוי: אף על פי שאמרו קטן המוטל בעריסה אין מזמנין עליו – אבל עושין אותו סניף לעשרה.

ואמר רבי יהושע בן לוי: תשעה ועבד מצטרפין.
מיתיבי: מעשה ברבי אליעזר שנכנס לבית הכנסת ולא מצא עשרה, ושחרר עבדו והשלימו לעשרה;
שחרר אין, לא שחרר לא!
תרי אצטריכו, שחרר חד ונפיק בחד . . .

אמר רב הונא: תשעה וארון מצטרפין.
אמר ליה רב נחמן: וארון גברא הוא?
אלא אמר רב הונא: תשעה נראין כעשרה מצטרפין . . .

אמר רבי אמי: שנים ושבת מצטרפין.
אמר ליה רב נחמן: ושבת גברא הוא?
אלא אמר רבי אמי: שני תלמידי חכמים המחדדין זה את זה בהלכה מצטרפין . . .

אמר רבי יוחנן: קטן פורח מזמנין עליו.
תניא נמי הכי: קטן שהביא שתי שערות מזמנין עליו, ושלא הביא שתי שערות – אין מזמנין עליו . . .

Talmud Bavli Berakhot 47b-48a
Said R. Yose: One makes a *zimmun* with a child resting in a cradle.

---

includes a *combination* of women, slaves and/or minors. As Koren herself points out, Talmud Bavli Berakhot 47b clearly understood the ban on counting minors to be absolute, not only operative in the context of counting women and slaves at the same time. Nonetheless, Koren advances her reading in part to explain the otherwise puzzling view of the medieval sage R. Yehudah HaKohen, who permitted a joint *zimmun* between men and women.

9. Other *zimmun*-specific issues may be at work as well, including a potential gender obligation gap in the blessing after a meal. See גרשון, "שלש דעות מזמנות," 9–19.

But doesn't the Mishnah say: "One does not make a *zimmun* with women, slaves and minors?"
[R. Yose] follows the view of R. Yehoshua b. Levi, for R. Yehoshua b. Levi said: Even though they said one does not make a *zimmun* with a child resting in a cradle, we do make him an adjunct to the ten.

And said R. Yehoshua b. Levi: Nine and a slave combine.
They challenged this from a *baraita*: "Once R. Eliezer came to the synagogue and did not find ten; he freed his slave and completed the quorum of ten."
He was only able to do so because he freed him, but an unfreed slave would not [have counted]!
They must have needed two; he freed one and counted one . . .

. . . Said R. Huna: Nine and an ark combine.
R. Naḥman said to him: Is an ark a person?
Rather, R. Huna said: Nine, when they look like ten, combine. . . .

Said R. Ami: Two and Shabbat combine.
R. Naḥman said to him: Is Shabbat a person?
Rather, R. Ami said: Two scholars who sharpen one another with [words of] *halakhah* combine . . .

Said R. Yohanan: One makes a *zimmun* with a "flowering" minor.
This is also taught in a *baraita*: One makes a *zimmun* with a minor with two hairs [that indicate the onset of puberty], but not with one who has not . . .

This text jumps back and forth freely between discussions of quorums of three and ten, among the categories of people, objects and times, as well as between the contexts of *zimmun* and prayer. Our passage begins with R. Yose allowing one to count an infant towards a *zimmun*. The gemara notes that this seemingly stands in direct contradiction to the Mishnah, which excludes minors (and certainly infants) from those who are counted towards a *zimmun*. The gemara deflects the challenge, by citing a view of R. Yehoshua b. Levi and molding R. Yose's statement to fit it: While an infant is not counted towards a *zimmun* of three (per the Mishnah), a baby may serve as an adjunct[10] to the quorum needed for a *zimmun* of ten, the ritual referred to in Mishnah Megillah 4:3.

10. It is not clear what is meant by סניף/adjunct here. Most commentators understood this to refer to counting a single infant along with nine adults. This approach is strengthened by assuming congruency with R. Yehoshua b. Levi's statement permitting a slave to join with nine free people. R. Tam argued for this reading, as we will see below. This reading seems to have been the original historical meaning of R. Yehoshua b. Levi; see Bereishit Rabbah 91:3. Others read the term סניף more broadly. See R. Ya'akov of Marvege in Responsa Min HaShamayim #53, who holds that two minors can be counted according to this view. R. Zeraḥiah HaLevi pushes

The passage continues with a statement by R. Yehoshua b. Levi that permits nine free people to join with a slave to form a quorum of ten. On its own, this might be a statement about *zimmun*, with no consequences one way or the other for prayer.[11] But once the sugya challenges it from the story about R. Eliezer in the synagogue, it is clear that we are meant to understand it as applying to prayer (as well). The sugya construes R. Eliezer's actions such that they do not conflict with R. Yehoshua b. Levi (i.e. there were two slaves in the story), leaving us with a viable position that counts a single slave towards the quorum of ten required for saying *zimmun* with God's name and for prayer. R. Huna continues this section on prayer, allowing the Ark in the synagogue to complete the quorum along with nine people. When this is dismissed as outrageous, R. Huna is cited for another proposal: When nine people look like ten, they can form a quorum.[12]

The sugya then returns[13] to play with the boundaries of the quorum for the *zimmun* of three. R. Ami allows a *zimmun* of two on Shabbat, counting the sacred day itself as the third. When this is dismissed as outrageous, R. Ami is cited for another proposal: Two scholars who are learning *halakhah* intensely during their meal are sufficient to form a quorum on their own. R. Yoḥanan then adds that the exclusion of minors from *zimmun* only applies to those not displaying the physical signs of puberty, and a *baraita* is cited to confirm this point.

What does this text tell us about the quorum of ten and who can count towards it? The story involving R. Eliezer assumes that slaves do not count equally in the *minyan* for prayer, as does R. Yehoshua b. Levi's second tradition, even as the latter allows for counting a single slave towards the quorum of ten. His language of סניף/adjunct also indicates that minors are not counted as equals towards the quorum of ten in *zimmun*. There is little reason to think he would include them any more broadly for quorum for prayer.

The gemara does not here or elsewhere spell out why minors and slaves are normally excluded nor why they might be included in these liminal situ-

---

the logic even further in Maor on Rif Berakhot 35b, allowing for counting up to four minors, since they are still a minority of the ten and can therefore be classified as adjuncts to the group. See Bereishit Rabbah 91:3 for an analogue to this sort of ruling. He clarifies that this is only true for minors, but that R. Yehoshua b. Levi clearly would not have counted more than one slave.

11. As we noted, we cannot tell from Mishnah Berakhot 7:2 alone whether its concerns about women, slaves and minors in the context of *zimmun* transfer entirely, partially or not at all to the realm of *tefillah*.

12. The gemara reports views that this may be when they are standing especially close together, or especially spread out.

13. In fact, the prior statement may already begin to return the conversation to *zimmun*. In Bereishit Rabbah 91:3, R. Asi is quoted as permitting nine that look like ten to form a *zimmun*, suggesting that this tradition might be about both contexts.

ations. It is possible that the latter section of this passage suggests that there was a tendency to "cheat" on the last member of the *minyan*, effectively considering nine to be like ten. In any event, these various lenient rulings were controversial, and our printed text of the gemara here ends with a rejection of these various statements: ולית הילכתא ככל הני שמעתתא – "The *halakhah* does not follow any of these traditions." While this legal rejection is in fact a later Geonic gloss that was added to the text,[14] it reveals that even toying with the margins of the definition of *minyan* was controversial.

An additional relevant passage engages another facet of the commandment to sanctify God's name: The obligation to martyr oneself when forced to violate certain *mitzvot* in certain contexts. The gemara reports a series of decisions that held that one must martyr oneself before violating *any mitzvah* in public, which is defined as a group of ten:

תלמוד בבלי סנהדרין עד.–עד:

וכמה פרהסיא? – אמר רבי יעקב אמר רבי יוחנן: אין פרהסיא פחותה מעשרה בני אדם. פשיטא, ישראלים בעינן, דכתיב: ונקדשתי בתוך בני ישראל. בעי רבי ירמיה: תשעה ישראל ונכרי אחד מהו? תא שמע, דתני רב ינאי אחוה דרבי חייא בר אבא: אתיא תוך תוך, כתיב הכא "ונקדשתי בתוך בני ישראל" וכתיב התם "הבדלו מתוך העדה הזאת" (במדבר ט"ז) מה להלן עשרה וכולהו ישראל – אף כאן עשרה וכולהו ישראל.

Talmud Bavli Sanhedrin 74a–b

And how many [people] form a public collection [such that a person is obligated in martyrdom because of the presence of a public collection – *parhesiya*]? Said R. Yaakov said R. Yoḥanan: "A *parhesiya* cannot be fewer than ten people." Obviously, we require Jews [for this number], as it says, "And I will be sanctified in the midst of *benei yisrael*." R. Yirmiyah asked: "Nine Jews and one non-Jew – what is the law?" Come and learn what R. Yannai the brother of R. Ḥiyya taught: We derive it from the double usage of "midst": It says here, "And I will be sanctified **in the midst** of the children of Israel," and it says there, "separate youseleves out **from the midst** of this congregation" (Bemidbar 16:21). Just as there all ten are Jews, also here all ten must be Jews.

The gemara here explores the margins of the quorum of ten for martyrdom, taking it as obvious that non-Jews are not primary members of this group. Nonetheless, **R. Yirmiyah** asks whether a Gentile could be the tenth member of a group triggering the obligation of martyrdom. The gemara then rejects

14. For confirmation of this point, see Otzar Hageonim Berakhot Teshuvot #314–316.

this possibility and insists that all ten members of the group must be Jews, invoking the Jewish identity of all ten of the wicked spies.

Neither of these passages weighs in on the question of whether women count toward the quorum of ten. It is hard to know whether the passage in Berakhot would take it for granted that women are included in the concept of *minyan* and therefore it explores only the cases of slaves and minors, or whether the total exclusion of women from *minyan* is so obvious that the liminal roles explored for these other groups are not even entertained for them. Though the Talmud's citation of Mishnah Berakhot 7:2 shows that a *zimmun* of three is not gender-blind,[15] we cannot tell from this passage what ramifications, if any, that has for the quorum of ten mentioned in Mishnah Megillah 4:3.[16] The passage in Sanhedrin would seem to push us in the former

15. When the Talmud on Berakhot 47b uses Mishnah Berakhot 7:2 to eliminate the possibility of counting a single minor towards a *zimmun* of three, it clearly reads the Mishnah as forbidding even a single member of the three classes mentioned to join in with free, adult males to make that *zimmun*. Almost all *Rishonim*, with the exception of R. Yehudah HaKohen and a few others, read the Mishnah in this way as well. See above, n8, for Koren's argument that the original meaning of the Mishnah is that women and men may in fact make a *zimmun*; only groups of women, slaves and minors are precluded from forming. We are less sure. Her evidence from Talmud Bavli Arakhin 3a presumes that all individuals fully obligated in *zimmun* can join to form a *zimmun* with all other similarly obligated individuals. This may not be the case; men and women might be fully equal in their obligations and nonetheless be forbidden from forming the core quorum of *zimmun* with one another. Nonetheless, R. Yehudah HaKohen's position must indeed be explained, and perhaps he felt that the dismissal of the legally binding nature of much of the material on Berakhot 47b–48a also rendered some of the assumptions of its literary give-and-take to be legally non-binding as well. Obviously, were one to accept her arguments, there would then be no evidence at all for excluding women and men from forming any sort of joint quorum, whether of three or ten.

16. R. Ephraim Halivni has suggested that Berakhot 47b *does* provide explicit evidence that women do not count in a *minyan*. His reasoning is as follows: R. Yehoshua b. Levi's second statement is about forming a *zimmun* of ten, but the gemara nonetheless challenges its validity from a text that speaks about the quorum of ten for *tefillah*. That should lead us to the conclusion that the quorums of *zimmun* and *tefillah* are interchangeable and knowing that a person is excluded from one teaches us that they are excluded from the other as well. Accordingly, a text that excludes slaves from the quorum for prayer (R. Eliezer) would be in conflict with a text that includes slaves in the quorum for *zimmun* (R. Yehoshua b. Levi). In this, Halivni follows an argument laid out in Tosafot Berakhot 48a s.v. *v'let*, which proposes that including a minor in *zimmun* of ten would lead us to include him in the ten of prayer as well, seemingly equating the two. Following this logic, Halivni argues that the gemara would thus derive from the Mishnah's exclusion of women from *zimmun* their exclusion from the quorum of ten for prayer. See הלבני, בין האיש לאישה, עמ' פ.

While Halivni's reading of the gemara is certainly *possible*, our goal here is merely to argue that it is by no means *necessary*, and therefore the Talmud does not definitively help later commentators resolve the question of gender and *minyan*. There are several problems with his line of analysis: (1) Perhaps R. Yehoshua b. Levi's second statement was *also* about prayer, as suggested by R. Tam in Tosafot Berakhot 48a s.v. *v'let*. Note the shift from מזמנין עליו to מצטרפין. [Though see the use of מצטרפין later in the sugya in the context of a *zimmun* of three.] If so, then that section is an internal dialogue between dueling sources on prayer and nothing can be learned from the model of *zimmun*. Perhaps the rules of quorums for *zimmun* and prayer do not cross their respective legal boundaries. Admittedly, this deflection is not strong, as Mishnah Megillah 4:3 itself suggests that the quorums for a *zimmun* of ten and other prayer rituals are most likely identical. But if we are asking whether the Talmud provides any conclusive evidence on the question of counting

direction: A plausible reading of that passage would claim that if the gemara is willing to entertain the liminal status of a non-Jew in such a quorum, then it clearly considers women to be included in those that the verse terms בני ישראל, and thus women would be included in *minyan*.[17] Furthermore, all other factors being equal, one might well assume that women count towards the

---

women towards the quorum of ten, these distinctions (even if unlikely) are important. (2) Even if R. Yehoshua b. Levi's second statement is *only* about *zimmun*, the gemara, strictly speaking, only concludes that being excluded from the ten for prayer implies an exclusion from the ten for *zimmun*. It does not make the converse claim. One could be excluded from the ten for *zimmun* and still potentially count for the 10 required for prayer. True, Bereishit Rabbah 91:3 *does* make the converse claim, suggesting it is harder to count for the ten of prayer than the ten of *zimmun*. But R. Tam points out that the Bavli's use of R. Eliezer to challenge R. Yehoshua b. Levi must indicate a different way of thinking than Bereishit Rabbah. If the Bavli thought like Bereishit Rabbah, it could not possibly challenge a lenient ruling on *zimmun* from a stringent ruling on *tefillah*. And if R. Yehoshua b. Levi's statement is indeed about *tefillah*, then we do have a case of someone (a slave) who is excluded from *zimmun* (by the Mishnah) and yet included in *tefillah*, which also contradicts Bereishit Rabbah's way of thinking. Thus, even if Mishnah Berakhot 7:2 is properly read as ruling that women do not count towards the ten of *zimmun*, it does not logically follow from this sugya that they do not count towards the ten of prayer. (3) Mishnah Berakhot 7:2 does not necessarily say anything about a *zimmun* of ten. Indeed, it is noteworthy that the gemara does not challenge R. Yehoshua b. Levi's inclusion of a slave from the Mishnah's ban on including him in a *zimmun*. The gemara's choice here might have been more literary than substantive, motivated by a desire to link two pre-existing sources (R. Yehoshua b. Levi and R. Eliezer) through a challenge. Nonetheless, the gemara's failure to set up a conflict between R. Yehoshua b. Levi and Mishnah Berakhot 7:2 makes it possible, if not plausible, that the Mishnah only excludes the slave from the quorum of three, but not from the quorum of ten. Again, Bereishit Rabbah 91:3 thinks differently and does seem to think that it is a bigger deal to count someone for the quorum of ten than for the quorum of three. But there is nothing to force a later reader to see that in the Bavli sugya. Indeed, Rosh Berakhot 7:20 assumes the exact opposite: דכולה שמעתתא מוכחא דזימון חמור מסניף עשרה – counting towards the quorum of ten is less weighty than counting towards the quorum of three. Absent a specific text excluding a woman from the quorum of ten, we would then have no dispositive evidence on that score from Mishnah Berakhot 7:2. (4) Whatever the evidence may be with respect to minors, we don't know that the concerns barring women from *zimmun* are identical, and there is good reason to think they are not. Berakhot 45b already seems clear that women make a *zimmun* on their own in a way that minors do not. Even if one concludes that exclusion from *zimmun* leads to exclusion from *tefillah*, we simply don't know whether that equation is only true for minors, for minors and slaves, or for minors, slaves and women. See the direct statement to this effect in Sefer Hameorot Berakhot 45a: וליכא משום פריצות הגדול עם הנשים דדוקא עבדים שהם פרוצים בעריות... אבל בבני חורין לא אמרינן הכי. (5) Mishnah Berakhot 7:2 says nothing about an all-female *zimmun*. Even if one follows Halivni's reading of the sugya – which is not necessary, given all the above – it maximally proves that men and women should not join to form a group. It says nothing about whether ten women are valid as a *minyan* on their own. Here the broader evidence of the Talmud is clear, as Berakhot 45b cites a *baraita* saying that women do form groups for *zimmun* on their own, and Arakhin 3a cites a *baraita* that mandates them to do so. Of course, following this line of analysis might lead one to require single-gender *minyanim* of ten. See pp. 107–108 below, n84–89) Perhaps the most significant point: Many later sources search for a basis for the claim that women do not count in a minyan for *tefillah*. None cite this sugya and several are explicit that there is no Talmudic evidence for the claim, despite it being reasonable in their eyes. See n25.

We reiterate our basic claim: There is nothing in the sugya on Berakhot 47b–48a that would force a later *posek*'s hand to exclude women from the quorum of ten required by Mishnah Megillah 4:3.

17. Similar reasoning is used by Urah Shaḥar, cited below n63–65.

minyan, given their equal obligation in prayer (in the context of which many of the situations requiring a *minyan* are clustered), and their explicit inclusion in the similar *mitzvah* of martyrdom.[18] But women's participation in *minyan* is nowhere directly addressed in classical rabbinic sources, leaving us simply to say that it impossible to prove from those sources either their normative exclusion or inclusion. In short, there is no dispositive evidence one way or the other.[19]

18. The latter point is made clear by the Talmud's initial assumption on Sanhedrin 74b that Esther ought to have been required to martyr herself rather than allow herself to be taken as Aḥashveirosh's wife.

19. Claiming that women are obligated in *tefillah* and martyrdom does not automatically positively dispose of the question of their inclusion in the *minyan* associated with those practices. Note that the Shulḥan Arukh at one and the same time held that women were obligated in prayer and that only men could constitute the *minyan*. Despite much argument to the contrary, by both proponents and opponents of counting women in a *minyan*, there is simply no good evidence for the notion that one counts in a *minyan* if and only if one is obligated in the respective *mitzvot* associated with that minyan. All of the rituals we have been discussing are in one way or another associated with the *mitzvah* of sanctifying God's name in public. While anyone obligated in this *mitzvah* (including women) may be eligible/obligated to engage in the relevant practice, it could well be that the requisite quorum to give these acts meaning must be made up of those with some sort of principal group identity that extends beyond obligation in these *mitzvot*. In other words, if the quorum is intended to assure that some microcosm of the Jewish community is present, it could be that women are sufficiently a *part* of that community to be obligated in the performance of the practice, but insufficiently *representative* of the community to create the quorum. Naturally, one could argue in the other direction as well.

Because the contrary argument has been advanced by so many, it is worth briefly engaging with one passage in the *rishonim* that is claimed to support the notion that obligation in a *mitzvah* and counting towards its quorum go hand in hand. Ran on Rif Megillah 6b s.v. *matnitin*, after positing that women can fulfill the obligation of men in the reading of the *megillah*, says the following: וי"א שאע"פ שהן מוציאות אין מצטרפות... וא"א... היאך אפשר שמוציאות אנשים ידי קריאה ואין מצטרפות עמהם למנין אלא ודאי מצטרפות. Some have taken this as a general principle that once one is obligated in a *mitzvah* one is eligible to count for all associated quorums. This is an overreading of the Ran. More likely the Ran is making a point local to the reading of the *megillah*. Whereas other quorums may be wrapped up in representing the community in microcosm, the ten for *megillah* (itself a disputed requirement in the Talmud) is required only in order to publicize the miracle of Purim and thus serves a different function from the quorum of ten required for *devarim shebikdushah*. Ran is making the claim that, *with respect to megillah*, there is absolutely no reason to think that there are any requirements beyond obligation for counting in the *minyan* for that *mitzvah*, since the only point of that quorum of ten is to get ten *megillah*-obligated people together to do this *mitzvah* more publicly. The voices he is arguing with apparently don't limit the quorum for *megillah* in this way and understand it to entail the same sorts of requirements as for other quorums. See the debate between Maor and Ramban on precisely this point. This reading of Ran is supported by the following passage from his teacher, Ritva, on Megillah 4a s.v. *ve-kheivan*, which is likely his source: הילכך הכא דעשרה אינם אלא לפרסומי ניסא בעלמא ולא חשיב צירוף כולי האי כיון דחיובות במקרא מגילה מצטרפות. There is therefore no solid support for the claim that anyone, including Ran, thinks that being obligated in a *mitzvah* automatically and generally validates one as counting towards the quorums associated with it.

II. MEDIEVAL RULINGS, INTERPRETATIONS AND ADDITIONS

Just as the question of a woman counting toward the *minyan* for public prayer and *devarim shebikedushah* does not arise in classical rabbinic sources, so too most *Rishonim* do not discuss it. They simply cite the language of the Mishnah, עשרה/ten, and add in the exclusions of minors and slaves that are explicit in Talmudic material.[20] However, several medieval authorities do say that a woman does not count for various functions. Some give no reason, such as **R. Sa'adiah Gaon** (Babylonia, 10th c., with reference to *devarim shebikdushah*), **Rambam** (with reference to Torah reading), **Tosafot** (public prayer and application to all requirements of ten),[21] **R. Meir b. Shimon HaMe'ili** (Narbonne, 13th c., the reading of Megillat Esther and application to all requirements of ten), **R. Menaḥem HaMeiri** (with reference to *devarim shebikdushah*) and **R. Tzidkiyah b. Avraham HaRofei** (Italy, 13th c., stated generally):

סידור רב סעדיה גאון פירושו על תפילת שחרית, אחר ישתבח

ואם צבור מתפלל את שלש התפלות האלה, ושיעור הציבור הוא עשרה זכרים שהגיעו לפרקם . . .

רמב"ם הלכות תפילה יב:ג

אין קורין בתורה בציבור בפחות מעשרה אנשים גדולים בני חורין

---

20. One typical example of this sort can be found in the language of Tur OḤ 55: ואומר קדיש וא"א אותו בפחות מעשרה דכל דבר שבקדושה כגון קדיש וברכו וקדושה א"א אותו בפחות מעשרה . . . ואלו היו"ד צריך שיהו כולם בני חורין וגדולים שהביאו ב' שערות.

21. Note that Tosafot claim that their interpretation is grounded in the claim on Berakhot 45b that "a hundred women are like two men", והא מאה נשי כתרי גברי דמיין. This line is part of a discussion exploring whether two men can exercise the option to form a *zimmun*, even though they are not obligated. A *baraita* authorizing an all-female *zimmun* is cited as proof, along with this tag line about 100 women being like two men. Tosafot read this as indicating the exclusion of women from all quorums, including those of 10. In other words, Tosafot assert that women have no capacity for group identity in halakhic discourse. The sugya would then be arguing that if women, with no group identity, can nonetheless form a *zimmun*, there should be no barrier to two men forming a *zimmun*, even if they lack the proper group identity. Rashi there, however, does not take this interpretation, and most other *rishonim* follow Rashi, seeing this line as specifically discussing *zimmun* and asserting that even the largest group of women is not obligated to form a *zimmun*. He reads "100 women are like *two* men" to indicate that they are short of the obligatory characteristics of a group of *three* men. Others, like Ritva, understand this line to mean that even the largest group of women is not more socially significant than two men; therefore, if women are allowed to form their own *zimmun*, two men should have the right to do so as well if they wish. Also note that the *baraita* coupled with this line is deflected by the sugya as ultimately irrelevant to the discussion. Given the broad interpretational dispute with the Tosafot, it is best to assess their position as a halakhic statement in its own right rather than engage Berakhot 45b directly as a relevant text for our topic. Because Berakhot 45b is plausibly only about a *zimmun* of three, we did not include it in our discussion of potentially dispositive Talmudic evidence above. See also above, n16.

תוספות מסכת ברכות מה:

"והא מאה נשי כתרי גברי דמיין" – לענין קבוץ תפלה ולענין כל דבר שבעשרה.

ספר המאורות, מגילה ה.

ונראה לומר שאף על פי שאשה כשירה להוציא את האיש ממקרא מגלה, שאין ראוי להשלים בה עשרה, דהיכא דבעינן עשרה, אנשים דוקא בעינן.

מאירי, בית הבחירה ברכות מז:

... ואין דבר שבקדושה מסור לנשים... אינה עולה למנין י' של מעמד ותפלה.

שבלי הלקט הלכות תפלה ט

ונשים ועבדים אינן משלימין לעשרה.

Siddur Sa'adiah Gaon, commentary following weekday *Yishtabaḥ*

If the community prays these three *tefillot* – the measure of a community for this being ten males who have reached puberty . . .

Rambam, Laws of Prayer 12:3

We do not read from the Torah in public with fewer than ten adult free males.[22]

Tosafot on Berakhot 45b

"But a hundred women are like two men" – for the matter of a prayer quorum and all other matters that require ten . . .

Sefer Hameorot Megillah 5a

It seems that though a woman may fulfill a man's obligation in reading the *megillah*, it is not proper to count her towards the ten for the reading, because wherever we require ten, we specifically need men.

Meiri, Beit Habeḥirah Berakhot 47b

. . . *devarim shebikdushah* are not the domain of women . . . she may not count [even as a tenth] for the necessary quorum for Torah reading and prayer.[23]

---

22. This follows our printed text of the Mishneh Torah. A number of commenators on this passage seem not to have had the word אנשים in their text, in which case there would be no explicit source from Rambam's writing excluding women from the *minyan* required for *devarim shebikdushah*. These include Sefer Hamenuḥah and Kesef Mishneh (but cf. Beit Yosef OḤ 199). But note that R. Avraham b. HaRambam's Sefer Hamaspik Leovdei Hashem, p. 190, indeed includes men as a criterion for who is eligible to count in a minyan. Regarding Rambam's approach to women and the ten required for *zimmun* with God's name, see Appendix C.

23. The first part of this passage in the Meiri is in the context of a discussion of whether 10 women can perform *zimmun bashem*, adding God's name into the introductory invitation to *birkat hamazon*. The immediate surrounding text reads as follows: אבל אם היו עשר אע"פ שמזמנות מכל מקום אין מזמנות בשם, שהזכרת השם דבר שבקדושה הוא, ואין דבר שבקדושה מסור לנשים. ויש חולקים בכך. It is syntactically possible to read this line in the Meiri as claiming that there are some who

Shibbolei Haleket Laws of Tefillah 9
Women and slaves may not complete the quorum.

Other *Rishonim*, especially several from Provençe, also specify men, but provide textual or logical support for this position. In each example of textual evidence, a particular *Rishon* focuses on one of the verses the Talmud cites to explain why some ritual requires ten, and explains that this verse must refer only to men. A summary of these various explanations is found in **R. Manoaḥ**'s Sefer Hamenuḥah.[24] After noting that Rambam's ruling in Hilkhot Berakhot 5:7 that ten women may not mention God's name in their *zimmun* has no explicit basis in the Talmud,[25] R. Manoaḥ offers three readings of Biblical verses to strengthen both Rambam's point and his assumption that women are generally excluded from the *minyan* for *devarim shebikdushah* as well:

וצ"ע... ועניין זה אינו בגמרא בפירוש, מיהו דינא הכי הוא... דהא כתיב "בְּמַקְהֵלוֹת בָּרְכוּ" (תהלים

---

disagree that *devarim shebikdushah* are not the domain of women and in fact permit ten women to perform rituals that require a *minyan*. In fact, there is a possibility, albeit unprovable, that R. Simḥah of Speyer subscribed to such a view, a point we will note below at n43. Nonetheless, given that there is no explicit evidence for such a view anywhere in the rishonim, it seems safer to read the view cited in the Meiri here as agreeing with the basic claim that *devarim shebikdushah* are not the domain of women. Rather, it rules that ten women doing a *zimmun* may mention God's name because adding God's name there is not a *davar shebikdushah*, and therefore, the agreed upon fact that women are not included in such rituals is irrelevant. This conservative reading is also supported by: 1) the fact that the next line in the Meiri cites a proof specific to the question of *zimmun bashem*, which seems to be arbitrating a dispute over ten women and *zimmun bashem*, as opposed to a broader debate over quorums of ten more generally, and 2) the second part of the passage we have quoted here, where Meiri takes for granted, even against the backdrop of the possibility that ten women might sometimes form a group, that ten women *never* add up to a quorum for *devarim shebikdushah*. This approach also comports with explicit evidence for views in the rishonim that *zimmun bashem* is *not* in fact a *davar shebikdushah*. See Ra'avan, Even Haezer #185 and Rashba Megillah 23b s.v. *ve'ein nos'in*. Note also that all manuscript witnesses to the text of Megillah 23b explain the reason for the quorum of 10 required to mention the Name in *zimmun* as לאו אורח ארעא, which might be taken as a claim that this ritual, unlike the first group of rituals in the Mishnah is not a *davar shebikdushah*. For more, see Benei Tziyyon 199:6. On the other hand, it might be that the gemara here is explaining that the whole notion of a quorum of 10 for a *davar shebikdushah* (including *zimmun*) is that it is לאו אורח ארעא to engage in such a serious ritual without significant numbers. We will return to the latter reading below, n63 and onward. For more on questions of *zimmun bashem* and the passage in Sefer Hamikhtam on which the Meiri referred to here is largely based, see Appendix C.

24. Commentary on Mishneh Torah Berakhot 5:7.

25. This is a point also noted by Sefer Hameorot 45a. He adds that, because this is the case, one should not protest against those who violate Rambam's ruling. This is an important text for helping to reframe an issue that often suffers from hot tempers and intolerance for divergent views, given that women's exclusion from the quorum of ten is nowhere explicated in classical rabbinic literature. R. Manoaḥ and Sefer Hameorot are important support for our final point in n16 above. See also Rashbatz on Berakhot 20b, who argues that Rambam drew this ruling from the Talmud's comment: והא מאה נשי כתרי גברי דמיין – a hundred women are like two men. This comment of Rashbatz is already heavily influenced by Tosafot Berakhot 45b s.v. *veha* and is unlikely historically to have been the source of Rambam's ruling. See above, n21.

סח:כז), והני לא איקרו קהל כלל. והכי נמי אמרינן בתפלה דאחייבי בה ואפילו הכי לא מצטרפי לעשרה, והן עצמן נמי לא אמרי' לא קדיש ולא קדושה, דכל דבר שבקדושה אינו בפחות מעשרה, דכתיב וְנִקְדַּשְׁתִּי בְּתוֹךְ בְּנֵי יִשְׂרָאֵל, ולא בנות ישראל. ו"עדה" נמי בזכרים היא ולא בנקבות, דהא מרגלים אנשי הוו. וכיון דדבר שבקדושה ליתי' בפחות מעשרה אנשים, והזכרת השם בברכת זמון ליתא אלא בעשרה משום דהוי דבר שבקדושה, ממילא אימעיטו להו נשים... ואף הסברא נותנת שלא יזמנו בשם, שהרי אין בהם דעת לגדל ולרומם שמו של הקב"ה כאנשים, וכתיב "גדלו לה' אתי".

This requires consideration . . . This matter is not explicit in the *gemara*, but nonetheless it is the law . . . for it is written, "bless in *mak'heilot*," and they [i.e., women] are not at all called a *kahal*. And we hold similarly with regard to prayer, in which women are obligated, but nonetheless they do not form the quorum of ten,[26] and they as a group on their own do not say *Kaddish* or *Kedushah*, for any *davar shebikdushah* may not be said in a group of fewer than ten, since it is written, "And I will be sanctified in the midst of *benei yisrael*" – and not *benot yisrael*. And "*edah*" also applies only to males, because the spies were men. And since a *davar shebikdushah* may not be said in a group of fewer than ten men, and the restriction on mentioning the Name in *zimmun* in a group of fewer than ten is because this act is a *davar shebikdushah*, women are thus excluded . . . and further, common sense tells us that they should not conduct *zimmun* with the Name, because they do not have the intellectual capacity to magnify and exalt the name of the Holy One as men do, and it is written: "Magnify God with me."

R. Manoaḥ begins by quoting Tehilim 68:27 – בְּמַקְהֵלוֹת בָּרְכוּ אֱלֹהִים/"Bless God in assemblies" – which appears in Mishnah Berakhot 7:3 as the basis for using increasingly elaborate language in praising God as the size of the gathering for *zimmun* increases further. He then proceeds to state that women are not considered a קהל, and since *zimmun* with God's name is associated with the term קהל,[27] ten women may not perform it. This notion that women

26. Note that R. Manoaḥ here makes explicit what we showed earlier, i.e., that obligation in prayer is irrelevant to – or at least, insufficient to answer – the question of counting towards the *minyan*.

27. While R. Manoaḥ here only seems to invoke קהל in the context of *zimmun*, others engage it more broadly. Eshkol, Hilkhot Keriat Shema 6a associates במקהלות ברכו אלקים with the ten required for ברכו more generally, influenced by the word ברכו in the verse. Ramban on Pesahim 85a associates it with all cases of *devarim shebikdushah*, likely influenced by R. Abahu's statement on Ketubot 7b that this verse is the basis for requiring ten for *birkat ḥatanim*. Since *birkat ḥatanim* is one of the rituals listed in Mishnah Megillah 4:3, it is a small step to suggest that במקהלות is a relevant associated text for all of them. R. Manoaḥ seems to have been the first to take this well-known association and use it to derive a point about gender in order to support Rambam. Ritva, a slightly later contemporary follows this gendered approach to קהל in his comments on Ketubot 7b, where he asserts that the 10 for *birkat ḥatanim* must be all male.

are not a קהל finds earlier roots in an exegetical tradition in Sifrei Bemidbar 109, which assumes that the term קהל only includes men. He then cites "And I shall be sanctified among the people [literally, 'sons'] of Israel" – "וְנִקְדַּשְׁתִּי בְּתוֹךְ בְּנֵי יִשְׂרָאֵל" (Vayikra 22:32), the core verse adduced in the Talmud to justify requiring ten for *devarim shebikdushah* (Megillah 23b). He explains here that the Torah intentionally specifies the "sons" of Israel, and not the daughters.[28] R. Manoaḥ is presumably basing himself on a tannaitic midrash, recorded in a number of places, that when the Torah commands "*benei yisrael*" with regard to certain procedures in Temple sacrifices, it means males specifically: בני ישראל סומכין ואין בנות ישראל סומכות.[29] R. Manoaḥ's innovation is to apply that reading to the context of *devarim shebikdushah* as well. His final Scriptural evidence is the word עדה/congregation: When the gemara demonstrates the necessity of ten for *devarim shebikedushah* from the story of the spies, it must mean men specifically, since all ten spies were men. He then concludes that common sense alone justifies a gendered practice around a *zimmun* of ten (and presumably other quorums of ten as well): women, he states, do not have the same intellectual disposition as men and cannot therefore serve as their equals and peers in these rituals.

As we noted above, R. Manoaḥ conveniently collects these scriptural associations and derivations, which are also found in other *Rishonim*. Do these actually reflect claims about objective Biblical interpretations of our topic, which generate law like any other classical midrash? Or do they function as *asmakhtaot* – *post facto* supports for a law already assumed, perhaps grounded primarily in intuitions and well-worn patterns of behavior? These midrashim all have analogues in classical rabbinic literature and the use of the spies' identity to derive law simply continues the legacy of the gemara on Sanhedrin 74b, which used the Jewish identity of the spies to exclude Gentiles from the *minyan*. Indeed, there is a significant tradition of sources that views various qualities of the spies as paradigmatic of various points of law about inclusion in *minyan*.[30] Nonetheless, there is an equally strong and compelling tradition that insists that such midrashim – *on a matter of rabbinic prayer* – must be

28. A century later, **Orḥot Ḥayyim** also cited this verse for the same point. A similar appeal to gendered language is made by Ritva on Ketubot 7b in the context of the 10 required for *birkat ḥatanim*. In addition to his gendered reading of קהל, he suggests that the word אנשים in Rut 4:2 specifies males and not females.

29. Sifra Dibbura DeNedava Parashah 2:2; Eruvin 96b and parallels. See also Sifre Bemidbar 39 and Sifre Zuta 15:25, where בני ישראל is understood to exclude converts, women and slaves.

30. Ra'avan, in Even Haezer #185, uses the fact that the spies were adults to exclude minors. Shulḥan Arukh HaRav 55:2 uses R. Manoaḥ's logic here as a basis for excluding women. R. Moshe Feinstein in Iggerot Moshe OḤ 2:19 argues that since the spies were wicked, it must be permissible to count one who violates Shabbat in a minyan.

understood as rich and authoritative language ("*asmakhta'ot*") for deeply-held religious convictions, and not as generative proof texts.[31]

A number of reasons recommend that approach in this instance:

First, despite Sifre Bemidbar's prior reading of קהל/assembly as a gendered term, several *mitzvot* in the Torah which equally apply to women and men also use that word. Examples are the Passover sacrifice – "The whole **assembly** of the congregation of Israel shall slaughter it at dusk" (וְשָׁחֲטוּ אֹתוֹ כֹּל קְהַל עֲדַת יִשְׂרָאֵל בֵּין הָעַרְבָּיִם, Shemot 12:6); the prohibition of a *mamzer* (child of an incestuous or adulterous relationship) from entering God's "assembly" (לֹא יָבֹא מַמְזֵר בִּקְהַל ה' Devarim 23:3); and, most strikingly, the commandment of "Assembly" ("הַקְהֵל"): "Assemble the nation – the men, the women, and the children" (הַקְהֵל אֶת הָעָם הָאֲנָשִׁים וְהַנָּשִׁים וְהַטַּף Devarim 31:12). Why favor the Sifre Bemidbar's gendered interpretation of קהל as the plain sense of that word to the exclusion of these other possibilities? Moreover, if we view the use of קהל as generative of the laws surrounding the identity of the *minyan* members, we might take the claim on Horayot 6b that *Levi'im* are not called קהל to exclude them from the *minyan* as well. No one would ever have suggested that. However, if we understand the use of this *asmakhta* as an expression of an assumption that women do not participate in corporate entities nor create communities, these *Rishonim* make quite a bit more sense – what could be a more appropriate verse to cite to this effect than one which invokes the notion of community?

Second, the appeal to בני ישראל as a gendered term in this context runs up against its use in other contexts that are gender blind such as the *mitzvot* regarding evaluative oaths (*arakhin*, Vayikra 27). Moreover, Sifre Bemidbar 115 states: ויאמר ה' אל משה לאמר דבר אל בני ישראל ואמרת אליהם ועשו להם ציצית, אף הנשים במשמע – "Tell בני ישראל and speak to them that they shall make themselves *tzitzit*: This suggests that women are included as well."[32] As we noted above, there is a clear tradition that explicitly excludes women from בני ישראל that cuts the other way as well.[33] But when asking what the *Rishonim* are doing, it remains unclear why they would favor one midrashic bias over another, given that no gendered conclusion on *minyan* is ever spelled out in classical literature. If, instead, we understand this use of the verse not as a formal proof, but as an allusive expression of a deeply-held belief – that the Jewish "community"

31. See Rosh Berakhot 7:20: **ואפילו הוי מלתא דרבנן כגון לשמוע קדושה וברכו שלא מצינו לו עיקר מן התורה**. See also Ran's statement about Mishnah Megillah 4:3 (found on Rif Megillah 13b): ומיהו הני מילי כולהו אסמכתא דרבנן נינהו דסדר תפלה גופה דרבנן – "All of these derivations are *post facto* supports for rabbinic laws, since the whole order of prayer is itself rabbinic.

32. This view is then followed by the dissenting view of R. Shimon, who exempts women from *tzitzit*, but not through an appeal to the terminology of בני ישראל.

33. See n29.

is not properly represented by its female members – then the use of a phrase about the Jewish people is a perfectly reasonable support.

Third, though the use of identities of the spies to derive law is well attested, it should also be clear how slippery and unreliable that usage can be. For instance, why not demand that the *minyan* be formed only by males over the age of thirty (as were Joseph's older brothers when they went down to Egypt)? Why not demand some tribal diversity among the participants, as was the case with the spies? Why not exclude male converts from the *minyan*? It seems more reasonable to see the use of these Biblical verses in the *Rishonim*, like many other exegeses found in rabbinic literature, as *post facto* support for an accepted practice. These scriptural citations, while weak as formal proofs, express the religious sensibilities of their authors and their communities.

Fourth, R. Manoaḥ also ends this passage with an appeal to reason. That suggests that he does not feel (nor does he intend others to feel) that the prior proofs are meant to be uncontested legal derivations that settle the matter. Indeed, this final sentiment, which grounds women's exclusion from *minyan* in common sense and the *posek*'s reality, may shed light on the deeper motivations behind the Scriptural anchors. The fact is that R. Manoaḥ did *not* consider the exclusion of women from *minyan* to be an oddity imposed on him by ancient texts. Rather, that exclusion rang true to him given his experiences with women, as a class, being insufficiently educated to form a community for the purposes of publicly praising God.[34] He considered this reality to be a relevant and, apparently, decisive factor toward the question of their participation.

All of this supports the general idea that those *Rishonim* who gender *minyan*, whether without justification, by recourse to scriptural anchors or by invoking common sense, all intuit and assume the exclusion of women as something obvious, rather than something counterintuitive imposed on them by a text. Indeed, given the absence of any dispositive source material in the Talmud, this would almost seem to be the only reasonable conclusion to draw.

---

34. These words burn in the ears of many contemporary readers and we in no way intend to minimize or dismiss that pain. At the same time, well-founded modern critiques of R. Manoaḥ's social setting as well as R. Manoaḥ's own troubling forumulation, should not lead us to a facile dismissal of his core point. If we consider a world in which education for women was minimal (even in comparison to the relatively spartan education of many Jewish men), then it should not surprise us that women would be viewed as intellectually inferior to men. In R. Manoaḥ's time, a group of women lacked the social capital that a similar-sized collection of men would have had. In the context of a reality very different from our own, R. Manoaḥ is emphasizing the weightiness of the sanctification of God's name – and the way in which this is played out through *devarim shebikdushah*. Perhaps his words can thus contribute something to our appreciation of the gravity of *devarim shebikdushah*, even if they do so in the context of a social reality that might be disturbing, and even if R. Manoaḥ's seeming complicity with this reality might be disappointing.

That women do not count is intuitive to these *Rishonim*, just as the exclusion of slaves and minors was intuitive to R. Yehoshua b. Levi. Their citation of verses is not meant to *prove* these religious intuitions, but rather to provide some allusive Scriptural context for them.

But however we read the gendering of *minyan* in these *Rishonim*, a core substantive question remains: Why? What is behind the exclusion of women that emerges clearly in the medieval period? How might we more precisely define the considerations at work in medieval discussions of this topic? And based on those considerations, how would we answer questions relating to gender and *minyan* in our own day?

III. WHAT IS *MINYAN* AND WHAT ARE THE IMPLICATIONS FOR GENDER?

We turn now to the question of understanding the essence of *minyan* and the criteria that stand behind some of the practical rulings we have seen so far.

A. Model I: Covenantal Belonging, Connection to *Mitzvot* and "Honor of Heaven" – R. Tam

The earliest (and only) thorough attempt in the rishonim to define what *minyan* is all about was proffered by **R. Tam**. Following R. Yehoshua b. Levi's ruling on Berakhot 47b that one baby – even an infant in a cradle – could be counted in a *minyan*,[35] R. Tam comments as follows:

תוספות ר"י שירליאון ברכות מז:
ואני מוסיף אפי' מוטל בעריסה, דאכל בי י' שכינתא שריא, דכי גמירי קדושה בעשרה מ"ונקדשתי", ל"ש גדולים ול"ש קטני', ובלבד שיהיו תשע גדולים, דטפי מחד לא, כדאמרי' גבי עבד, דליכא יקרא דשמיא כולי האי, ועבד נמי איתי בכלל ונקדשתי, דשכינה שריא אכל מחוייבי מצות ובני ברית...

Tosafot R. Yehudah Sirleon on Berakhot 47b
And I add even an infant in his cradle, for God's presence dwells among all groups of ten, for when they learn that matters of sanctity are done in a quorum of ten from the verse "I will be sanctified," no distinction is made between minors and adults. But there must be nine adults, because more

35. R. Tam arrives at this view by arguing that the statement ולית הלכתא ככל הני שמעתתא – already an integral part of his text – only applied to the immediately prior statements and not to R. Yehoshua b. Levi's rulings on counting a slave and a minor. See Tosafot Berakhot 48a s.v. *v'let*. This, of course, is just a return to possibilities of the the original text of the gemara prior to the incorporation of the Geonic gloss.

> than one [minor] may not be counted, as it is taught with respect to a slave, for [with more than one] *there is insufficient honor for heaven.* And a slave also comes under the principle "I will be sanctified," for God's presence dwells among all who are obligated in commandments and members of the covenant . . .

Recall that the Talmud's source for the numerical make-up of *minyan* was Vayikra 22:32: ונקדשתי בתוך בני ישראל – "And I shall be sanctified among the children of Israel." R. Tam explains that this "sanctity" inhabits all who are מחוייבי מצות ובני ברית – obligated in *mitzvot* or members of the covenant. His point is to argue that slaves (who are obligated in *mitzvot* – to the same extent as Jewish women – despite not being Jews) and children (who are Jews but not yet obligated in *mitzvot*) are essentially eligible to count in the *minyan*,[36] as evidenced in his eyes by the Talmudic phrase כל בי עשרה שכינתא שריא/"The divine presence dwells in all groups of ten" (Sanhedrin 39a). However, even the most inclusive opinion in the Talmud allows counting only one slave, and not many.[37] Therefore, R. Tam explains that the reason a *minyan* should not include more than one child or slave is because more than that would be "insufficient honor for Heaven" ("ליכא יקרא דשמיא כולי האי"). R. Tam does not appeal here to precedent or a formal definition; he is expressing that it is inappropriate to form the *minyan* – the representative microcosm of the community for the task of exalting God's name – with such peripheral, undignified members. He argues that this is the case even though, from a theological perspective, God's *Shekhinah* does descend on any group of ten members who are connected to the Jewish people either through obligation (slaves) or birth (minors). For R. Tam, *minyan* is nothing less and nothing more than a convocation of ten people anchored to the Jewish people through ancestry or obligation and any such group is theoretically an appropriate manifestation of בני ישראל– the group in which God's name is sanctified. Beyond that, a *minyan* must not violate the standard of יקרא דשמיא/ "the honor of heaven," which

36. This assumes the *vav* of ובני ברית is disjunctive. If one, however, reads the *vav* as conjunctive – which seems to be the reading of Rosh Berakhot 7:20 – one would have to say that infants are obligated in mitzvot because they will be obligated in mitzvot as adults. Slaves would be considered בני ברית in the sense that they are circumcised (an interpretation advanced by R. Yom Tov Lippman Heller's commentary on the Rosh, Ma'adanei Yom Tov on Rosh Berakhot 7:20, likely influenced by Bava Kama 15a and driven by the Rosh's reading of R. Tam's two criteria as jointly necessary rather than individually sufficient). The first reading seems stronger to us.

37. It is plausible that R. Yehoshua b. Levi's statement about making an infant a סניף also only imagined counting one, and this is how R. Tam clearly understood him. Others, however, understood him to be more liberal on infants, possibly permitting counting up to four towards the minyan. See n10.

captures the notion of a gathering that is objectively dignified and worthy of God's serious attention.

Now, we have no record of R. Tam discussing the question of women and *minyan*, but his conceptual framework can further our understanding. His description of what *minyan* is about would include women, who were obligated in all the same *mitzvot* as slaves in his context, and were also considered part of the covenant.[38] Purely following R. Tam's logic, we might well conclude that ten women can constitute a *minyan*. There is no rabbinic source that limits the participation of women, as there is regarding slaves and minors, and no indication that counting more than one woman would violate יקרא דשמיא, the honor of heaven.[39] At that point, we could revert to R. Tam's original definition of where the Divine Presence dwells, about which he says לא שנא גדולים לא שנא קטנים; i.e., ten minors (and ten women) could theoretically make up a *minyan*.

Indeed, this basic conceptual extrapolation was made by **Rabbenu Simḥah of Speyer** (Germany, 13th c.), who ruled that a woman could count towards the ten. From the context in which his ruling is cited, however, it seems that he limited the extrapolation to a more conservative extension from R. Tam's actual ruling regarding one slave or one minor and only allowed one woman to count towards the *minyan*:[40]

מרדכי ברכות קעג

מצאתי בשם רבינו שמחה: עבד ואשה מצטרפין בין לתפלה בין לברוך א-להינו, ומעשה דר' אליעזר ששחרר עבדו והשלימו לי' דמשמע דוקא בשחררו אבל אי לא שיחררו לא והוא הדין לאשה, יש לומר תרי הוו ושחרר חד ומילא בחד.

Mordekhai Berakhot #173

I found in the name of R. Simḥah: A slave or a woman can join towards the ten required for prayer and for [the formula mentioning God's name in *zimmun*]. And regarding the case where R. Eliezer freed his slave in order to complete the quorum, which makes it sound as if an unfreed slave may not count towards the ten – and the same restriction would apply to a woman – we can say that there were two slaves present; one he freed [in order to count as the ninth] and one he counted as the tenth [while still a slave].

---

38. If the term "covenant" is meant generally to refer to Jews, then women are obviously included – for a usage of בת ברית to refer to a woman in this sense, see Sifre Zuta 35:12 – and if it refers to circumcision, the Talmud considers women to be already circumcised (Avodah Zarah 27a).

39. R. Tam never applies the concern of יקרא דשמיא to women, which just reflects the fact that there is no Talmudic statement that limits counting women in a *minyan*, in contrast to slaves and minors, who are so limited.

40. This conservative reading of R. Simḥah is maintained by Beit Yosef OḤ 55 and many others. See n43.

According to one version, R. Simḥah acted upon this ruling:[41]

מרדכי ברכות קנח=מרדכי גטין תא

... גם רבינו שמחה היה עושה מעשה לצרף אשה [לי'] לזימון, ואפילו אם תמצא לומר דאשה לא מיחייבא האשה אלא מדרבנן ... ה"מ לאפוקי אחרים י"ח, אבל לצרוף בעלמא להזכרת שם שמים, שפיר מצטרפת.

Mordekhai Berakhot #158 = Mordekhai Gittin #401

R. Simḥah used to count a woman toward the [ten required for][42] *zimmun*. Even if you say that a woman is only rabbinically obligated [in *birkat hamazon*] . . . that is only a concern for her fulfilling the obligation of others, but there is no problem with her counting towards the ten needed to mention the Name.[43]

---

41. It should not be surprising to find this kind of leniency specifically in the writings of R. Tam and the Tosafists, who, by and large, lived in tiny Jewish communities in northern France and Germany. Making a *minyan* is much more difficult when the pool of potential participants is so small. Perhaps of additional significance is the greater financial independence enjoyed by women in these communities as opposed to those in Southern Europe and the Mediterranean. For the broader religious context, see A. Grossman, *Pious and Rebellious: Jewish Women in Medieval Europe*, Waltham, 2004.

42. The word לי', which is added here by a later hand to clarify that the context is a *zimmun* of ten, is no doubt influenced by the final words in this passage, which speak of הזכרת שם שמים/ mentioning God's name. That suggests that R. Simḥah was only dealing with a quorum of ten, and not a quorum of three. However, Agur #289 quotes R. Simḥah, in the name of the Mordekhai, as counting a woman towards the quorums of both three and ten: וכן רבינו שמחה בין לעשרה בין לג'. R. Simḥah's positions seem to have been filtered through various later editorial layers that interpreted him differently. Indeed, the whole final clause here – beginning with ואפילו – may be a later addition. Traditions allowing a woman to count towards the quorum of three were attacked by Maharam of Rothenberg in his Responsa IV:2227. The language here in our version of the Mordekhai seems to account for Maharam's attack while still defending a more modest version of R. Simḥah, applied to the less radical case of counting women towards the quorum of ten. See n16 for more on the relative hierarchy of the quorums of three and ten and see n43 for further reflections on the processing of R. Simḥah's positions in these sources.

43. R. Simḥah's position on counting women towards the *minyan* is reported here second hand, filtered and repackaged along with other sources. The language in this latter source actually sounds as if R. Simḥah allowed women to count as equals towards the ten of *zimmun*. This opens the possibility that R. Simḥah permitted women to count as equals towards the quorum of ten, even as he limited slaves and minors to one of the ten slots, in keeping with R. Tam's rulings on the matter. Indeed, R. Moshe Blau seems to understand R. Simḥah – and R. Tam – similarly in his edition of Sefer Hameorot, p. 135 n9, as does R. Shmuel Dikman in his edition of Bet Habeḥirah, Jerusalem, 1960, p. 179 n152. It might be that only a later hand bringing his positions on women and slaves together in the first passage in the Mordekhai cited above assumed that the rulings were identical and that R. Simḥah permitted only one woman to count in a *minyan*. This reading of R. Simḥah is unprovable, but it is important to establish its historical possibility given the later views that we will see that in fact establish the theoretical plausibility of counting ten women towards a *minyan*. In the discussion here, however, we will assume, so as to be as cautious as possible, that R. Simḥah *practically* permitted counting only one woman towards the *minyan*, even as we will maintain that he *theoretically* permitted ten women to count, following R. Tam's criteria.

Even if R. Simḥah restricted his practice of counting women in the *minyan* to a single woman, the basic claim is clear: R. Tam's definition of *minyan* includes them in principle, with the only remaining question being whether, and to what degree, the honor of heaven limits this being carried out in practice.

B. Model II: Only Maximally Obligated Members of the Community can Represent it in Microcosm – Levush

While R. Tam's theory of *minyan* is the only such explicit articulation in the medieval period, there are possible hints of another approach that eventually flowers more fully in the modern era. As we noted above, a Geonic-era gloss on Talmud Bavli Berakhot 48a dismissed R. Yehoshua b. Levi's rulings that were inclusive of slaves and minors. Another definition of *minyan* built on this tradition and suggested that minors and slaves were excluded from *minyan* not on account of honor alone, but on account of a more fundamental deficiency: Insufficient obligation in *mitzvot.*

In discussing *minyan*, a number of authorities use the term מצוה/*mitzvah* to get at the essence of what it means to count towards a minyan. For instance, **R. Yonah of Gerona** (Spain, 13th c.) explains why one might count minors toward the *zimmun* but not towards the ten required for aspects of public prayer:

רבינו יונה על הרי"ף ברכות לה:
ודוקא לענין בהמ"ז עושין אותן סניפין מפני שכל אחד בפני עצמו יכול לפטור עצמו מחיוב ברכת המזון אבל לקדיש ולקדושה ולברכו שכל אחד ואחד לא היה יכול לפטור עצמו מחיוב בשום ענין צריך שיהו כולם **בני מצוה**...

> Specifically with regard to the blessing after the meal, we can add minors as adjuncts, because each person that makes up the *zimmun* can fulfill his own obligation in the blessing after the meal. But with respect to *Kaddish*, *Kedushah* and *Barekhu*, where each person cannot in any way fulfill his own obligation, the group must be entirely ***b'nei mitzvah*** . . .

R. Yonah here appeals to the minor's lack of obligation in *mitzvot* to justify his exclusion from the *minyan* required for *devarim shebikdushah.*[44] This may hint at a broader theory that, contrary to R. Tam, minors are not even theoretically eligible for *minyan* on account of this lack of obligation.[45] While

---

44. Note that R. Yonah thinks there is some sort of individual obligation in *devarim shebikdushah*, though the exact nature of his view is unclear. See our discussion above, Part One, n121–141.

45. Use of the term בני מצוה to exclude children from being the tenth can also be found in Sefer HaOrah II:156=Maḥzor Vitry #81. The term is also used to define the normal group required for a

the precise meaning and intent of R. Yonah on this front is far from clear, an explicit articulation of a *mitzvah*-centered approach to *minyan* is delivered by **R. Mordekhai Jaffe** (Poland, 16th c.):

לבוש או"ח נה:ד

ועבד ואשה וקטן אין מצטרפין שאינם חייבים במצות. ויש מתירין בט' וצירוף קטן כיון שיכול להגיע לכלל חיוב מצות . . .

Levush OḤ 55:4

Neither a slave nor a woman nor a minor may count towards the *minyan*, because they are not obligated in *mitzvot*. And some permit joining nine adults with one minor, since the minor will eventually become obligated . . .

Levush is clearly operating with a different definition of *minyan* from that of R. Tam, despite some of the linguistic similarities. Though both authorities talk about obligation in *mitzvot* as a criterion for counting in a *minyan*, they mean very different things. R. Tam thought this criterion *included* slaves (and, by extension, women), since they are obligated in many *mitzvot*. Levush, by contrast, uses this criterion to *exclude* slaves and women. For him, "obligation in *mitzvot*" clearly means *maximal* obligation and excludes those, like women and slaves, who, though obligated in many *mitzvot*, are exempt from a range of others (those of the positive, time-bound variety explored above).[46] This paints a significantly different picture of *minyan*. R. Tam is able to conceive of a "community" that comprises free adult males as well as more marginal types, such as slaves, minors, and, most likely, women, but he feels that most such convocations are not so respectful to the honor of Heaven. However dishonorable, such a group nonetheless does constitute the עדה/קהל/בני ישראל grouping that is the essence of *minyan*. Levush cannot even conceive of such a convocation being considered a representation of the larger community. By his logic, how can someone exempt from a whole category of *mitzvot* possibly help constitute a microcosm of the Jewish people? Justifying a gender-blind

---

minyan in Or Zarua II:3370: מיהו הא מספקא לי [מגילה] שלא בזמנה שצריכה עשרה אם צריכ' עשרה שיהו בני מצוה כמו כל הטעונים עשרה. See also R. Ya'akov Mölin (Germany, 14th-15th c.) in Responsa Maharil #106: וחרש שמדבר ואינו שומע אם יש לצרפו לעשרה, לא ידענא מאי קא [מבעי] ליה למר . . . אי משום דבור הוא, מאי נפקא מינה הואיל ובר דיעה ו**בר מצוה** הוא, אכל בי עשרה שכינתא שריא. . . . "With respect to the question of whether a deaf person who can speak can count towards a *minyan* of ten, I am not sure what you are asking . . . If you are concerned that he is unlearned, why would that matter? Given that he has intelligence and is a ***bar mitzvah***, the Divine Presence dwells on all groups of ten . . ." But this source may simply be saying that this deaf person, once he is obligated in *mitzvot* on account of having the power of speech has no other basis for being disqualified.

46. Levush is here borrowing language of the sort used in Tosefta Berakhot 6:18: שאין הנשים חייבות במצות. That formulation clearly refers to an absence of *maximal* obligation, not to an absence of any obligation whatsoever.

minyan according to the Levush would require claiming that contemporary women *are* obligated in (all) *mitzvot* and are thus – unlike slaves, minors and women of the past – indeed fitting representatives of the community. Pursuing gender equality in *minyan* through this model would require addressing not only issues of honor, but more fundamental inequalities of obligation.

C. Weighing the Two Models

As we noted earlier, most of the *Rishonim* who exclude women from the *minyan* do so without articulating any support for that view, and even those who cite verses and midrashim to support their positions do not offer a theory of *minyan* different from those we find either in R. Tam or in the Levush. Many authorities, in both the medieval and the modern period, reject R. Tam's ruling on minors and slaves, but the theoretical implications are unclear. Those who exclude minors and slaves even as the tenth might be doing one of two things:

1. Perhaps they accept R. Tam's theoretical model but reject implementing it for even a single minor or slave. In other words, even if minors are the theoretical equals of adults in constituting a *minyan* and count towards בני ישראל, it might offend the honor of heaven to count *even one* towards the quorum of ten. Whereas R. Tam agreed to a modest infraction on the dignity of Heaven (relying upon one minor or slave), these authorities would not allow even that level of infraction. Under this reading of the silence in the *Rishonim*, even those who ban minors and slaves entirely agree with R. Tam that the only criteria to count in a *minyan* are:
    a) Evincing sanctity through some basic connection to the Jewish people and;
    b) Not creating a situation that offends the dignity of heaven.

The disagreement regards only criterion b) and whether some degree of adjunct participation is tolerated.

2. Perhaps their rejection of R. Tam's practical ruling is bound up with a rejection of the theory that undergirded it. In this reading, any authority who refuses to count a minor or a slave even as a tenth has also made a claim that *minyan* has more robust requirements than posited by R. Tam. Since it is silly to speculate about theories of *minyan* that no one ever bothered to articulate, the most straightforward reading would be that such positions are proto-versions of the Levush. In other words, the wholesale exclusion of minors and slaves from *minyan* in practice

would thus indicate a definition of *minyan* that excludes them in essence as well.

An honest analysis will concede that there is no way to tell which of these two interpretations is correct when dealing with a source that simply excludes minors and slaves without explicating that decision further. The exclusion might be minor and local, focused on the proper boundaries of the honor of Heaven/ יקרא דשמיא. Alternatively, it might be over the very notion of whether minors and slaves can even theoretically represent the community in microcosm – a rejection of R. Tam's more fundamental principle of לא שנא גדולים לא שנא קטנים, that the essence of *minyan* does not depend on the presence of ten free adult males. On the one hand, R. Yosef Karo in Beit Yosef OḤ 55 takes no issue with R. Tam's model in theory; he simply explains the opposition to using that model to count women as an issue of ingrained practice: וכיון דר"ת בעצמו לא רצה לעשות מעשה מי יקל בדבר – "But since R. Tam himself did not want to do such a thing, who can be lenient regarding it?" This suggests a more modest, practical dispute between R. Tam and his opponents. On the other hand, **R. Shneur Zalman of Liady**, among others, reads the Levush's model back into these rishonim, setting up a more fundamental divide:

שולחן ערוך הרב או"ח נה:ה

(יז) יש מתירין לומר דבר שבקדושה בט' וצירוף עבד או אשה או קטן לפי שעל כל עשרה בני ברית השכינה שורה אלא שאינו כבוד שמים לומר דבר שבקדושה בפחות מט' בני מצות – שט' נראים כי' . . . (יט) וי"א שאין אשה ועבד או קטן מצטרפים בשום ענין אלא צריך שהיו כל עשרה זכרים בני חורין גדולים שהביאו שתי שערות ובפחות מכן אין השכינה שורה ואין אומרים דבר שבקדושה . . .

(יז) רב האי ור"ת ורז"ה כריב"ל ברכות מ"ז ב'

(יט) ר"י רא"ש רמב"ם . . . רשב"א הרר"י ראב"ד ראבי"ה

Shulḥan Arukh HaRav OḤ 55:5

Some permit saying a *davar shebikdushah* with nine joined together with a slave, a woman or a minor, because the *Shekhinah* dwells on any ten members of the covenant – nonetheless it would not be honoring heaven to say a *davar shebikdushah* with fewer than nine *b'nei mitzvot*,[47] because nine look like ten . . . and some say that a woman, slave or minor may not count at all and all ten must be free male adults who have reached puberty, and

47. Note that Shulḥan Arukh HaRav's reading of R. Simḥah fits the more conservative reading we offered above: Only one woman can count towards the ten and any additional women would present a problem of יקרא דשמיא/כבוד שמים. But we noted that R. Simḥah himself is less clear on this matter and there is nothing in R. Tam himself to suggest that כבוד שמים applies to gender as well, even though this would be a reasonable claim, as we will explore further below.

with fewer than that, the *Shekhinah* does not dwell and one may not say a *davar shebikdushah* . . .

Note that Shulḥan Arukh HaRav's formulation here considers slaves, minors, and women to be בני ברית – members of the covenant – but *not* בני מצות, which here must mean fully obligated adults. Minors are exempt by dint of their age, whereas women and slaves are exempt from a whole class of *mitzvot* (those positive *mitzvot* caused by time that we explored above). This is a different usage from that of R. Tam, who explicitly puts slaves in the category of מחוייבי מצות. In any event, Shulḥan Arukh HaRav's characterization of R. Tam's position is clear: Ten women are theoretically valid for a *minyan*, but in deference to the honor of heaven, we must reserve nine slots for free, adult males.[48] This lays bare the contrast between R. Tam and Levush. The core dispute is whether in fact the divine presence can dwell amidst anything other than a group of ten free adult males, on account of the issues of maximal obligation raised in Levush. R. Tam says yes; Levush says no.

We will return to this "debate within a debate," the question of whether to see the practical disagreement between R. Tam and his opponents in theoretical terms as well, as we turn to the considerations of practical *halakhah*. For now, we note that the difference between the models of R. Tam and the Levush is stark as it relates to assessing the role of gender in contemporary *minyanim*. If one understands the dignity of Heaven to be the only possible obstacle to counting women as equals in the *minyan*, then a determination that claims such a concern does not apply closes the issue. If, however, one understands the question of gender and *minyan* to be a subset of the question of gender and *mitzvot*, women's inclusion in the *minyan* would hinge on a broader reformulation of the role of gender in halakhic discourse.

---

48. Note that Shulḥan Arukh HaRav was so influenced by Levush's model of *minyan* that he reads it back into R. Tam's position as well. R. Tam himself thought that a basic level of obligation and membership in the covenant make one a fitting vehicle for the divine presence but that the factor of יקרא דשמיא – seemingly unrelated to issues of obligation – prevents allowing more than one such undignified member from counting towards the quorum. Shulḥan Arukh HaRav sees membership in the covenant (an attribute he assigns to women, slaves *and* minors) as the criterion for being a theoretically fitting vehicle for the divine presence and mentions nothing about *mitzvah* obligation. But he then assumes that the concern of יקרא דשמיא is *itself* about obligation: it is the lack of maximal obligation that makes someone an undignified candidate for more than one *minyan* slot. Thus, according to Shulḥan Arukh HaRav's reading of R. Tam, even the latter's model would require a wholesale reevaluation of contemporary women's obligations in order to have a gender-equal *minyan*. This does not seem like a very plausible reading of R. Tam. The latter only engages one level of obligation, which is the level of obligation that makes one theoretically eligible for the *minyan*. As we will see, most other interpreters of R. Tam did not read him as Shulḥan Arukh HaRav does so here. Nonetheless, this passage is a good example of the conceptual power of the Levush's model, as demonstrated by the tendency of some to read it back into earlier positions.

D. Aftermath of R. Simḥah and Gender Inclusivity in *Minyan* in Practice

If we follow R. Tam's definition of *minyan*, then its application to women becomes a live halakhic question, beginning with R. Simḥah's ruling above. The subsequent history of this ruling – at least in practice – is somewhat checkered. **R. Ya'akov Landau** (Germany/Italy, 15th c.), in Agur #240, does not formally reject R. Simhah's practice on *zimmun*, but he states: ואני המחבר לא ראיתי מעולם נוהגים כך ולא שמעתי מקום שנוהגין כן – "I have never seen anyone practice this way nor have I heard about a place that practices this way."

R. Yosef Karo curiously does not cite any of the authorities who explicitly exclude female participation, but he does mention R. Simḥah's position to count one woman in the context of *tefillah* and rejects it, arguing that it would be unseemly to practice that way since R. Tam himself never did so, nor did common custom include even one woman:

בית יוסף או"ח נה

וכתוב במרדכי בשם רבינו שמחה דעבד ואשה מצטרפין לתפלה ולברכת המזון בעשרה ופשוט הוא שזהו לפירוש ר"ת דפסק כרבי יהושע בן לוי בעבד אחד מצטרף וסובר רבינו שמחה דהוא הדין לאשה דבכל דוכתא אשה שוה לעבד וכיון דר"ת בעצמו לא רצה לעשות מעשה מי יקל בדבר וכן נהגו העולם שלא לצרף אשה כלל:

Beit Yosef OḤ 55

And it is written in the Mordekhai in the name of R. Simḥah that a slave or a woman may be included for *tefillah* and for the grace after meals in the ten; and clearly, this is according to the explanation of R. Tam, who ruled like R. Yehoshua b. Levi that one slave may be included, and R. Simḥah opined that this is also the law for a woman, for in every situation, a woman is equal to that of a slave [with respect to ritual roles]. But since R. Tam himself did not want to do such a thing, who can be lenient regarding it; and it is also the universal practice not to include a woman at all.

Based on this reasoning,[49] he states summarily in the **Shulḥan Arukh** that the *minyan* consists of ten free, adult males.

---

49. It is also possible that R. Karo was influenced to reject R. Simḥah in light of what he understands to be behind Rambam's ruling in Hilkhot Berakhot 5:7, that ten women may not mention God's name in *zimmun*. In Beit Yosef 199:7, R. Karo explains Rambam as rejecting the possibility of ten women forming this quorum because *zimmun* with God's name is a *davar shebikdushah*, and a *davar shebikdushah* can only be done in the presence of ten adult, free males. But see Sefer Hameorot Berakhot 45a, who understands Rambam differently, as well as yet another analysis of Rambam in Benei Tziyyon 199:6, based on differing manuscript traditions of Megillah 23b. See above n25 and Appendix C, especially n15.

שולחן ערוך או"ח נה:א

אומרים קדיש. וא"א אותו בפחות מי' זכרים בני חורין גדולים שהביאו ב' שערות, וה"ה לקדושה וברכו שאין נאמרין בפחות מעשרה.

Shulḥan Arukh OḤ 55:1

Kaddish is said. And it is said only in the presence of ten free, adult males who have reached puberty, and the same is true of *Kedushah* and *Barekhu*, which are not said with fewer than ten.

Not all rejected R. Simḥah, however. **R. Yoel Sirkes** (Poland, 16th c.) rules like R. Simḥah on *zimmun* and permits counting one woman towards a *zimmun* of ten.[50] **R. Shlomo Luria** (Poland, 16th c.), **R. Ḥayyim Benveniste** (Turkey, 17th c.), and **R. Aharon Shmuel Kaidonover** (Russia/Poland/Moravia, 17th c.), all cite R. Simḥah on *zimmun*, suggesting that they endorse his ruling as valid as well.[51]

In principle, R. Simḥah's ruling applied to *zimmun* and *tefillah* equally and we find various authorities who discuss the ramifications of his position for public prayer as well. **R. Yaakov Emden** (Germany, 18th c.), while affirming the Shulḥan Arukh's exclusion of women, asserted that the only barrier to their exclusion pertains to the honor of heaven, following R. Tam and R. Simḥah:

מור וקציעה או"ח סימן נה

כתוב במרדכי דעבד ואשה מצטרפין לתפלה ולברכת המזון בעשרה. עכ"ל. נראה דבודאי יש יסוד גדול לדברי רבינו שמחה גם בדרך הסוד, מלבד דרך הנגלה, שבלי ספק האשה מצטרפת בין למנין עשרה בין למנין שבעה, המבין יבין. ולכן אמרו חז"ל בפירוש שהיא עולה למנין שבעה הקורין בתורה. **אלא שמכל מקום אמרו שלא תקרא בצבור מפני כבוד צבור, והוא הדין לדברים הצריכים עשרה, בודאי שכן הלכה, שאין מצרפין אותה מפני הכבוד בלבד**, ואין אחר הסכמת הפוסקים כלום. אף על פי שהיה מקום לומר, לפי מה שכתבתי, שיש להקל לענין צרוף עשרה יותר מקריאת התורה דלא אפשר אלא עם הצבור במקום אחד ובמעמד אחד בתוכם ממש, מה שאין כן בצירוף לעשרה, דאפשר לאשה לעמוד מן הצד או בחדר, ובחצר קטן הפרוץ במלואו לגדול, שבאופן זה כבר תוכל להצטרף עם שמירת כבוד הצבור במקומו עומד, אף על פי כן אין לזוז מהכרעת הרב"י עדותו נאמנה, שפשט המנהג שלא לצרפה כלל.

50. Baḥ OḤ 199. He quotes Rambam's view that ten women must not make a *zimmun* with God's name and explains Rambam's objection as grounded in a requirement that *devarim shebikdushah* can only be done with ten, free men. Baḥ does not seem to reject this core point about *devarim shebikdushah* in general, but he does not accept it in the context of a *zimmun* of ten, preferring R. Simḥah's position: מיהו להצטרף בעלמא להזכרת שם שמים כתב רבינו שמחה דשרי באשה ומשמע ודאי דהוא הדין בעבד דשרי להצטרף לעשרה להזכיר שם שמים והכי נקטינן. Baḥ's ruling is even more remarkable given that he rejects counting a child as a tenth later on in his commentary on Tur OḤ 199.

51. Maharshal's notes on Tur OḤ 199 and testimony that he ruled this way in Ateret Z'keinim 199:1; Shiyarei Kenesset Hagedolah on OḤ 199, citing the Baḥ; Tiferet Shmuel on Rosh Berakhot 7:5.

Mor Uketziah OḤ 55

It is written in the Mordekhai that a slave and a woman can count towards the ten required for the *Amidah* and *birkat hamazon*. R. Simḥah's position clearly has solid Kabbalistic, as well as halakhic, grounding, because a woman clearly counts towards the quorum of ten and towards the quorum of seven.[52] Therefore, *Ḥazal* explicitly said that a woman counts toward the seven who read from the Torah. **But they nonetheless said that she may not read in public because of the honor of the community, and that is also the problem with counting women towards the quorum of ten. It is clearly the law that the only obstacle towards counting her is the issue of honor**, but no more can be said now that all the authorities agree [to exclude women entirely]. Even though we might have said, according to what I have written, that one could be lenient in counting her towards the quorum of ten, more than in the case of reading from the Torah, which is possible only in one [clearly visible and central] location, because in the case of counting towards the ten, she could stand on the side or in an adjoining room such that she could join without impinging on the community's honor. Nonetheless, one should not depart from the decision of the Beit Yosef, whose testimony is faithful, that custom has become widespread not to count her at all.[53]

R. Emden forcefully argues that we accept R. Tam and R. Simḥah's definition of *minyan* in theory, even as he does not allow for any practical deviation from the Shulḥan Arukh's decision. A similar analysis was offered by an anonymous rabbi, in the context of the question of whether it is permissible to count a

---

52. The point here about Kabbalah seems to be that *Malkhut* is the *sefirah* that corresponds to the female qualities of the Godhead and it is both one of the ten *sefirot* as well as part of the seven lower *sefirot* that are often grouped separately. Women therefore have an appropriate part to play in the quorums of ten and seven, which correspond to these groupings.

53. R. Aryeh Frimer, in פרימר, "מעמד האשה בהלכה", argues that R. Emden here was only suggesting that *kevod hatzibbur* prevented counting one woman towards the *minyan*; the exclusion of women from the other nine slots is due to other, unspecified reasons. In our estimation, this is an unsustainable reading: (1) There is no indication of another factor at work here excluding women, and the entire conversation is built around R. Simḥah's extension of R. Tam, which aims to give a fundamental definition of who counts towards a *minyan* in theory and in practice. (2) The Kabbalistic argument that kicks off this paragraph appeals to the numbers 7 and 10 as a way of justifying women's inclusion in Torah reading and the *minyan* for prayer. R. Emden, in his glosses on Megillah 23a, s.v. *aval amru* and Mor Uketziah #282 rules clearly that women may read all *aliyot* under certain circumstances. His logic thus intends to support the notion that once the feminine aspect of the Godhead is included in the count of either seven or ten, femininity has been admitted to the quorum, and there is no basis for arguing that the theoretical inclusion of women in a *minyan* does not extend to all ten slots, just as it allows for all seven Torah readers to be women. Also, as we will demonstrate, other Aharonim also state that the only barrier to counting women as equals in a *minyan* is that of honor and dignity. There is thus no reason to resist reading R. Emden in this straightforward way as well.

hermaphrodite towards the *minyan* for public prayer. The **anonymous *posek*** advances the claim that ten hermaphrodites can indeed make a *minyan*, basing himself on R. Tam. The hermaphrodite, he says, is both obligated in *tefillah* and in *mitzvot* in general and is also a בן ברית, a member of the Jewish people. Regarding his potential exclusion on account of יקרא דשמיא – the honor of Heaven – he argues that there is no reason to think this applies to the hermaphrodite. At that point in the argument, he says the following:

שו"ת אורח לצדיק סימן ב

...ואם תאמר, אי הכי, מהאי טעמא נמי נצטרף לאשה, דהא היא גם כן בת ברית כעבד, והא לא קיימא לן הכי, ובהדיה מצאנו דאינה מצטרפת! יש לומר, שאין הכי נמי דמן הדין מצטרפת... ובהדיא כתב המרדכי בשם הרב שמחה, הביאו הבית יוסף בסימן נ"ה, דאשה מצטרפת לתפלה. **אבל אין לנו לצרפה מפני כבוד הציבור**... וכן נראה דברי הבית יוסף על ההיא דהרב שמחה שכתב "וכן נהגו העולם שלא לצרף אשה כלל," ע"כ **מנהג בעלמא**... ואם באשה מצאנו בהדיא שמצטרפת אי לאו משום כבוד הציבור, כל שכן בנדון דידן שעדיף טפי דלא שייך האי טעמא... והאנדרוגינוס פשיטא שמחוייב בתפלה כשאר בני ישראל דמינה שאין להוציאו מכללם אלא לצרפו לכל דבר שבקדושה **או אחד או יותר** בכל מקום ובכל זמן.

Responsa Oraḥ LaTzaddik #2[54]

... You might object: According to my logic we would have to count a woman towards the quorum of ten, because she also is a member of the covenant[55] just like a slave, and yet we explicitly hold that a woman does not count! I would respond that, in fact, a woman should by all rights count ... and the Mordekhai wrote in the name of R. Simḥah – cited in Beit Yosef 55 – that a woman counts towards the ten needed for *tefillah*. **But we may not actually count her because of the honor of the community** ... and this seems to be the point of Beit Yosef when he writes in reaction to R. Simḥah

54. This collection of responsa belongs to R. Avraham Ḥayyim Rodrigues (Italy, 18th c.), though this specific responsum is the work of an anonymous sage. R. Rodrigues cites this opinion in order to attack it. We will turn to his attacks below; for now we seek to understand this view on its own terms.

55. The author here refers to both slaves and women as "members of the covenant." There are a few possibilities for understanding this locution: 1) This is an imprecise way of referring to both criteria of מחוייבי מצות *and* בני ברית laid out in R. Tam, but he simply only mentions one of them. Slaves are considered "members of the covenant" via circumcision, as are women, as they are considered already circumcised (without foreskin). 2) This is an imprecise way to sum up R. Tam's approach of requiring *either* being part of the Jewish people or being obligated in *mitzvot*. The author here would then be saying that what truly matters is a connection to the Jewish people – being a member of the covenant – which can be attained through birth or an acquired obligation in the commandments. These two readings correspond to the conjunctive and disjunctive readings of R. Tam we explored above in n36. It is not viable to read the author here as claiming that slaves and women are in through circumcision *alone* (a version of the disjunctive reading), since babies would qualify under this criterion as well and there would then be no place for the מחוייבי מצות terminology we find in R. Tam.

> that "the custom everywhere is not to count a woman at all" – **on account of custom alone** . . . and if it is the case that a woman can clearly count were it not for the problem of *kevod hatzibbur*, we can obviously count a hermaphrodite, where that concern does not exist . . . It is obvious that a hermaphrodite is obligated in *tefillah* like all other Jews, and from this we can deduce that there is no reason to distinguish him from other Jews, rather, we should count such a person towards all *devarim shebikdushah*, **whether one or many**, anywhere, anytime.[56]

In other words, women meet the theoretical definition for being full members of the *minyan*, but it would violate standards of honor and dignity to count them in practice, even as a tenth.

Others maintained the legitimacy of sometimes practically following a narrow reading of R. Simḥah, defending the legitimacy of counting a woman as a tenth in pressing circumstances. Indeed, the continued viability of applying R. Tam's inclusive model even in the context of *tefillah* is attested to by **R. Shneur Zalman of Liady**. Though he prefers the Shulḥan Arukh's ruling insisting on a *minyan* of ten men, he says not to protest against those who are lenient in dire situations, since they have authorities on whom to rely:

שולחן ערוך הרב או"ח נה:ה

יש מתירין לומר דבר שבקדושה בט' וצירוף עבד או אשה או קטן . . . וי"א שאין אשה ועבד או קטן מצטרפים בשום ענין אלא צריך שהיו כל עשרה זכרים בני חורין גדולים שהביאו שתי שערות . . . וכן עיקר ואעפ"כ אין למחות באותן שנוהגין להקל בשעת הדחק . . . כיון שיש להם על מי שיסמכו . . .

Shulḥan Arukh HaRav OḤ 55:5

Some permit saying a *davar shebikdushah* with nine joined together with a slave, a woman or a minor . . . And some say that a woman, slave or minor may not count at all and all ten must be free male adults who have reached puberty . . . the latter opinion is correct. Nonetheless, one should not protest against those who are lenient in pressing circumstances . . . they have authority on which to rely.[57]

56. Note that the argumentation here fundamentally assumes that R. Simḥah – at least in theory – would have counted ten women towards a *minyan*, in keeping with the broader reading we offered above at n43.

57. For Shulḥan Arukh HaRav, this latitude is clearly limited to counting a single woman. See n43. However, note that while he tolerates R. Simḥah's position on counting a single woman in the context of prayers in the synagogue, he seems to take a harder line in forbidding it in the context of a meal, since sexual impropriety is a greater threat there, though perhaps he would not object strongly there either and is only giving his preferred position. See Shulḥan Arukh HaRav OḤ 199:7.

Later authorities, even when not authorizing counting women in a *minyan*, continue to affirm R. Tam's and R. Simḥah's model as a viable way of thinking about it. **R. Ya'akov Ze'ev Kahana** (Lithuania, 19th–20th c.) struggles to find a basis for *not* counting women in a *minyan* and concludes that issues of honor and shame are ultimately at the root of the matter:[58]

תולדות יעקב, אורח חיים סימן ה

נסתפקתי אם נשים מצטרפות לעשרה לתפילה יען דמחויבות המה בתפילה כמו אנשים . . .

ולכאורה משמע דאינן מצטרפות ליו"ד מדהוצרך רבי אליעזר לשחרר עבדו להשלים ליו"ד . . . טפי היה לו להצטרף לאשתו או לבתו ולא לעבור על עשה דלעולם בהם תעבודו. ודוחק לומר שלא היה לו אשה אז . . .

הגם שיש לדחות ולומר דאין הכי נמי דהצטרף לאשתו אך בכל זה לא היו יו"ד ונצטרך גם לשחרר עבד. אבל האמת יורה דרכו דלא רצה להצטרף לאשה. ואפשר דנהי דאשה מצטרפת ליו"ד אבל זילא בהם מלתא להצטרף לאשה דומיא דאין אשה מוציאה את הרבים במגילה משום דזילא בהו מילתא טובא . . .

Toledot Ya'akov OḤ 5

I am unsure as to whether women count towards the ten for prayer, since they are obligated in prayer just like men . . .[59]

It seems that they do not count towards the ten, since R. Eliezer had to free his slave in order to get a tenth . . . [if it had been an option to count a woman as the tenth] he should have counted his wife or his daughter rather than violate the commandment to work slaves forever [and not to emancipate them].[60] It is difficult to say that he had no wife at that time . . .

Nonetheless, we might deflect that objection by saying that he *did* count his wife, but he was still one short and he needed to free his slave as well. It seems more honest to admit that he did not want to count a woman. Then again, perhaps women do indeed count towards the quorum of ten, but it would have been shameful for them to count a woman, just as a woman cannot fulfill men's obligations in *megillah* because it would be extremely shameful.[61]

58. We do not know why R. Kahana does not engage with the Shulḥan Arukh's explicit ruling on this front. One could potentially suggest that the Shulḥan Arukh only *explicitly* excludes women from the *minyan* required for *Kedushah, Kaddish,* and *Barekhu*, whereas R. Kahana is asking about the ten for the *Amidah* alone. That seems forced, especially given that the public *Amidah* includes *Kedushah*. It instead seems that he is examing the essence of the law here, trying to understand the essential principles that might lie behind the restrictive rulings he is well aware of.

59. Here is further evidence for our analysis in Part I above.

60. This refers to Berakhot 47b's discussion which wonders how R. Eliezer could have violated this law, which is articulated elsewhere.

61. The back and forth here is a striking example of how the Talmud's silence on the matter of gender and *minyan* leaves it open to such different interpretations. The language of זילא בהו מילתא/"it would be shameful for them" used here is taken from Tosafot Sukkah 38a, where it is

Even though it would be a shameful departure from normal practice to count women towards the *minyan*, argues R. Kahana, there is nothing essentially gendered about the quorum of ten. It is not surprising, then, that he tentatively suggests counting women towards the quorum of ten needed for *birkat hatanim* when there are insufficient men available.[62]

R. Natan Nata Landau (Poland, 19th–20th c.) also affirms R. Tam and R. Simḥah's basic theoretical analysis of *minyan* and explains that women don't count toward the *minyan* in practice because לאו אורח ארעא/"it is not the way of the world," not because they lack any essential religious quality necessary for *minyan*. In fact, he argues that the Talmud's implicit inclusion of women in the quorum of ten that triggers an obligation in martyrdom leads us to this conclusion. He even entertained the notion that ten women might form a *minyan* for *devarim shebikdushah*:

עורה שחר, קדושה (אות ק, ו)

ובב"י... מביא דעת רש"י [צ"ל: ר' שמחה] דאשה או עבד מצטרף לעשר', וכתב הב"י דזהו לפיר"ת ...ובסנהדרין ס"פ בן סורר מבעיא לן לענין מצות קידוש השם תשעה ונכרי אחד מהו, משמע דאשה ועבד ודאי מצטרפין. ולא עוד אלא דמשמע בתוך עשרה נשים שייך "ונקדשתי בתוך בני ישראל" ... **ואפשר הא דאשה אינה מצטרפת לתפילה משום דלאו אורח ארעא**... אבל בקידוש השם ודאי מצטרפת... ועיין בר"פ ג' שאכלו גבי והא מאה נשי כתרי גברי דמיא, ולשיטת רש"י שם אפשר דעשרה נשים יכולות להצטרף לומר דבר שבקדושה...

Urah Shaḥar s.v. *kedushah* (letter *kof*, #6)

And in the Beit Yosef... he cites the opinion of [R. Simhah] that a woman or a slave can be included in the ten, and the Beit Yosef wrote that this is according to the explanation of R. Tam ... And on Sanhedrin 75a, we ask regarding the *mitzvah* of *kiddush hashem*: Nine [Jews] and one non-Jew, what is the law? – which implies that a woman or a slave certainly are included. And not only this, but it also implies that amidst ten women, [the principle/verse] "And I will be sanctified" applies[63] ... **And it is possible, that this situation that a woman is not included for the purpose of *tefillah***

used to describe why it might be inappropriate and shameful for women to fulfill the obligations of men even when they share equal obligations. This clearly has to do with the social shame of men being led by women, in contrast to an earlier suggestion in the Tosafot that has to do with gaps in religious obligation. See Tosafot Harosh there for a clearer parallel. Tosafot themselves seem to take the term זילא בהו מילתא from Kiddushin 32a, where the term מאירה/"curse," local to Sukkah 38a, appears in conjunction with it. Ritva and R. Avraham min HaHar express the Tosafot's idea of זילא בה מילתא through the Tannaitic language of מאירה itself; see Part One, n84–96.

62. Toledot Ya'akov EH 5.

63. This obviously stands in tension with the tradition that excludes women from the term בני ישראל and supports our claim above that that derivation should be seen as *post-facto* support for an already assumed practice, rather than an obvious interpretation of the language of the verse.

> **is because it is not the way of the world**... but regarding *Kiddush Hashem* they certainly are included... And see the beginning of Berakhot chapter 7 regarding [the statement]: "And a hundred women are like two men." And according to the opinion of Rashi there,[64] it is possible that ten women can be included to say a *davar shebikdushah*...[65]

R. Landau's main contribution here is to engage the broader context of קידוש השם – the sanctification of God's name – as reflected not only through rules surrounding *tefillah,* but martyrdom as well. Women are clearly obligated in martyrdom, and several other *Aḥaronim* are also explicit that they count towards the quorum of ten required to trigger an obligation to give up one's life even for the smallest of violations.[66] However, some authorities who count women towards the quorum of martyrdom reject their participation in the quorum for *tefillah,* even though the two are derived from the same verses and fall under the same religious obligation to sanctify God's name in public.[67] Why?

Though the verses about formal *kiddush hashem* (martyrdom) are the same as those used by at least some sages to define *minyan,* R. Landau accepts that we might not, in practice, simply equate these two categories.[68] Thinking that it is dangerous to violate *mitzvot* in front of a given group of people certainly does not imply that said group represents the community in microcosm when calling down God's presence in the synagogue. Though there is not an iron wall dividing these two issues, they are easily enough separated. We can surely understand the many *Aḥaronim* who consider women part of the quorum for

64. Because Rashi interprets this line differently, this phrase is irrelevant to *minyan,* thus eliminating any possible Talmudic hook for the exclusion of women from *minyan,* as we noted above.

65. The rest of this passage notes the various sources that argue against allowing this in practice, but he ends with ועדיין צ"ע, unsatisfied with articulating a blanket ban and seeming to hold minimally that any *minyan* that did count women would be valid after the fact.

66. **R. Shmuel Aboab** was in doubt about this possibility in Responsa Devar Shemuel #63, but see **R. Yosef Ḥayyim Al-Ḥakham** in his Responsa Rav Pe'alim II OH #62 and **R. Reuven Margaliyot** in Margaliyot Hayam on Sanhedrin 74b for clear rulings that women count towards this quorum. Those who oppose counting women towards the ten of martyrdom either think that concerns about insufficient social and religious capital apply to these situations as well or are working with something like the Levush's model of *minyan*: One is not considered to have engaged in a public violation unless the Jewish community – defined by its fully obligated members – is out in full force.

67. For one contemporary example, see Yabia Omer IV OḤ #9.

68. We disagree here with R. David Golinkin's responsum on this matter; the inclusion of a set of people in one quorum does not necessarily lead to their practical inclusion in the other given their different social functions and resonances. R. Golinkin is certainly correct that the logic employed by R. Moshe Feinstein in Iggerot Moshe OH 2:19 does presume the equation of the two quorums. Nonetheless, we feel it is important to account for views, such as that of R. Ovadiah Yosef in Yabia Omer IV OḤ #9, that apply different standards for the quorum of martyrdom than for the quorum for prayer.

martyrdom while unequivocally excluding them from the quorum required for prayer: Conventional hierarchies and perceptions of dignity dissolve in times of communal stress, as marginal members of a community get persecuted along with the more central citizens. Furthermore, communal destabilization and desecration of God's name – which the demand for martyrdom is intended to avoid – is potentially much more gender-blind than a society's definition of a sufficiently august group whose presence is fitting for an active, public sanctification of God.

Nonetheless, R. Landau notes that the shared verses and themes that these two categories hold in common do reveal significant overlap, if not congruity. Though martyrdom and public prayer invoke different concerns and priorities, they are by no means unrelated; they fall under the same rubric of קידוש השם – the sanctification of God's name. This controlling idea permeates both categories and influences the rulings of numerous authorities as they borrow principles and details from one topic to elucidate the other.[69] Indeed, those who include women not only in the obligation of martyrdom but also in the quorum required to trigger this obligation effectively think about *minyan* as did R. Simḥah. It cannot be that women are *ontologically* excluded from the *minyan* of prayer even as they count for the *minyan* of martyrdom, seeing as these are two aspects of the same *mitzvah*. If women are fitting vehicles for the sanctification of God's name anywhere, they must, at least in theory, be fitting for its sanctification everywhere.

One can embrace the coherence of a position that excludes women from the *minyan* for prayer without endowing it with metaphysical power. The inclusion of women in the rubric of *kiddush hashem* does not automatically resolve the question of whether they count in the synagogue, but it does limit their exclusion in the synagogue to a secondary factor, as opposed to writing them out of the definition of ונקדשתי בתוך בני ישראל – "I shall be sanctified in the midst of the children of Israel." Or, in other words, the obstacle to counting women as equals in a *minyan*, according to this view, is nothing more and nothing less than יקרא דשמיא/כבוד ציבור/זילא בהו מילתא/אורח ארעא – a sense that the community is doing a disservice to the honor of heaven, to its own dignity and to common-sense standards that define "the way of the world."[70] Indeed, more recently, **R. Ahron Soloveichik** has been cited[71] as explicitly saying that

69. See Iggerot Moshe OḤ 2:19. While R. Feinstein's practical conclusion is not accepted by R. Ovadiah Yosef, his analysis is important evidence for how closely linked these two areas of *halakhah* are for many poskim.

70. Sperber, "Congregational Dignity," p. 5, offers yet another translation of this concept: "As the Yiddish expression has it, *es passt nicht.* [It is unseemly.]"

71. Aryeh Frimer and Dov Frimer, "Women's Prayer Services – Theory and Practice", *Tradi-*

the only reason women do not count in a *minyan* is because of *kevod hatzibbur*.

Even after all this, though, we must note that aside from the few exceptions we noted above, very few *poskim* – even among those who embrace R. Tam's analysis – practically allowed for gender-blind *minyanim*.[72] Can the concerns of יקרא דשמיא/כבוד הציבור/אורח ארעא that bar the practical implementation of R. Tam's theory be addressed, such that women could count as equals in a contemporary *minyan*?

Here we return to our conversation of *kevod tzibbur* in our analysis of Torah reading.[73] There, we saw that some authorities defined *kevod tzibbur* as a protection for the community's honor, a communal prerogative subject to the community's waiver. This understanding of *kevod tzibbur* cannot be the meaning of יקרא דשמיא as that term is used in R. Tam's analysis of *minyan*.

---

tion 32:2 (1998), footnote 85 (http://www.daat.ac.il/daat/english/tfila/frimmer1.htm). They write: "Interestingly, R. Ahron Soloveichik, in conversation with Dov I. Frimer, July 8, 1997, maintains that men and women share the same obligation (or lack thereof) in both *tefilla betzibbur* and *keriat haTorah*. However, even were women personally obligated, R. Ahron Soloveichik posits that they are, nonetheless, specifically excluded by *Ḥazal* from counting towards a *minyan* or serving as a *ḥazzan* or *ba'alat keri'a* because of *kevod hatzibbur*. Further discussion of this position is beyond the scope of this paper." In fact, R. Soloveichik's points seem to be central to any discussion of this topic and run counter to what the authors argue throughout their paper. Our analysis both of prayer leadership and *minyan* accords entirely with R. Soloveichik's position and shows the rich set of halakhic sources that help us understand it.

72. We will mention one other interesting train of thought here that led to some interesting practical rulings. Tashbetz Katan 201 reads Tosafot Berakhot 48a s.v. *v'let* as holding that since a minor can read from the Torah, a minor can surely count as a tenth for the required quorum for Torah reading. (This interpretation of the Tosafot is disputed, so we do not cite this view in their name. See Yabia Omer IV OḤ #9, sec. 9.) Magen Avraham 55:4 cites this view, though suggests it is problematic. **R. Tzvi Hirsch Grodzinski**, in Mikraei Kodesh, Sha'arei Kedushah 4:1, argues that Magen Avraham's resistance to this view (and what ought to be our rejection of it) is grounded in the fact that minors have no obligation to hear Torah reading. (We engaged the question of obligation in Torah reading above at length; see Part One, n58–80.) Women, he argues – citing Magen Avraham 282:6 – have an equal obligation to men in public Torah reading and that this obligation is fundamental, different even from their obligation in *megillah* reading, which is grounded in the more derivative formulation of אף הן היו באותו הנס. He also notes that the Shulḥan Arukh mentions the requirement for males in OḤ 55, where Torah reading is not mentioned, and does not mention males when discussing the requirement for Torah reading in OḤ 143. R. Grodzinski uses this inconsistency in the text and Massekhet Soferim's claim that women and men are equally obligated to hear Torah reading to say that women count towards the ten of Torah reading, but not towards the ten for other *devarim shebikdushah*! **R. Hillel Posek** (Romania/Israel, 20th c.), in Responsa Hillel Omer #187, put this theory into practice, recommending that a small community that would otherwise not read Torah ought to count women for Torah reading rather than cancel it. But he does not permit counting women towards the other quorums of 10 spelled out in SA OḤ 55, since that would contradict the Shulḥan Arukh. These are highly technical arguments that are not of great practical use to a discussion about more thoroughgoing egalitarian practice. They are nonetheless significant in complicating the history of gender and *minyan*, demonstrating further that there have been some *poskim* who have been willing to take a practical stance on some of the theory explored here. They are also important indicators of the absence of any clear Talmudic exclusion of women that would have shut this sort of conversation down immediately.

73. See above, Part One, n97–112.

Even those authorities, such as the anonymous *posek* cited in Oraḥ LaTzaddik #2 and R. Landau in Urah Shaḥar, who equate יקרא דשמיא with the terms כבוד צבור and אורח ארעא, cannot have thought that יקרא דשמיא is subject to communal waiver. First, the language of יקרא דשמיא/"the honor of Heaven" itself indicates a factor that is not subject to communal discretion. Second, there is no record of anyone – including those who embrace R. Tam's definition of *minyan* – suggesting that an individual community is entitled to waive its honor and thereby allow counting minors for half the *minyan*. The only practical rulings to emerge from R. Tam's school are those that did not tamper with יקרא דשמיא by suggesting it was some kind of relative concern. Rather, יקרא דשמיא is an objective claim about honor and dignity, which is apparent to anyone willing to honestly assess the situation. A *minyan* made up mostly of children is something everyone would agree we do not and ought not to take seriously.

When later *Aḥaronim*, such as those we cited above, translate יקרא דשמיא as כבוד ציבור, they are therefore using the latter term in the sense we saw it used by the Baḥ. *Kevod tzibbur* here means an objective assessment of communal action when viewed from afar: Is the act in question something you would do when presenting yourself to an earthly sovereign? Would it meet your standards for seriousness in other realms of life? If not, then it is inappropriate to settle for something less in a communal, ritual context. יקרא דשמיא is not a force subject to communal discretion, it is a demand that communities live up to the standards of dignity and seriousness that they are capable of. The same is true of Urah Shaḥar's rendition of יקרא דשמיא as אורח ארעא/"the way of the world." The honor of Heaven demands that we not serve God in a manner that would be recognized as mediocre, unseemly and falling short of broadly recognized standards.

The honor of Heaven can only be appeased when the quorum in question quite obviously and objectively presents no indignity whatsoever. We would suggest an even more conservative standard: The inclusion as equals in the *minyan* of previously marginal members is consistent with יקרא דשמיא when their exclusion *would* offend it. Groups consisting mostly of minors were not taken seriously in the ancient world, nor in the medieval world, nor today. The same was true of groups made up mostly of women, until very recently in modern times.[74] In this sense, a highly-gendered definition of *minyan* exactly matched the standards for seriousness in the broader society. But the times have now changed so dramatically that there are almost no groups that are taken seriously that do *not* include women as equals. In fact, groups defined

74. Note that in the United States, women, even after they possessed the right to vote, could be rejected for a line of credit on the grounds of their gender until 1974.

by male membership are limited to sports and caricatured private clubs that generally have racist backgrounds as well. Communal bodies that do not count women and men as equals are increasingly marginalized and mocked or at best treated as nostalgic accommodations to men looking for some escape from contemporary society. They are bodies that neither command respect nor evoke "the honor of Heaven."

If one follows R. Tam's definition of *minyan* but maintains its all-male nature in practice on the basis of יקרא דשמיא, one may in fact be undermining the very value one intends to uphold. יקרא דשמיא certainly cannot be waived; but society's changing standards can affect how we do and don't experience it. R. Tam's analysis shows that women count in theory. The question has only been whether the realities of Jewish life could and should support the theory's practical implementation. It has never and likely will never support the practical implementation of the theory with respect to minors (nor would it to slaves if they still existed in our contexts), and there may be communities where that reality will persist for women as well. The question before the communities that grapple with this issue today is what the consequences are of perpetuating that reality. The very existence of this moral dilemma for certain communities and the intensity with which it is engaged there demonstrates a conviction that the message that says women compromise the honor of heaven is today palpably false and distorting, perhaps even threatening to the vitality of the Jewish community. Communities who count women as equals in the *minyan* based on R. Tam's theoretical approach to *minyan* and a contemporary, gender-neutral assessment of יקרא דשמיא in practice, have strong halakhic grounds on which to base themselves.

E. Those who Reject R. Tam and the Consequences for Gender and *Minyan*

Our entire analysis in this last section was predicated on R. Tam's definition of *minyan* as theoretically including all those obligated in *mitzvot* and those who are members of the covenant. As we noted, the Levush demurred from this definition and excluded women (and slaves and minors) from *minyan* in a more fundamental way, based on their lack of maximal obligation in *mitzvot*. We thus also find practical discussions surrounding gender and *minyan* that draw much more fundamental lines when it comes to gender equality.

We already saw the words of R. Shneur Zalman of Liady above, who acknowledged R. Tam's theory of *minyan* and granted it some legitimacy under certain circumstances, while nonetheless arguing that the Levush's approach was superior and correct. Other *Aḥaronim* similarly considered R. Tam's approach and rejected it, some with great force. Recall the position we cited above of one anonymous rabbi who argued that the exclusion of women from *minyan* was about one factor and one factor alone: *Kevod tzibbur*. That *posek* used this claim to argue for counting hermaphrodites as equals in a *minyan*, based on the theory that *kevod tzibbur* would not apply as a concern to these otherwise qualified members of the *minyan*. As we saw above, **R. Avraham Ḥayyim Rodrigues** (Italy, 18th c.)[75] cites this anonymous view in his collection of responsa, Oraḥ LaTtzaddik. He then proceeds to rebut it in strident fashion:

שו"ת אורח לצדיק סימן ג

... דאטו משום שחייב בתפלה משום דרחמי נינהו יתחייב להתפלל בעשרה? הא אשה חייבת בתפלה מהאי טעמא ואינה חייבת להתפלל בעשרה, ומינה דאינה מצטרפת!... אחר כך יגע ולא מצא שהביא ראיה מהא דכתב הבית יוסף בשם המרדכי דטעמא דמאן דשרי לאיצטרופי קטן נראה דהיינו משום דכל בי עשרה שכינתא שריא ואמאי נוציא האנדרוגינוס מכלל זה כיון דהוי זרע קדש וכו'. כל דבריו אינם אלא דברי תימא, דהא הודה ולא בוש שכל ראיותיו שהביא מקטן ואשה לאו הלכתא נינהו, ואם כן טעמא דבית שמאי אתא לאשמעינן וההיא טעמא לאו בר סמכא הוא כיון דלא קיימא לן הכי ... ולפי דבריו בואו ונצרף לנשים לעשרה לתפלה, בין אחת או יותר, כיון שחייבות בתפלה וגם הן זרע קדש, ולכל דבר שבקדושה. חי נפשי שמתבושש אני ונכלם להשיב על דברים אלו.

Responsa Oraḥ LaTzaddik #3

... Do you mean to say that because one is obligated to pray the *Amidah*, on account of its being a personal request for mercy, he is obligated to pray with a *minyan* of ten? A woman is obligated to pray the *Amidah* but is not obligated to pray with a *minyan* of ten, and we can deduce from this that she may not count towards that *minyan*! ... Then you tried, without success, to cite proof from the Beit Yosef's citation of the Mordekhai that those who permit counting a minor do so because the *Shekhinah* dwells in any group of ten; why would we exclude the hermaphrodite, who is also of holy stock? Everything you say is surprising; you yourself admit without shame that your proofs are drawn from rejected positions regarding minors and women! If so, are you coming to teach me the reasons for Beit Shammai's opinion? Those reasons have no authority given that we do not follow their practical implementation ... According to your logic, we should count women towards the quorum of ten for *tefillah*, whether one or many, based on the fact that they are obligated to pray the *Amidah* and are of holy stock, and towards the quorum needed for every *davar shebikdushah*. By my life, I am ashamed and embarrassed even to have to respond to such an argument.

75. R. Rodrigues taught, among others, R. Malakhi HaKohen, author of the great methodological work Yad Malakhi.

R. Rodrigues makes a number of arguments here. First, while conceding that women have a full obligation in prayer, he claims that they do not have an obligation to pray in a *minyan* and if one is not obligated to pray in a *minyan*, then one certainly does not count in that *minyan*.[76] But then he proceeds with a more direct attack. He argues that the entire argument for theoretically including women and minors in the *minyan* stems from a theory (R. Tam's) that is not followed in practice. Since it is common practice not to count a minor or a woman even as a tenth, this indicates, argues R. Rodrigues, that this theory is rejected as well. R. Rodrigues refers to R. Tam's theory as "Beit Shammai's opinion" in that our refusal to implement it in practice is reflective of our rejection of it in theory as well, just as we treat the many views of Beit Shammai that are largely discarded as legally inoperative. *Minyan* is not, for R. Rodrigues, simply a collection of individuals with some basic connection to *mitzvot* and the covenant as it was for R. Tam. As a result, he ends with his shock that a person would ever entertain that ten women could count for a *minyan*, since this would be based on a rejected theory of what *minyan* is all about.

In truth, R. Rodrigues' attack on his interlocutor here is not entirely fair. The anonymous *posek* did *not* argue that women could be counted for a *minyan* in practice. Indeed, he would have strongly opposed counting even one. He only argued that this exclusion was due to *kevod tzibbur* as opposed to more fundamental issues of identity, responsibility and belonging. He would have agreed with R. Rodrigues that counting a woman towards the *minyan* would be unthinkable *in practice in his time and place*. But he would likely advocate for resisting the notion that just because something is wildly inappropriate in a *given* social context, it is therefore theoretically unimaginable in *any* possible context. This approach flows directly from R. Tam's model. The real gulf here is that the anonymous *posek* – like R. Ya'akov Emden – felt that R. Tam's theory remained live even when not implemented in practice. By contrast, R. Rodrigues rejects R. Tam entirely and works with a different definition of *minyan*, almost certainly that of the Levush. The hermaphrodite would then

76. This claim is unsourced here and has no precedent in the *Rishonim*. While there are views in the *Rishonim* that think that individuals have an obligation to pray in a *minyan*, there is no ancient or medieval source that suggests that such an obligation to pray with a *minyan* would be gendered. See Appendix B for more on the topic of the obligation to pray with a *minyan*. In particular, see the Shevut Ya'akov there, who seems to assume that we learn that women are not obligated to pray with a *minyan* from the fact that they do not count towards it! That claim is unprecedented in the medieval period as well. Nonetheless, it is of course not an unreasonable position to see linkage between one's ability to constitute a quorum and the expectation that one be present to help make it a reality. R. Rodrigues seems to be making that sort of claim here: Of course anyone who would count in a *minyan* would be obligated to help constitute one; from the fact that we don't expect women to come, it must be that they don't count.

not be included as an equal in the *minyan* because he is not unambiguously maximally obligated like adult, free men.[77]

Anyone following the approach of the Levush and others who define *minyan* as a group of ten bearing maximal Jewish obligation would have to make a different argument in order to justify a gender-equal *minyan*. Since, for the Levush, only a Jew obligated in the full range of *mitzvot* can count as a member of the *minyan*, one would have to claim that contemporary women (at least in some communities) are no longer exempt from the category of positive commandments caused by time.

F. Are Contemporary Women Maximally Obligated?

Throughout our analysis, we have reached various points in the discussion where fully gender-equal practice in a given ritual context has been linked to the broader obligation gaps between men and women in classical sources. We saw this most clearly in the Ran's analysis of Torah reading and the Levush's definition of *minyan*. We noted that in order to make an argument for gender equality that would address the concerns of these authorities, one would have to claim that contemporary women, unlike their female ancestors, are indeed maximally obligated in *mitzvot* no different than men.

Is it possible to make such a claim? We can only briefly outline the contours of such an argument here. As is the case with any legal term, one must carefully examine its original context before assuming what it means in a different context. While it is possible to read *Ḥazal*'s term נשים as applying across history to all those who are biologically female, it is also possible – particularly when נשים is juxtaposed with the categories of slaves and minors – that this term is intended to refer to adjunct members of society who are dependent on and subservient to their husbands and a larger patriarchal structure for support. Indeed, **R. Yoel Bin-Nun** has recently been advancing precisely this argument, suggesting that those women in our day and age who understand themselves to be בנות חורין, freed from earlier patriarchal structures, are thus subject to all the traditional ritual obligations of men:[78]

77. Tosefta Bikkurim 2:4 states that hermaphrodites indeed have all the same obligations in positive *mitzvot* as men. But the larger context there indicates that this may well be because they are treated with the dual stringencies of both men and women, such that their maximal obligation in practice is in fact derivative of a more doubtful claim about their maximal obligation in theory. This matches rulings elsewhere that do not allow a man to fulfill his obligations through the agency of a hermaphrodite. See Tosefta Rosh Hashanah 2:5.

78. י. בן־נון, תגובה ל"ברכת חתנים: האם מניין גברים הוא הכרחי?", *גרנות* 3 (תשסג): 172–173.

רוב הנשים של ימינו בנות חורין הן ... ואינן דומות לעבדים בשום פנים, שהרי אין רשות אחרים עליהן. לפיכך, כל מי שמצטט פסקי חכמים, שהתבססו על כך ש"אישה דומה לעבד" בכל מקום, אינו מבין שהוא מעביר הלכה ממציאות אחת למציאות אחרת, בלי יסוד. "נשים שלנו", לא רק שכולן חשובות, כדברי הרמ"א, אלא שהן "בנות חורין" ... פשוט לא מדובר באותו סוג של נשים.

Most women in our day are independent/liberated [*benot ḥorin*] . . . and they bear no resemblance to slaves, because there is no higher power over them. Therefore, anyone who cites the rulings of the Sages, which are based on the notion that "a woman is similar to a slave" in all arenas, fails to understand that he is transferring a *halakhah* from one reality to another without any basis whatsoever. "Our women" are not only all important – as the Rema already said – but they are independent/liberated . . . it is obvious that we are not speaking about the same category of *nashim*.

For R. Bin-Nun, the entire terminology of אשה/*ishah* must be revisited, particularly when the term is used in conjunction with terms like עבד/slave. This juxtaposition suggests the legal categories share some fundamental characteristics and that the term אשה may map better in such contexts onto sociology (being a social adjunct) as opposed to biology (having a certain chromosomal makeup). If the terms of the local *halakhah* are driven by sociology, then contemporary females – at least those in societies that afford them full rights and equality – in fact have no exemption from positive commandments caused by time.[79] In this reading, נשים עבדים וקטנים/"Women, slaves, and minors" is best translated as "social adjuncts" or "not full citizens" and may map onto biology differently in a society where the correlation between biology and power has undergone transformation or revolution. For instance, telling a contemporary neurosurgeon who happens to be biologically female that she is exempt from reciting the *Shema* might be a *violation* of the Torah's values, which would expect all of those who wield power to be subject to the command to accept the yoke of heaven twice a day.[80]

79. In a personal communication, R. Bin-Nun confirmed that he would extend this logic to the realm of vicarious fulfillment; i.e., a woman in this category could blow *shofar* for a man. Interestingly, in discussing the concept of *minyan*, R. Bin-Nun says: לכן, לכאורה, היה אפשר בימינו להיאחז בשיטת רבנו תם – "Therefore, it would seem that one can, in our day, follow the position of R. Tam." R. Bin-Nun means this in the practical sense that R. Tam's position theoretically allows for ten women to constitute the *minyan*. But the essence of R. Bin-Nun's argument is in fact that contemporary women often have a different status than the women spoken of by *Ḥazal*, such that, according to R. Bin-Nun's analysis, ten women can constitute a *minyan* even under the Levush's theory.

80. This sort of linguistic redefinition is well attested in halakhic literature. Though a full survey of this phenomenon is beyond the scope of our discussion, two important examples should suffice to convince the reader that this is a plausible argument with an established pedigree. (1) R. Menaḥem HaMeiri, of 13–14th century Provençe, argued that various *halakhot* regarding

In order to count women as equals in the Levush's *minyan*, one would have to take this broader step, arguing that women not only have the social capital they would need for R. Tam, but also the broader religious equality that would enable them to constitute the community in microcosm.[81] Indeed, there are already many communities where men and women are functionally equal in this regard, where women do not make room for men when a *sukkah* is too small, where women are no more lenient about the *mitzvot* of *lulav* and *shofar* than are men, and where *sefirat ha'omer* reveals no trace of any gendering. Such communities may already be implicitly adopting R. Bin-Nun's model and could, with integrity, make explicit the implicit theory behind their practice. R. Bin-Nun's model supports allowing women to count as equals in the *minyan* even according to Levush's definition of a quorum of ten as being comprised of

---

interactions between Jews and non-Jews related only to lawless pagans and not the civilized Christians he knew and interacted with regularly. Meiri's approach essentially redefined the term נכרי or גוי in areas of civil and criminal law. Though an unreflective application of these terms to all non-Jews would have been understandable, Meiri argued that these terms were in fact aiming to get at the negative sociological traits of certain non-Jews – i.e., lawless pagans – but not all non-Jews, and in particular not the Christians among whom the Meiri lived. Some of the halakhic consequences of this analysis were merely greater stringencies on the Jew, demanding equal treatment of the non-Jew in civil and criminal law. But Meiri took his rereading of the terms גוי and נכרי seriously enough to justify violating Shabbat – a capital crime in Jewish law – to save the lives of his contemporary Christians, whereas classical rabbinic sources assume that this is not permitted. For more on this interpretational shift, see מ. הלברטל, *בין תורה לחכמה: ר' מנחם המאירי ובעלי ההלכה המיימונים בפרובנס*, ירושלים תשסג, 80–108. (2) A deaf-mute (חרש) is generally classed in rabbinic literature with the mentally incompetent and is therefore exempt from various *mitzvot*. When sign-language was developed in the modern period, a number of *poskim* advocated understanding חרש not as a physical description, but rather as an indicator of mental incompetence, such that a deaf-mute able to communicate with the outside world and to learn would not fall into this halakhic category. For more on this topic, see א. אנצ'ילובץ, "מעמד החרש במציאות זמננו", *תחומין* כא (תשסא): 141–152. Both of these redefinitonal approaches are controversial and neither attracted unanimous support. Nonetheless, they are a part of the halakhic conversation and can serve as important parallels to the contemporary debate surrounding gender and Jewish practice. For a fuller analysis of these sorts of "category shifts" and the possible application to gender, see E. Tucker, "Category Shifts in Jewish Law and Practice," at https://www.mechonhadar.org/torah-resource/category-shifts-jewish-law-and-practice.

81. R. Joel Roth, in the context of the conversation regarding the ordination of women as rabbis in the Conservative movement, also attempted to square the desire for a gender-equal *minyan* with the Levush's standard of ten maximally obligated individuals. He suggested that women could electively obligate themselves in all *mitzvot* and thereby be eligible to be treated identically to men, even according to the Levush. See his paper, cited in Introduction, n1 above. Engaging this approach of self-obligation and its effectiveness is beyond the scope of our discussion. Note that R. Bin-Nun's argument is different, arguing that women are *automatically* obligated in the *mitzvot* from which they were traditionally exempt, as a result of their changed social status. Therefore, for R. Bin-Nun, women's actual record of performing those *mitzvot* or their theoretical commitment to them is not relevant to their ritual status as citizens and leaders. This, of course, was always the case with Jewish men, whose actual record of *mitzvah* observance was never relevant to their status. Nonetheless, a community that adopts R. Bin-Nun's theory without having gender-equal *mitzvah* observance in practice will not have as much self-evident religious integrity.

ten maximally obligated Jews.[82] We find this model to be honest and plausible as a halakhic pathway and are drawn to its emphasis on ritual gender equality as a stringency rather than a leniency. But we also acknowledge that this mode of halakhic thinking remains novel and is still being considered and digested in many quarters. For those who are not yet prepared to accept it, gender equal *minyanim* would depend on R. Tam's approach and a reassessment of the honor of heaven in contemporary settings.[83]

IV. THE PROPRIETY OF MIXED-GENDER QUORUMS

Whether following the approach of R. Tam or the Levush, one might still engage the question of the propriety of having men and women join together to create a public ritual space.

Ra'ah (R. Aharon HaLevi of Barcelona, 13th c.), cited in Ritva Megillah 4a, advances the argument that women, as an extension of their obligation in *megillah* reading, ought to be able to count towards the quorum of ten that is ideally required for reading it. He contrasts the case of the quorum of ten needed for *megillah* reading with Mishnah Berakhot 7:2's apparent ban on women joining with men to form a *zimmun*, which Ra'ah understands to be motivated by concerns about sexual impropriety.[84] Why wouldn't such sexual impropriety be a concern in the context of the *minyan* for *megillah* reading? Ra'ah proposes that we are only concerned about sexual impropriety when the dual-gender nature of the quorum is obvious from the form of the ritual itself – צירוף כולי האי' or צריכי גברי לצירוף דידהו לגמרי. Specifically, when two men and one woman join for a *zimmun*, an entire introductory section is added to the blessings after food. All are thus aware that the *zimmun* ritual is happening only because the men and women present have been melded into a group and are dependent on one another's presence. By contrast, *megillah* reading looks the same when done for one person or for ten. Since the quorum of ten in that case is a requirement with no effect on the form of the liturgy,[85] it

82. Note that adopting an approach like R. Bin-Nun would make women eligible to perform other rituals that we are not addressing in our current analysis, such as fulfilling men's obligations in *shofar* blowing and in the recitation of the full *Hallel*. See Introduction, n7.

83. The same would be true for a fully gender-equal Torah reading, which, absent R. Bin-Nun's sort of analysis, requires following R. Tam's approach, which largely sidelines the relevance of the identity of the leader.

84. This interpretation of Mishnah Berakhot 7:2 is not universal. See Koren's article cited above, n8 and see Appendix C.

85. Either Ra'ah does not subscribe to the view taken by some *Rishonim* that the final *berakhah* after the *megillah* is only done in a group of ten, or he does not consider this sort of addition to be significant enough to trigger a *peritzut* problem. Depending on how one answers this question, one would reach a different conclusion as to whether, for the Ra'ah, a mixed group of ten men

is not as obvious that men and women are forming a group and thus is not inappropriate.[86]

Ra'ah's logic would obviously extend to mixed quorums of men and women for *devarim shebikdushah*, which are only done in a group of ten, such that the interdependence of the members of the *minyan* is obvious. Ra'ah's opinion was far from universal.[87] R. Simḥah and those who followed in his wake clearly reject it. Others, like R. Ya'akov Emden, did not consider this to be a factor in the ban on counting women as equals. Yet others, such as Sefer Hameorot, dispute the notion that concerns about sexual impropriety are the issue with a male-female *zimmun* in the first place.[88] And even for those, like Ra'ah, concerned about potential sexual improprieties in mixed-gender quorums, that concern is anchored in a broader social reality in which male-female interactions in public spaces are obviously inappropriate. That assessment would need to be evaluated in each time and place according to its character. As we noted, we are not exploring those issues in depth in the context of this analysis.

Nonetheless, the Ra'ah's concerns may continue to be compelling for many contemporary communities. Those communities, even if following the pathways to a gender-equal *minyan* that we outlined above, might choose to avoid mixed quorums and allow for *minyanim* composed of ten men *or* ten women.[89]

---

and women could perform *zimmun* with God's name, given that the fundamental structure of the *zimmun* is already in place via the presence of three men and/or three women.

86. This line of thought is then also cited in Ran on Rif Megillah 6b. This is a novel articulation of the nature of the concern of *peritzut*. All sources earlier than the Ra'ah assume that *peritzut* is a problem of interaction in the context of the ritual, such that it would theoretically apply to any case of a man or a woman performing rituals one for the other. Indeed, based on such an assumption, Sefer Hameorot on Berakhot 45a argues that *peritzut* cannot be an area of concern when dealing with free adults of mixed gender, since men perform rituals for women all the time and women, were it not for *kevod hatzibbur*, are eligible to read Torah for a community that includes men. Ra'ah is the first to advance the notion that though leading a ritual for someone else is devoid of *peritzut*, being *dependent on the presence* of the other person in order to do so is, and said concern applies to mixed-gender groups of free adults as well. In part because earlier sources implicitly reject this notion and in part because it doesn't necessarily translate easily into intuitive notions of how *peritzut* would actually work in a human context, it seems best to understand Ra'ah here as coming up with a *post facto* defense of his ruling that women count as equals for the ten of *megillah* in order to defend it from any challenges from the realm of *zimmun*.

87. Note the tacit disagreement of all authorities prior to Ra'ah on his novel definition of *peritzut*.

88. Ra'ah also does not address Sefer Hameorot's evidence from women's principled inclusion in Torah reading. For more on the view of Sefer Hameorot and the question of *zimmun*, see Appendix C.

89. A number of *Aḥaronim* resist mixed-gender quorums even when it can be demonstrated that women have identical obligation to men. For one example, see R. Simhah Bamberger (Germany, 19th c.), in Responsa Zekher Simḥah #75, who argues that women and men can never form a group because of R. Yonah's reason for the problem of mixed-gender *zimmun*: אין חברתן נאה. While not an issue of sexuality, this is a claim that there is simply never a proper sense of group when men and women are both involved.

Indeed, a similar approach is taken by R. Yoel Bin-Nun, who draws a sharp distinction between

V. ARE GENDER-EQUAL *MINYANIM* WISE?

Beyond our analysis here, some may argue that counting women in the *minyan*, though theoretically appropriate today, is too destabilizing to countenance, while others will argue that counting women does not entail any more risks than the benefits it would bring. This argument echoes the dispute we saw above between the rabbis of Amsterdam, who had no objection to women saying *kaddish*, and the Ḥavvot Yair, who thought such a practice would be disruptive of norms,[90] and the contemporary dispute between R. Mendel Shapiro and R. Daniel Sperber, who see women reading Torah and having *aliyot* as appropriate, and R. Yehuda Henkin, who thinks that such a practice will inevitably correlate with a more lax standard of observance and is therefore unwise. We of course have precedent in the halakhic tradition for recognizing that these concerns, as well, are contextual. As we noted previously, R. Aharon Soloveichik permitted women to say *Kaddish,* precisely because, in his community, to refuse to do so would lead to the weakening of Jewish observance via the abandonment of Orthodox communities by Jewish women searching for synagogues that would allow such a practice. Any assessment of risk and benefit will ultimately be made by each community based on what it experiences on the ground. In communities where distinctions between men and women remain strong generally, tampering with an all-male definition of *minyan* may weaken the status of communal prayer and the seriousness with which it is approached. But as we have noted repeatedly, maintaining all-male *minyanim* in an increasingly gender-equal society has its own risks, including the relegating of communal prayer to a nostalgic activity decoupled from the real data of life. And as R. Bin-Nun points out, such a standard may not only be unwise, but might even be a distortion of the *halakhah* as it is meant to

---

contemporary women's equality to men and the permissibility of women and men collaborating to create a shared ritual space:

> אבל יש דבר שלא נשתנה כל עיקר, והוא "יצר לב האדם". ולכן, כל צירוף של גברים ונשים יחד בדברים שבקדושה אין לו מקום, מעצם העובדה שהוא מכניס מתח מיני אל הקודש, חס ושלום, וכל הטענות, הנכונות כשלעצמן, של שינוי במעמד הנשים שבזמננו, אינו קשור כלל ליצרי מעללי איש. אפשר אף להפך: השינוי הדרמטי מחייב זהירות מיוחדת בדברים שבקדושה. תפילת נשים – כן, על פי רצונן והחלטותיהן. צירוף גברים ונשים יחד בתפילה או בזימון – לא ולא.

> "But there is one thing that has not changed at all, which is the human sexual drive. Therefore, there is no place for men and women to join together for the *minyan* for *devarim shebikdushah,* on account of the fact that this would introduce sexual tension into sacred space, God forbid. All the claims about the change in the status of women in our time, which are correct, have no connection to the sexual desires of human beings. Indeed, it might be that just the opposite is true: The dramatic shift [in the social status of women] necessitates heightened vigilance around sacred rituals (*devarim shebikdushah*). Women's prayer – yes, subject to their desire and decision. Joining men and women together in *tefillah* or in *zimmun* – absolutely not."

90. See above, Part One, n159.

be applied to a contemporary community that treats men and women in the public realms with equal seriousness and respect.

Summary

A *minyan* is the manifestation of the Jewish community in microcosm. The earliest sources demand ten members for this purpose, though they minimally define who is eligible to constitute this group. Talmudic sources clarify that slaves and minors are clearly marginal members at best, but they are silent on the question of counting women. The middle ages brought a mix of views: Some continued silence, some unsourced exclusion of women from *minyan*, some attempts to ground the exclusion of women in verses and terms that evoke microcosmic Jewish community and some appeals to common sense for the obviousness of the female exclusion. In addition, at least one medieval source advocated including women at least partially in the *minyan*.

Peering behind the data to discover the theory underlying them, we discovered two main conceptions of *minyan*:

1) R. Tam argued that all those attached to the Jewish community through *mitzvah* obligation and covenantal membership are theoretically eligible to count towards the *minyan*. The only bar to doing so in practice is יקרא דשמיא/"the honor of Heaven."
2) Levush argued that the essence of the *minyan* is ten maximally obligated Jews. As such, women, slaves and minors, with their varying exemptions from many or all *mitzvot*, cannot ever constitute a *minyan*.

These two theories present two distinct pathways for assessing the validity and legitimacy of gender-equal *minyanim*. R. Tam's theory – which is followed by a range of medieval and modern authorities, even if they reject implementing it in practice – allows for the counting of women as equals provided that no offense results to the honor of Heaven. Jewish communities of today still share this instinctive feeling about counting children as equals in the *minyan*. For a significant communal act such as public prayer the community should bring out its finest, its full citizens, not its peripheral members. We discussed this concept of "the honor of Heaven," demonstrating that it is not a communal prerogative to be waived. Rather, it demands an honest assessment: Will the de-gendering of *minyan* be experienced as a cheapening of communal prayer in order to lower standards and increasing the participation of marginal members? Or will it be experienced as raising the dignity of communal prayer to keep it in line with the standards of gender equality that reflect dignity and seriousness in the rest of society? If the honor of Heaven will honestly be advanced, rather than compromised, by embracing a gender-equal standard for *minyan*, then R. Tam's theory is a strong basis for egalitarian practice in this area.

Levush's theory can only countenance counting women as equals if accompanied by the claim that contemporary women have a broader set of obligations than those described in classical rabbinic sources. One would need to argue that the term אשה/"woman" in classical literature is sometimes used as a placeholder for a sociological status that women shared with slaves and minors in most times and places in human history. Under that reading, contemporary changes in the status of women have resulted in corollary shifts in their religious obligations such that they now are, through proper application of *halakhah*, maximally obligated Jews and thus self-evidently included in a *minyan* just like men. Pursuing this approach with integrity would demand educational and religious messages that communicate equal expectations of men and women, treating gender equality not just as an excuse for greater flexibility but also as a source of redoubled religious commitment. Communities that manifest that application of *halakhah* to their contemporary lives can reasonably claim not only R. Tam but also the Levush as support for their egalitarian practice.

According to either model, the delicate questions of whether equality should be played out through gender-mixed practices as opposed to gender-segregated ones can and must be assessed community by community, with great sensitivity to the social context.

At the end of the day, we and others grapple with these questions because much of human society has recently experienced seismic shifts in the role of gender in our lives. It was crystal clear to so many of our ancestors that women do not represent a microcosm of the body politic, on account of their adjunct status, whether in the social sphere or on account of their less central role in certain areas of Jewish ritual practice. And yet for many of us, almost the opposite of that is true: When we confront structures that place limits on female citizenship, we are uncomfortable and become concerned that the community is not fully represented when half of its members are excluded.

Human society sometimes has a more difficult time with gender equality than does God. God may tolerate and even, in certain cultural settings, endorse social arrangements that discriminate based on gender. But our tradition also tells us that many such distinctions are contextual and contingent. They are not necessarily, in their essence, divinely ordained. Our Sages of blessed memory expressed this point in their midrashic expansion on the story of the daughters of Tzelofeḥad:

ספרי במדבר קלג

"וַתִּקְרַבְנָה בְּנוֹת צְלָפְחָד" (במדבר כז:א): כיון ששמעו בנות צלפחד שהארץ מתחלקת לשבטים, לזכרים ולא לנקבות, נתקבצו כולן זו על זו ליטול עצה. אמרו, 'לא כרחמי בשר ודם רחמי המקום: בשר ודם רחמיו על הזכרים יותר מן הנקבות אבל מי שאמר והיה העולם אינו כן אלא רחמיו על הזכרים ועל הנקבות רחמיו על הכל', שנאמר ["נֹתֵן לֶחֶם לְכָל בָּשָׂר וגו'" (תהלים קלו:כה), "נוֹתֵן לִבְהֵמָה לַחְמָהּ וגו'" (שם קמז:ט) ואומר] "טוֹב ה' לַכֹּל וְרַחֲמָיו עַל כָּל מַעֲשָׂיו" (שם קמה:ט).

Sifre Bemidbar #133

"And Tzelofeḥad's daughters drew near" (Bemidbar 27:1): When Tzelofeḥad's daughters heard that the land would be divided according to the tribes – to males and not to females – they all gathered to take counsel with one another. They said, "The goodness of God is not like the goodness of flesh and blood. Flesh and blood show greater goodness to males than to females, but the One-Who-Spoke-the-World-into-Being is not so, but is good to all, as it is said . . . 'The Lord is good to all and shows kindness to all creatures'" (Tehillim 145:9).

We pray that our investigation of this topic can lead Jewish communities to a deeper understanding of their own practices, a sense of the underlying values that have guided these conversations throughout the centuries and a profound desire to properly apply God's eternal *mitzvot* to our personal and communal lives.

Appendix A: Talmud Bavli Berakhot 20b

MISHNAH Berakhot 3:3 discusses women's obligation in *tefillah*, and there are many variants in the Talmud Bavli's analysis of this Mishnah on Berakhot 20b. Here is a synopsis of various textual witnesses:

Soncino (1484)

מאי שנא ק"ש ותפילין דמצות עשה שהזמן גרמ' וכל מצות עשה שהזמן גרמ' נשים פטורות' תפלה ומזוזה וברכת המזון דמצות עשה שלא הזמן גרמ' נשים חייבות' ק"ש פשיטא' מצות עשה שהזמן גרמ' הוא וכל מצות עשה שהזמן גרמא נשים פטורות' מהו דתימ' הואיל ואית בה מלכות שמים קמ"ל" ומן התפילין פשיטא' מהו דתימ' הואיל ואתקוש למזוזה' קמ"ל" וחייבין בתפלה דרחמי נינהו' מהו דתימ' הואיל וכתי' בה ערב ובקר וצהרים כמצות עשה שהזמן גרמ' דמי קמ"ל" ובמזוזה' פשיטא' מהו דתימ' הואיל ואתקש לתלמוד תורה' קמ"ל" ובברכת המזון פשיטא' מהו דתימ הואיל וכתי' בתת יי לכם בערב בשר לאכל ולחם בבקר לשבע' כמצו' עשה שהזמן גרמא דמי קמ"ל"

Paris 671

מאי שנא קרית שמע וכל מצות עשה שהזמן (ש) גרמה נשים פטורות משום דכתי' ביה בשכבך ובקומך הוייא ליה מצות עשה שהזמן גרמה תפלין נמי לילה לאו זמן תפילין הוא הוו להו מצות עשה שהזמן גרמה נשים פטורות אבל תפלה ומזוזה וברכת המזון כיון דהוייא להו מצות עשה שלא הזמן גרמה חייבות מאי טעמ' כל מצות עשה שלא הזמן גרמה נשים חייבות פטורין מקרית שמע פשיטא דהא מצות עשה שהזמן גרמה הוא מהו דתימ' כיון דמלכות שמים (הוא) היא הכל חייבין קמ"ל ומן התפילין פשיטא מהו דתימ' הקיש תפילין למזוזה מה מזוזה מיחייבי תפילין נמי מיחייבי קמ"ל וחייבים בתפלה פשיטא מהו דתימ' הואיל וכתי' ערב ובקר צהרים כי מצות עשה שהזמן גרמה היא קמ"ל כיון דרחמוי נחילא ובמזוזה פשיטא מהו דתימ' אקיש מזוזה לתלמוד תורה מה תלמוד תורה פטירי אף מזוזה נמי פטירי קמ"ל דמחייבי וברכת המזון פשיטא מצות עשה שלא הזמן גרמה היא ס"ד אמינ' הואיל וכתי' בתת יי"י לכם בערב בשר לאכול ובבקר תשבעו לחם כי מ()[צ]וות עשה שהזמן גרמה היא קמ"ל

Oxford Opp. Add. fol. 23

פשיטא מהו דתימא הואיל ואית בה מלכות שמים אימא לא קמ'ל ומן התפילין פשיטא מהו דתימא הואיל ואיתקש למזוז' אימא לא קמ'ל וחייבין בתפלה פשיטא מהו דתימא הואיל וכתיב ערב ובקר וצהרים אשיחה ואהמה הויא לה מצות עשה שהזמן גרמה וכל מצות עשה שהזמן גרמה נשים פטורות קמ'ל ובמזוזה פשיטא מהו דתימא הואיל ומזוזה איתקש לתלמוד תורה ליפטרינהו קמ'ל וברכת המזון פשיט' דמצות עשה שאין הזמן גרמה היא סד'א הואיל וכתי' ויאמר משה בתת יי"י לכם בערב בשר לאכול ולחם בבקר לשבע תהוי כמצות עשה שהזמן גרמה קמ'ל מאי שנא ק'ש ותפילין דהויא להו מצות עשה שהזמן גרמה וכל מצות עשה שהזמן גרמה נשים פטורו' אבל תפלה ומזוזה וברכת המזון מצות עשה שלא הזמן גרמה היא ומשום הכי נשים חייבות

Munich 95

(מאי טעמ' דק"ש ותפילין הוי להו מצות עשה שהזמן גרמא וכל מצות עשה שהזמן גרמא נשים פטורות תפלה ומזוזה וברכת המזון דהוו מצות עשה לא הזמן גרמא נשים חייבי') [אינו מלשון התלמ.. ?...?.. אין צריך לפרש אלא גרסינן פשי?ט..? כו'] ופטורין מק"ש פשיטא מצות עשה שהזמן גרמא הוא מהו דתימ' הואיל ואית ביה מלכות שמים ליחייבינהו קמ"ל ומן התפילין פשיטא מהו דתימ' הואיל ואיתקש תפילין למזוזה מה מזוזה מיחייבי אף תפילין מחייבי קמ"ל ובמזוזה פשיטא מהו דתימא הואיל ואיתקש מזוזה לתלמוד תורה מה תלמוד תורה פטירי אף מזוזה פטירי קמ"ל וחייבין בתפילה (פשיטא דמצות עשה שלא הזמן גרמא הוא ?) (? [מהו דתי'] הואיל וכתי') [גירס' רש"י תפלה דרחמי ננהו וא"ד פשיטא מ"ד הואיל דכתיב ערב ובקר וצהרים אשיחה כמצות עשה שהזמן גרמ' דמי קמ"ל מתנית?ין? ובברכת המזון פש.. מ"ד הואיל וכתיב] ויאמר משה בתת ייי לכם בערב בשר לאכול כמצות עשה שהזמן גרמא הוא קמ"ל (מאי שנא ק"ש ותפילין דלא דמצות עשה שהזמן גרמא הוא וכל מצות עשה שהזמן גרמא נשים פטורות תפלה ומזוזות וברכת המזון מצות עשה שלא הזמן גרמא הוא ומשום הכי חייבות) [אינו תלמוד]

Florence II-I-7

פשיטא מצות עשה שהזמן גרמא הוא ונשים פטורו' מהו דתימא הואיל ואי(ן)[ת] בה מלכות [שמים] (לא) [חייבות] קמ"ל [נ"א קרית שמע ותפילין דהויא לה מצות עשה שהזמן גרמה וכל מצות (לא) תעשה שהזמן גרמה נשים פטורות תפילה ומזוזה וברכת המזון דהויא להי מצות עשה שלא הזמן גרמה וכל מצות עשה שלא הזמן גרמה נשים חייבות] מן התפילה פש' מהו דתי' הואיל וכתי' בה ערב ובק' וצה' כמצות עשה שהזמן גרמא הוא [דדמיא] קמ"ל [תפילה רחמי היא] מן התפילין פשיטא מצות עשה שהזמן גרמא הוא ונשים פטור' [נ"א לגי' מה מזוזה מיחיבי אף תפילין נמי ליחייבי קמ"ל] מהו דתימא נקיש תפילין למזוזה קמ"ל מתני' (...) ומזוזה [פשיטא מהו דתימא ניקוש מזוזה (לתפילה) לתלמ' תורה מה תלמ' תורה פטירי אף מזוזה נמי פטירי קמ"ל וברכת המזון פשיטא מצות עשה שלא הזמן גרמה היא איצטריך סד"א הואיל וכת' בתת ה' לכם וכו' תהוי כמצות עשה שהזמן גרמה קמ"ל (האומ' רב אדא בר)] (פשיטא מצות עשה שלא הזמן גרמא וכל מצות עשה שלא הזמן גרמא נשים חייבות מהו דתי' נקיש מזוזה לתלמוד תורה קמ"ל)

* Transcriptions taken from The Saul and Evelyn Henkind Talmud Text Databank of The Saul Lieberman Institute of Talmud Research of the Jewish Theological Seminary of America

A quick look at these parallels reveals two basic versions of the gemara here.

1) A statement explaining why the different *mitzvot* are treated differently: Those that are caused by time are obligatory for women and those that are not are not. This version appears in bolded text above.
2) A series of short פשיטא exchanges on all five *mitzvot* in the Mishnah, with an expression of shock that one might ever have thought otherwise. In the case of the obligatory *mitzvot*, we imagine how they might have been considered caused by time (*tefillah* and *birkat hamazon*), or how they might have been closely linked to another *mitzvah* from which women are exempt (*mezuzah*). In the case of the exemptions, either the value at stake is high enough (*Keriat Shema*) or the *mitzvah* is similar enough to an obligatory *mitzvah* (*tefillin*) that we might have thought women were obligated. This version appears in highlighting above. There are also a few sections of plain text, which reflect later additions from other sources and processes.

Though there is much to say about these manuscripts, the following picture emerges: The Florence manuscript lacked the bolded version in the body of the text and bears witness to a version of the gemara with five פשיטא passages and no general explanation. A later hand then added the other version of the gemara into the margins. The double appearance of the bolded text in the body of the Munich manuscript suggests that it was a marginal gloss to a textual ancestor of this text that crept into the body in two separate places. A later hand, however, clearly possessed something like the body of ms. Florence and was careful to note that the bolded version ought not to be considered an original part of the gemara (in his opinion, at least). The parallel nature of these two versions of the gemara is confirmed by *Rishonim*, with both Rashba and Tosafot R. Yehudah Heḥasid stating that they knew of texts that lacked the פשיטא passages entirely and only featured the general statement in the bolded text. The other textual witnesses thus represent a hybrid picture, reporting both versions of the gemara together. Mss. Oxford and Paris nonetheless switch the order of the two versions, a classic sign that one of them is a later addition that crept in from the margins (a process we described above in ms. Munich). The first printing solidifies this process, with both versions of the text achieving canonical status until today, even though they were originally dueling versions.

It is thus clear that when the Rif offers his summary statement of the reasoning behind the Mishnah's ruling, he is citing his version of the Talmud Bavli, which itself offers this sort of blanket statement and does not engage the

פשיטא structure at all (the bolded text above). The same is true of many other rishonim, including Talmidei R. Yonah, who offer their own explanations of their version of the Talmud, which asserts without explanation that *tefillah* is not a time-caused commandment.[1]

The next significant change to the text comes about as a result of Rashi:

רש"י מסכת ברכות דף כ עמוד ב
הכי גרסינן תפלה דרחמי נינהו ולא גרס פשיטא דהא לאו דאורייתא היא

Rashi clearly had the version of the gemara that featured multiple פשיטא passages, like the italicized section of ms. Oxford. Rashi assumed two points that created a problem for him:

1) That the term מצות עשה refers to something Biblical, and
2) that *tefillah* had no Biblical component and was entirely rabbinic in provenance.[2]

He therefore considered this passage as the work of an unlearned copyist and argued for its erasure. In place of the פשיטא passage on *tefillah*, he suggested the phrase דרחמי נינהו an assertion of the basis for obligating women in *tefillah* independent of the question of its status as a time-caused commandment.[3] In other words, the word "פשיטא" in Rashi's comment above, meant פשיטא... covering that word and the entire conceptually-linked section that followed it, through the קמ"ל.[4] We can see this process at work in ms. Munich. The base text there begins with a text that reads identically to the italicized section of ms. Oxford, but which gets cut off in the middle due to a copyist's error caused by the next section of text.[5] A later hand adds a note that Rashi replaced

---

1. This confirms the instinct of Ma'adanei Yom Tov letter *tzadi* on Rosh Berakhot 3:13, who said that Talmidei R. Yonah seem not to have had anything in their gemara. To put it more precisely: they did not have a version with any פשיטא statements, just a blanket statement about the nature of these different obligations.

2. The first assumption seems to be a linguistic point, though it is disputed by Tosafot Berakhot 20b s.v. *peshita*; the second point is supported by Berakhot 21a: אלא: קריאת שמע וברכת המזון – דאורייתא, ותפלה – דרבנן.

3. The phrase is borrowed from Sotah 33a, where it is used to explain why *tefillah* can be said in any language. The phrase also appears on Pesahim 117b, where it helps explain why blessings in the *Amidah* are formulated with present tense verbs. Other passages describe tefillah as רחמי with different phrasing; see Berakhot 26a for one example. The concept that *tefillah*'s essence as a personal request for mercy is at the core of women's obligation in it is already found in the Yerushalmi parallel to our sugya: כדי שיהא כל אחד ואחד מבקש רחמים על עצמו.

4. That this is Rashi's intent is clear from Tosafot Berakhot 20b s.v. *peshita*.

5. The copyist seems to have jumped from the words מהו דתימא הואיל וכתיב in the section on תפילה to the same words in the later section on ברכת המזון, a common type of scribal error.

this section with the words דרחמי נגהו and that the alternative he was arguing against read as does the italicized section of ms. Oxford. In ms. Florence, we see how Rashi's version is suggested as an alternative in the margins to a passage virtually identical to the italicized section of ms. Oxford. In ms. Paris, this alternative has already crept into the base text.[6]

Our printed version represents the final stage of this process. Either the manuscript used by the printer or the printer himself wanted to update the text of the gemara to reflect Rashi's emendation. But this editor did not properly understand Rashi's comment. He thought that when Rashi wrote, ולא גרס פשיטא, he was merely referring to the *word* פשיטא as opposed to the *entire phrase that begins with that word*. As a result, the first printing features a text that replaces the *word* פשיטא with the words דרחמי נינהו, and then continues on with the rest of the פשיטא text. This hybrid doesn't really make any sense – having a מהו דתימא without a prior expression of surprise is syntactically awkward – but we can now understand how it came about.[7]

6. See also Meiri s.v. *mahloket*. Note that some versions of Halakhot Gedolot report the phrase דרחמי היא in their summary of this sugya. But see Halakhot Gedolot, ed. Hildesheimer, vol. I, 17, n82, which demonstrates that this is not the original text of Halakhot Gedolot, but rather a later addition based on Rashi's highly influential correction.

7. Note that the process of conceptual hybridization – asserting that one might obligate women in prayer *even if* it were a positive *mitzvah* caused by time, because it is a personal request for mercy – already gets underway in the rishonim. See Talmidei R. Yonah and Rosh Berakhot 3:13 for two examples. All such efforts, however, result from an attempt to synthesize an earlier text with Rashi's emendation. Everyone before Rashi (and even Rashi himself) understands the gemara's text to be saying that *tefillah* is *not* caused by time and therefore is obligatory on women. They may then disagree over *why* prayer belongs in this category, but not *that* it does.

Appendix B: The "*Mitzvah*" of Public Prayer

A NUMBER of Talmudic sources engage with the question of public prayer ("praying with a *minyan*"). The Talmud discusses R. Eliezer's decision to free his slave so that the ex-slave could be the tenth in a *minyan*:

תלמוד בבלי ברכות מז:

מעשה ברבי אליעזר שנכנס לבית הכנסת ולא מצא עשרה, ושחרר עבדו והשלימו לעשרה.

... והיכי עביד הכי? והאמר רב יהודה: כל המשחרר עבדו עובר בעשה, שנאמר, "לְעֹלָם בָּהֶם תַּעֲבֹדוּ" (ויקרא כה:מו)!

לדבר מצוה שאני.

מצוה הבאה בעבירה היא!

מצוה דרבים שאני.

ואמר רבי יהושע בן לוי: לעולם ישכים אדם לבית הכנסת כדי שיזכה וימנה עם עשרה הראשונים ...

Talmud Bavli Berakhot 47b

It happened that R. Eliezer entered the synagogue and did not find ten, so he freed his slave and rendered him the completion of the ten.

... How could he act thus? Did not R. Yehudah say, "Anyone who frees his slave transgresses a positive commandment, as it said, 'forever treat them as slaves' (VaYikra 25:46)"?!

... For a *mitzvah* it is different.

[But] it is a *mitzvah* that is performed through a transgression!

A communal *mitzvah* is different.

And R. Yehoshua ben Levi said, "A person should always get up and go early to the synagogue in order to merit and be counted with the first ten ..."

The critical phrase in this passage is מצוה דרבים, literally, "a *mitzvah* of the many." This quality of praying with a *minyan* is what justified R. Eliezer's violation of the gemara's assumed ban on freeing slaves. There are multiple ways to interpret this phrase, each interpretation having different consequences for how we understand the practice of public prayer and its relationship to the individual:

1) מצוה דרבים means an individual obligation possessed by many people. R. Eliezer's action was warranted because he enabled multiple people to fulfill their individual obligations in public prayer. This reading supports the notion of an individual obligation to pray with a *minyan.*
2) מצוה דרבים means a communal obligation to have a *minyan* and, as such, devolves on all individuals, though not as a specifically individual obligation. Once the community has assured the presence of a *minyan,* no individual obligation to be present remains. According to this reading, all individuals who count in a *minyan* are responsible to do what they can to make sure the community has a *minyan,* but there is no individual obligation beyond that communal imperative.
3) מצוה דרבים simply means a praiseworthy act that involves many people, but does not signify a neatly quantifiable personal obligation. The term מצוה is used here to mean something like "a good deed" or "the ideal way to do things."[1] This reading maintains that while it is certainly praiseworthy, beneficial and possibly even of deep importance to pray in a *minyan,* it is not a formal obligation like other *mitzvot.*

Various sources within the Talmud Bavli can be marshaled to support these various readings. **R. Abbahu** cryptically says in the name of Reish Lakish: לגבל ולתפלה ולנטילת ידים: ארבעה מילין – "for a kneader, for prayer, and for the washing of the hands: Four *mil.*" **Rashi** explains "prayer" there to refer to the degree one must inconvenience oneself to pray in a synagogue:

רש"י פסחים מו.
וכן לתפלה, אם מהלך אדם בדרך ובא עת ללון ולהתפלל, אם יש בית הכנסת לפניו ברחוק ארבע מילין הולך ומתפלל שם ולן שם.

Rashi on Pesahim 46a
And so, too, for prayer: If a person is traveling along the way and the time comes to sleep and to pray, if there is a synagogue ahead within a distance of four *mil,* then one should go on and pray there and sleep there.[2]

---

1. For a similar usage of מצוה, see Makkot 10b.
2. There is a parallel passage containing both R. Abbahu's statement and a similar comment by Rashi on Hullin 122b.

This may argue for an individual obligation to pray in a *minyan*, even when one is on the road, outside of one's local community, though it may be speaking more about importance of setting – where one can pray in a sacred location, one should do so.[3] It might also be *specific* to a case of one who is traveling who can easily reconfigure his itinerary to end up at a synagogue. In any event, Rashi's interpretation is disputed by **R. Hananel**, who explains "prayer" here to refer to the distance that one needs to travel to find *water* so that one can wash one's hands before praying.[4] If one adopts this reading, there is certainly no clear source formally mandating the individual to pray in a *minyan*.

Other sources seem to militate against the notion of an individual obligation, even as they may leave room for the notion of a communal imperative. When **Reish Lakish** says, on Talmud Bavli Berakhot 8a, כל מי שיש לו בית הכנסת בעירו ואינו נכנס שם להתפלל נקרא שכן רע – "Anyone who has a synagogue in his city and does not enter there to pray is called a bad neighbor," the emphasis is not on fulfilling an individual obligation, but rather on the need to make sure that the community can live out its collective obligations.

Yet other passages suggest that the act of public prayer should not be engaged on the axis of obligation at all. These sources suggest that public prayer is to be judged by its metaphysical value, not by its ability to fulfill personal obligations.[5] It is a spiritual means rather than a personal or communal end. Theological expression for this value can be found in the following passage:

תלמוד בבלי ברכות ז:–ח.

אמר רבי יוחנן משום רבי שמעון בן יוחי, מאי דכתיב, "וַאֲנִי תְפִלָּתִי לְךָ ה' עֵת רָצוֹן ..." (תהלים סט:יד) – אימתי עת רצון – בשעה שהצבור מתפללין.

רבי יוסי ברבי חנינא אמר, מהכא: "כֹּה אָמַר ה' בְּעֵת רָצוֹן עֲנִיתִיךָ ..." (ישעיהו מט:ח).

רבי אחא ברבי חנינא אמר, מהכא: "הֶן אֵל כַּבִּיר וְלֹא יִמְאָס ..." (איוב לו:ה), וכתיב: פָּדָה בְשָׁלוֹם נַפְשִׁי מִקֲּרָב לִי כִּי בְרַבִּים הָיוּ עִמָּדִי (תהלים נה:יט).

תניא נמי הכי, רבי נתן אומר: מנין שאין הקדוש ברוך הוא מואס בתפלתן של רבים, שנאמר: "הֶן אֵל כַּבִּיר וְלֹא יִמְאָס ..." (איוב לו:ה), וכתיב: פָּדָה בְשָׁלוֹם נַפְשִׁי מִקֲּרָב לִי וגו' (תהלים נה:יט): אמר הקדוש ברוך הוא כל העוסק בתורה ובגמילות חסדים ומתפלל עם הצבור – מעלה אני עליו כאילו פדאני, לי ולבני, מבין אומות העולם.

---

3. A series of statements at the beginning of Yerushalmi Berakhot 5 seem to evince this perspective.

4. The interpretational advantage of this reading is obvious: all three portions of the statement then deal with water, with "washing of the hands" referring to the water required before eating bread. Of course, R. Hananel may also be pushed to this perhaps less intuitive reading of the the word "*litfillah*" by the total foreignness of the idea that one would be obligated to pray with a *minyan*.

5. The exhortatory tone of R. Yehoshua b. Levi's statement in the passage we opened with fits with this framing as well.

Talmud Bavli Berakhot 7b–8a

R. Yoḥanan said in the name of R. Shimon b. Yoḥai: What is the meaning of the verse, "I am my prayer to you, God, at a time of goodwill" (Tehillim 69:14)? When is a time of goodwill? When the community is praying.

R. Yose b. R. Ḥanina derives it from here: "So says the Lord: At the hour of favor I answer you . . ." (Yeshayahu 49:8).

R. Aḥa b. R. Ḥanina derives it from here: "See, God is great and is not contemptuous . . ." (Iyov 36:5), and it is written: "[God] redeems my life in peace from the battle against me, as though there were many with me" (Tehillim 55:19).

So was it also taught [in a *baraita*]: R. Natan said, From where do we learn that the Holy One never despises the prayers of the many? As it is said, "See, God is great[6] and is not contemptuous . . ." (Iyov 36:5), and it is written: "[God] redeems my life in peace from the battle against me, etc." (Tehillim 55:19). Said the Holy One: Anyone who engages in Torah and acts of lovingkindness and who prays with the community, I relate to that person as though he had redeemed Me – Me and My children – from the nations.

Prayers are more likely to be accepted in an עת רצון/"time of favor," interpreted here by these Sages as synchronizing one's prayers with those of the community. Similarly, R. Natan argues that though individuals risk God not hearing their prayers because of the offending consequence of their sins, a community's prayers will always be heard: The corporate voice drowns out individual shortcomings. These paeans to communal prayer are focused on its metaphysical efficacy, not on any notion of personal obligation.

Indeed, classical sources never clearly articulate a full-fledged personal obligation for an individual to pray in a *minyan*. This is likely explainable, in part, because of a person's inability to fulfill such a "*mitzvah*" on his or her own. Moreover, we find views that some commitments trump praying with a *minyan* if there is a conflict. For example, in the material surrounding the above Talmudic passage, we find R. Naḥman justifying not bothering to go to the synagogue because he was "unable" and not convening a *minyan* where he was, because that would be "difficult." A few lines later, we find several sages concluding that those deeply engaged in Torah study should pray where they are, in the *beit midrash*, rather than interrupting their study to join the community:

6. This translation reflects the contextual meaning of the verse. The proof is based on reading the word for "great" as referring to the greatness – in quantitative terms – of the community.

תלמוד בבלי ברכות ז:-ח.

אמר ליה רבי יצחק לרב נחמן: מאי טעמא לא אתי מר לבי כנישתא לצלויי?

אמר ליה: לא יכילנא.

אמר ליה: לכנפי למר עשרה וליצלי.

אמר ליה: טריחא לי מלתא.

ולימא ליה מר לשלוחא דצבורא, בעידנא דמצלי צבורא ליתי ולודעיה למר.

אמר ליה: מאי כולי האי?

אמר ליה: דאמר רבי יוחנן משום רבי שמעון בן יוחי . . .

ואמר אביי: מריש הוה גריסנא בגו ביתא ומצלינא בבי כנישתא, כיון דשמענא להא דאמר רבי חייא בר אמי משמיה דעולא: מיום שחרב בית המקדש אין לו להקדוש ברוך הוא בעולמו אלא ארבע אמות של הלכה בלבד – לא הוה מצלינא אלא היכא דגריסנא.

רבי אמי ורבי אסי אף על גב דהוו להו תליסר בי כנישתא בטבריא לא מצלו אלא ביני עמודי, היכא דהוו גרסי.

Talmud Bavli Berakhot 7b-8a

R. Yitzḥak asked R. Naḥman: Why didn't you come to synagogue to pray?

He said to him: I couldn't.

He said to him: Then gather ten and pray.

He said to him: That would be difficult for me.

Then why not tell the *ḥazzan* to inform you of when they are praying?

He said to him: Why should I go to such lengths? He said to him: Because R. Yoḥanan said in the name of R. Shimon b. Yoḥai . . .[7]

And Abaye said: Originally, I would study in the house and pray in the synagogue. When I heard that which R. Ḥiyya b. Ami said in the name of Ulla – "From the time the Temple was destroyed, the Holy, Blessed One has only the four cubits of *halakhah*" – I would pray only where I studied.

R. Ami and R. Asi – even though there were thirteen synagogues in Tiberias, would pray only between the columns where they studied.

Various *Rishonim* cite these voices and weigh them differently. As noted above, **Rashi** may well argue for some sort of personal obligation in public prayer.[8]

7. Here, the gemara continues with the passage we cited above about the positive values associated with praying with the community.

8. R. Ya'akov b. Asher (Spain, 14th c.) in Tur OḤ 90 favors Rashi's reading of the gemara over that of R. Hananel. Nonetheless, he seems not to embrace the obligation in nearly as full terms, in principle accepting the notion that other values – such as praying where one learns – can trump the value of praying in a *minyan*. Tur, following Rosh, doubts whether contemporary scholars are truly so engaged in Torah study as to justify such an exemption from supporting the community, and out of concern that the masses would misunderstand the nature of the exemption. He therefore rules that this exemption no longer applies. [Rambam, whom we will cite shortly, limits the exemption for scholars by saying that sages may pray in their places of study only when there is a *minyan* there.] But the idea that praying with a *minyan* is ultimately a highly-valued, strongly preferred act rather than a hard and fast obligation seems to prevail for the Tur. This explains

Rambam, by contrast, quite clearly emphasizes the metaphysical benefits highlighted on Berakhot 8a while pointedly avoiding any language suggesting a personal obligation. It is fairly clear that for him there is no concrete individual obligation in play at all here:

רמב"ם הלכות תפילה ח:א, ג

תפלת הציבור נשמעת תמיד ואפילו היו בהן חוטאים אין הקדוש ברוך הוא מואס בתפלתן של רבים, לפיכך צריך אדם לשתף עצמו עם הציבור, ולא יתפלל ביחיד כל זמן שיכול להתפלל עם הציבור, ולעולם ישכים אדם ויעריב לבית הכנסת שאין תפלתו נשמעת בכל עת אלא בבית הכנסת, וכל מי שיש לו בית הכנסת בעירו ואינו מתפלל בו עם הציבור נקרא שכן רע... בית המדרש גדול מבית הכנסת, וחכמים גדולים אף על פי שהיו להם בעירם בתי כנסיות הרבה לא היו מתפללין אלא במקום שהיו עוסקין שם בתורה והוא שיתפלל שם תפלת הציבור.

Rambam, Laws of Prayer, 8:1, 3

The prayer of the community is always heard, and even if there are sinners in it, the Holy One does not reject the prayer of the many. Therefore, a person needs to participate with the community, and not to pray alone when one could pray with the community, and a person should always arrive early and leave late from the synagogue ... and anyone who has a synagogue in one's city and does not pray with the community is called a bad neighbor... A *beit midrash* is greater than a synagogue, and great sages, even though they have in their city many synagogues, would pray only in the place where they would engage with Torah – and this is provided that there is communal prayer there.

Others make clear that, while the community may have an obligation to constitute a *minyan*, this not an individual obligation *per sé*. For example, **Maharil** addressed the legitimate parameters for establishing an *eruv teḥumin*, the placing of a food source far out in one direction of one's home in order to enable one to extend the distance permissible to walk on Shabbat:

ספר מהרי"ל, הלכות עירובי חצרות

תנן אין מניחין עירוב תחומין רק לסמוך עליו לילך לדבר מצוה כגון לבית האבל או לבית המשתה. אמר מהר"י סג"ל דלא ראה בשום פוסק שמותר לערב תחומין לילך לבה"כ כדי להתפלל בעשרה רק בסמ"ק ובספר אגודה. א"ל הר"ר איקא ולא יהא פחות מבית המשתה, א"ל הרב להתפלל בעשרה אינה כ"כ מצוה דיכול לכוון תפלתו בביתו, **דלא אשכחן אשר הצריכו חכמים להתפלל בי'**...

Tur's language of צריך להשתדל בכל כחו – "One should try with all one's might" to pray with the community, plaintive language not normally used with straightforward, individual obligations. Shulḥan Arukh borrows this language.

Sefer Maharil, Laws of Eruvei Ḥatzeirot

It is taught: We set an *eruv teḥumin* only to rely on it for a *mitzvah*, such as to go to a house of mourning or to a wedding celebration. [Maharil] said that he did not see in any authority that it is permitted to make an *eruv tehumin* to go to synagogue in order to pray with ten, except for the Semak[9] and the Agudah.[10] R. Ika said to [Maharil], "And should it be of less status than a wedding?" [Maharil] said to him, to pray with ten is not truly a *mitzvah*, because one can direct one's prayer in one's house, **for we do not find that the Sages required one to pray with ten.**

Maharil's North African contemporary **R. Shimshon Tzemaḥ Duran** concisely summed up this conception of praying with a *minyan*:

שו"ת תשב"ץ א:צ

... שחובת צבור היא להתפלל בעשר' אבל אם יש שם יותר מעשרה כל אחד יכול לומר לו והלא יש עשרה חוץ ממני וא"כ הריני יכול להשמט מלבא אצלך באותה שעה ...

Responsa Tashbetz I:90

It is an obligation on the community to pray with ten, but if there are there more than ten, each one can say, "But without me there are still ten, and if so, I can refrain from coming to join you at that time ..."

Four centuries later, **R. Yair Ḥayyim Bachrach** explicitly rejected the notion that there is a personal obligation to pray in a *minyan*. In that case, why did R. Eliezer free his slave to be a tenth in a *minyan* and why did the gemara justify this on the grounds that this was a "*mitzvah*"?

שו"ת חוות יאיר סימן קטו

ונ"ל דאין הכוונה דהמצוה נהוגה בכל ישראל רק ר"ל שהוא קידוש השם ודווקא ברבים ואם לא שחררו היה בטל המצוה מכל הרבים ההם שהיו נאספין יחד.

Responsa Ḥavvot Yair #115

... It seems to me that the intent is not that such a *mitzvah* [of praying in a *minyan*] is incumbent on every Jew, rather it means to suggest that it is

9. Siman 282.

10. We have not found a passage in the Agudah that states this explicitly. However, Agudah Berakhot 2:41 and Pesahim 3:44 both reveal an understanding of R. Abahu's statement on Pesahim 46a as requiring praying with a *minyan*. Maharil may just be noting that someone who reads the Talmud in this way would naturally extend that interpretation to considering praying with a *minyan* to be sufficiently required to validate the use of an *eruv tehumin*. As the end of this passage in the Maharil indicates, the latter rejects any notion that there is a Talmudic passage outlining such an individual obligation.

> the sanctification of God's name, and only among the many, and had he not freed him, this *mitzvah* would have been unfulfilled by all of the people gathered together.

This claim, that praying in a *minyan* is a public responsibility, but not an individual *mitzvah*, seems to be the dominant perspective on this important activity. Not being a personal obligation does not mean it is value-less, of course. Far from it: If a community must convene public prayer, each citizen has a certain categorical imperative to contribute toward its successful formation, even if there might not be a full-fledged personal obligation. This explains the language of the codes, such as the **Shulḥan Arukh**: "A person **should make great effort** to pray in the synagogue with the community" – "**ישתדל** אדם להתפלל בבית־הכנסת עם הציבור" (OḤ 90:9). Nonetheless, many authorities also codify the expectation that individuals will normally go out of their way to attend public prayer, whether or not this can be formally classified as an individual obligation.[11]

In sum, there are *Rishonim* whose words suggest an idea that individuals are obligated to pray in a *minyan*. [12] Others expect individuals to attend as part of their civic duty to help the community fulfill its *communal* obligation, but balk at the notion that the individual is obligated *per sé*, allowing individuals to absent themselves when a *minyan* is otherwise present. Finally, other voices suggest that a discourse of obligation misses the point and that the community gathers in prayer as an effective strategy for communicating with God.

No gender gap is ever articulated with regard to this responsibility – such as it is – before the late 17th century. Some recent authors have cited a few *Aḥaronim* to buttress the claim that there is such an obligation, that women are exempt from it, and that said exemption prevents them from leading the community in prayer. Of particular prominence in these claims is the statement of **R. Yaakov Reischer** (Prague/Galicia/Alsace-Lorraine, 17th-18th c.) that "a woman is not commanded at all to pray with ten" – האשה אינה מצוה כלל להתפלל בעשרה. Here is a fuller citation:

שו"ת שבות יעקב ג:נד

נשאלתי מישוב אחד שבעל הבית אחד יש לו חדר בתוך ביתו והניח ליכנס הצבור בתוך החדר

11. For instance, Shulḥan Arukh OḤ 90:16, after using the language of ישתדל/"make great effort" earlier in the Siman, follows Rashi in articulating expectations on travelers going out of their way to pray in a *minyan*. Mishnah Berurah 90:52 codifies later views that explicitly apply this to someone who is at home as well.

12. For a later adherent of this approach, see Iggerot Moshe OH II:27: הנה להתפלל בעשרה הוא חיוב מצוה על האדם ולא רק הדור ומעלה בעלמא.

אנשים לחוד ונשים לחוד להתפלל ועכשיו נולד קטטה גדולה בין בע"הב עם אחד מאנשים ואשתו שרגילין לבוא לבה"כ שלא יבואו עוד לבה"כ . . . עליהם להביא הראיה אך שהם טוענים כיון שחדר זו שהי' שייך לבעלים הראשונים נכנסו ג"כ בחדר זו להתפלל כמה וכמה שנים ע"כ הוא בחזקת הצבור ומסתמא השאילו להם ומידי ספיקא לא נפקא ופסקתי שלא יוכל לאסור מספיקא על אחד מן הקהל להסתפח מנחלת ה' אבל על אשתו המתחלת תמיד במריבה יוכל לאסור עליה שלא תבא לבה"כ כלל כי אע"פ שהאשה ג"כ מחויבת בתפלה כמבואר בא"ח סי' ק"ו מ"מ כיון שהאשה אינה מצוה כלל להתפלל בעשרה ואינה מצטרפת למנין ולא לקדושה כלל כדאמרינן "אשה בעזרה מנין?" [קדושין נ"ב:] ו"בתולה ציילנית מבלי עולם" ע"ש בסוטה דף כ"ב וכבר כתב המ"א בסי' ק"ו ס"ק ב' וז"ל ולכן נהגו רוב נשים שאינן מתפללים בתמידות משום דאומרים מיד סמוך לנטיל' איזה בקשה ומדאורייתא די בזה עכ"ל המ"א לכן נ"ל דיכול למחו' בידה עד שיפייסו וימחול זה לזה כי הנשי' עלולת להרבה בקטטות ומריבות וכן דנתי למעשה . . .

Responsa Shevut Yaakov, 3:54

I was asked by a certain community regarding a homeowner who had a room in his house, and he had given permission to the community to enter into that room, men and women separately, to pray. And now, a great dispute had come about between the homeowner and one of the men and his wife who were accustomed to go to this synagogue such that [the owner determined that] they should no longer go to the synagogue . . . The community must bring proof [that they have rights to pray there] even though they claim that they used to pray in this room for many years in the time of the prior owners of the house, such that the room has the status of a public space [which would prevent the current owner from excluding specific people from coming there]. Nonetheless, the matter is still in doubt, and I ruled that he could not forbid one of the members of the community from joining on to the Lord's portion [in this case, where there is doubt as to whether prior owners of the prayer might have explicitly and clearly licensed it for public prayer use], but regarding his wife, who was always starting arguments, he could forbid her from going to [that] synagogue at all, because even though the woman is obligated in prayer, as is clear in [Shulḥan Arukh] Oraḥ Ḥayyim 106, nevertheless, since the woman is not commanded at all to pray with ten, and she does not count toward the *minyan*, nor for *Kedushah* at all, as we say, "What would a woman be doing in the Temple Court?" [Kiddushin 52b][13] and "a young woman who prays excessively destroys the world" – see

13. Here, the Shevut Yaakov quotes R. Yehudah's words in a *baraita* in which he accuses R. Meir's students of badgering him with irrelevant and picayune questions, such as regarding the status of a marriage transaction of a *kohen* with the parts of the sacrificial meat which are his portion. Rashi understands R. Yehudah's point to be that this is a foolish question because the meat is useless if it leaves the Temple court, and women are not allowed in the Temple court. The Shevut Ya'akov imports this sense of the words to bolster his rhetorical point about women's presence in the synagogue being unnecessary: if they weren't even allowed in the main Temple

> Sotah 22[14] – and Magen Avraham has written [that perhaps women are not obligated in the daily *Amidah*, but only in one freeform prayer a day][15] . . . therefore it seems to me that he can prevent her [from going to the synagogue in his house] until they reconcile and forgive each other, for women are likely to bicker and fight a lot. So have I ruled . . .

In order to understand Shveut Ya'akov's logic here, we need a little background. One of the many ordinances promulgated by **R. Gershom** (Germany, 10th–11th c.) pertained to an individual who allows the community to use his home as a synagogue space. R. Gershom legislated that when a person lends their house out to community for public prayer, he cannot then exclude a specific individual from praying there unless he forbids the entire community from using the space at all.[16] This ordinance seems to have been set up to make sure that those with resources and power not use their leverage to isolate people from the communal experience of public prayer. **R. Meir Katzenellenbogen of Padua** (Bohemia/Italy, 15th–16th c.) later ruled that this ordinance only applied when the homeowner's space had been explicitly lent to the community. In cases where a homeowner merely allowed people to gather in his house for prayer but never formally "leased" the space, he would retain total control over who could enter, as he would with respect to guests in his home more generally.[17]

---

court, and the synagogue is in some way an imitation of the Temple, then their presence there is extraneous as well, giving license to the homeowner to exclude a difficult woman. However, note that Tosafot s.v. *ve-khi* attack this interpretation of Rashi, pointing out that, counter to Rashi's claim, no mishnah stipulates that women are excluded from the Temple court. Moreover, they argue, Mishnah Zevaḥim 3:1 assumes women's legitimate presence there, as it teaches that a sacrifice slaughtered by a woman is legitimate, and further, a *sotah* (woman accused of adultery) and a female Nazirite *must* bring offerings in the Temple Court. Tosafot, therefore, interpret the *baraita*'s words more modestly, to mean "What would a woman be doing getting betrothed in the Temple Court?!" That is, "This whole case is so preposterous and remote that you shouldn't be wasting my time with it." Both the Tosafot's point as well as the observation that women were rarely found in the Temple Court is summed up by Tosefta Arakhin 2:1: לעולם לא נראית אשה בעזרה אלא בשעת קרבנה בלבד. Shevut Ya'akov is using the paradigm of the Temple here to emphasize that there is a long tradition of women being more marginal in public sacred spaces and thus they can be more easily excluded when a problem arises on their account.

14. This opaque statement displays an aversion to excessive piety in female figures, though it is immediately challenged by another source in the gemara that features R. Yoḥanan praising a young woman whom he finds praying. Rashi understands the core problem here to be one of sorcery and witchcraft being dressed up as genuine religious expression. In any event, the passage is not referring to the *Amidah* and Shevut Ya'akov's use of the phrase here is clearly part of a larger rhetorical flourish he is building to make his case for excluding this woman from the prayer space.

15. See our lengthy discussion of Magen Avraham above, Part One, n28–33.

16. For one citation of this ordinance, see Orḥot Hayyim, Dinei Beit Kenesset #25: כתב הר' רבינו גרשום בתקנותיו שעשה איש שהשאיל ביתו לבית הכנסת ויש לו מריבה עם אחד מהקהל שאינו רשאי לאוסרה לו אלא אם כן יאסור אותה לכל הקהל כאחד.

17. Responsa Maharam Padua #85: כי לשון התקנה הוא וז"ל ואם אדם משאיל לרבים כו' ואלו היתה התקנה

With this background in mind, Shevut Ya'akov confronts the case of a homeowner who wants to exclude a married couple from the *minyan* being held in his home. The facts of the case are under dispute: The owner of the house never formally leased the space to the community for public prayer, but the community claims that they had an arrangement in place prior to the current owner's purchase of the house. Because the matter is in doubt, Shevut Ya'akov will not allow the community to potentially violate R. Gershom's ordinance by excluding an individual man from praying there while allowing the rest of the community to do so.

Nonetheless, he argues that the homeowner may exclude the man's wife from coming. He perceives the woman in this case to be the troublemaker and sees women in general as more prone to bickering and fighting. He justifies this exclusion of the wife specifically by appealing to a number of points that indicate a more marginal application of communal prayer obligations to women, perhaps suggesting that they are not protected by R. Gershom's ordinance in the same way as are men:

1) Women, though they are obligated to pray, are not obligated to pray with a *minyan*, whereas men are.
2) Women do not count in a *minyan*.
3) According to Magen Avraham, maybe they are not even obligated in the *Amidah* at all.

All of these factors, which place the woman on a different footing than her husband with respect to public prayer, lead Shevut Ya'akov to justify removing the woman from this home-based synagogue.

Point 2) is straightforwardly based in Shulḥan Arukh OḤ 55's holding that women do not count in a *minyan*. We dealt with this issue at length above.[18] Shevut Ya'akov here seems to appeal to the notion that one who cannot help form a *minyan* cannot possibly be essential to that space. Point 3) is based on the reading of Magen Avraham that we dealt with at length as well. As we noted, building any firm legal argument based on Magen Avraham's analysis – particularly given that he seems to have abandoned it himself – is difficult. Any use of Magen Avraham to bolster an argument for female exemption from the *Amidah* must be balanced against the overwhelming evidence to the contrary that we amassed in our discussion of his view.

Point 1) is our main concern here. Shevut Ya'akov makes the unsourced

---

אפילו בסתם היה לו לומר ב"ה של יחיד שרבים נכנסים שם כו' אלא ודאי ר"ל משאיל בפירוש.

18. See Part Two.

claim that women, as opposed to men, are exempt from public prayer. As we saw above, this claim is grounded in a contentious assumption, given that men's obligation to pray in a *minyan* is by no means universally agreed upon. Moreover, the notion that public prayer is gendered has no antecedent that we can find, whereas the values attached to praying with a *minyan* by the Talmud seem to apply to anyone who is required to pray.

Indeed, other *Aḥaronim* emphasize the gender-blind aspects of praying with a *minyan*. **R. Eliyahu Ragoler** (Lithuanua, 19th c.) writes as follows:

יד אליהו, פסקים א:ז

שאלה: אם יש באיזה בית הכנסת קטן או מנין של ששה או שבעה אנשים שלא התפללו ושלשה התפללו, ונמצא שא"א לקיים רק מצות קדיש וברכו וקדושה, אבל אין זה עולה לתפלה בציבור כי אם בעשרה ממש . . . אכן נסתפק לי לכאורה אם יש בבית הזה ג' נשים שמתפללים אם יש לצרף הנשים עמהם, אם נחשבת תפלת הנשים בכלל הציבור?

ונראה לי לפשוט מהא דאמר . . . תשעה ועבד מצטרפין, ומקשה מעובדא דר"א דשחרר עבדו, ומתרץ תרי הוי חסר, ושחרר אחד וצירף אחד עיין שם, והשתא אי אמרת דתפלת נשים אינם בכלל תפלת הצבור כמו דלא מצטרפין אותם לקדיש ולקדושה, אם כן הוה ליה לתלמודא לשנויי דלכן שחרר עבדו בכדי להתפלל בציבור – דהא אשה ועבד שקולין לענין צירוף וחיוב מצוות עשה . . . **אלא על כרחך דתפלת נשים** ועבדים **מצטרפים לתפלת הציבור**, ולא היה צריך ר"א לשחרר עבדו בשביל זה . . .

Yad Eliyahu, Pesakim I:7

Question: In a small community, when there are only six or seven men who have not prayed and three who have, one can only fulfill the *mitzvah* of *Kaddish, Barekhu* and *Kedushah*, but praying in such a group does not count as public prayer unless there are actually ten [who have not prayed] . . . What I am unsure about is what if there are three women in this house who have not prayed, do the three women join with them such that the prayer of the women is considered part of the community?

It seems to me we can answer this from the fact that it says . . . nine and a slave join [to make a *minyan*] and then it challenges this point from the case of R. Eliezer, who freed his slave, and then resolves by saying that they needed two additional participants and so he freed one and counted the other slave as the tenth. If you claim that the prayer of women is not a part of the public prayer just as they are not joined to the *minyan* for *Kaddish* and *Kedushah*, then the Talmud should have resolved that R. Eliezer freed his slave in order to have public prayer – given that a woman and a slave have the same status with respect to joining a *minyan* and in their obligations in positive commandments . . . **rather it must be that the prayer of women** and slaves **counts towards public prayer**, and R. Eliezer had no need to free his slave for this purpose . . .

Though Yad Eliyahu would have excluded women from the *minyan* required to recite *devarim shebikdushah*, he thought the *mitzvah* of public prayer – *which he understands to be the recitation of the private Amidah in a group of ten*[19] – was equally applicable to men and women (and slaves).

R. Ya'akov Ariel (Israel, 20th–21st c.) addresses the case of a woman who arrives late to synagogue on Shabbat morning, such that she can either pray in the usual order by beginning with *Shaḥarit*, or she can begin with *Musaf* in order to synchronize her prayer with that of the community. R. Ariel concludes that this comes down to the question of whether she is obligated to pray with the community:

שו"ת באהלה של תורה ב:כז

ואם כי אשה חייבת בתפילת המוסף, אך השאלה היא אם היא חייבת להתפלל **בציבור** דוקא... מיהו נראה שגם אשה חייבת להתפלל בציבור, שנאמר "הן קל כביר ולא ימאס"... ועדיין י"ל שהאשה יכולה להתפלל מוסף עם הציבור ושחרית אחרי מוסף...

Responsa Be-Aholah shel Torah II:27

But even if a woman is obligated in the *Musaf* prayer, we must still address the question of whether she is obligated specifically to pray it **with the community**[20] ... it seems that a woman is also obligated to pray communally, as it is said: "See God is mighty, but not contemptuous ..."[21] [Therefore,] a woman who arrived late should pray *Musaf* with the community and then pray *Shaḥarit* after *Musaf*...

R. Ariel notes that the core basis given for praying with a *minyan* in the Talmud – the greater effectiveness of prayers uttered as a community – is a gender-blind consideration. To the extent that communal prayer leads to better, more acceptable prayer, then this obligation in communal prayer will devolve on anyone obligated to *pray*. Thus, since women are obligated to pray, they must also be obligated to pray with a *minyan*.

Alternatively, perhaps Shevut Ya'akov means to link points 1) and 2) here, suggesting that one's exclusion from the quorum for *minyan* not only means that the public prayer space does not depend on them, but that they themselves have no real need of that space. In other words, he might be arguing that the whole notion of requiring people to pray in *minyan* devolves from the communal imperative to make sure that people show up to make a *minyan*. This would then be legal expression of that sense that many people in

19. We will return to this point below.
20. R. Ariel's emphasis.
21. This verse, from Iyov 36:5, is cited in the passage on Berakhot 8a that we cited above.

non-egalitarian communities have, in which many men feel driven to go to *shul* during the week "to help make the *minyan*," whereas women in the same communities are much less likely to make that effort, since they are not "needed." Here, the Shevut Ya'akov seems to be saying that in such a community, the homeowner may not restrict a troublemaking man from the synagogue in his home, since the man's presence fulfills more than his own personal desire to come to *shul*. His presence represents his portion of the communal duty to sustain the *minyan*; his absence weakens the community. A troublemaking woman, on the other hand, could be restricted: Since she shoulders no part of the communal duty, her presence reflects just her own personal desire to attend and participate in the life of the community, which can be forfeited because of anti-social behavior. Obviously, this claim would fall away in any context in which women were potential members of the required quorum, per our discussion above.[22]

All of this helps clarify why there might be a debate about the gendered nature of an obligation to pray with a *minyan*. But even if one posits such a gender gap in the "obligation in communal prayer," one point is particularly central: Whatever the obligation in communal prayer may be, it seems to be about *attending* communal prayer and is something that cannot and need not be fulfilled vicariously through the prayer leader. Note that Shevut Ya'akov nowhere suggests that the leader somehow fulfills the obligations of *others* in communal prayer. An assumption that women need not go to *shul* in the same way as men do is irrelevant to the obligations of others in the *Amidah*; nothing in Shevut Ya'akov argues this point. Indeed, Yad Eliyahu's analysis makes clear that תפילה בציבור refers to the *private Amidah*, and this obligation, such as it is, is in no way fulfilled through the prayer leader. Questions of obligation in public prayer, while possibly relevant for our expectations of who should

22. This conversation continues among later authorities as well. **R. Avraham Ḥayyim Rodrigues** (Italy, 18th c.), in Responsa Oraḥ Latzaddik #3, also asserts, as we saw above, that women are exempt from praying with a *minyan*. He also does not source this claim, though he makes clear that it is *not* derivative of women's exclusion from *minyan*. His insistence on the gendered nature of public tefillah is thus all the more puzzling. See Part Two, n75–76. **R. Ovadiah Yosef**, in Yalkut Yosef Siman 106, offers the analysis we are suggesting for Shevut Ya'akov here: women are not obligated to pray with a *minyan* because only those who count in a *minyan* are expected to be there. R. Menachem Nissel in Rigshei Lev, chapter 7, cites **R. Yosef Shalom Elyashiv** as ruling that women *are* obligated to pray with the community and **R. Ḥayyim Pinḥas Scheinberg** and **R. Eliyahu Greenblatt** as opining that women should do so, while **R. Shlomo Zalman Auerbach** and **R. Moshe Shternbuch** rule that women usually have no special responsibility to pray with the community. See also R. Aryeh and R. Dov Frimer's citation of R. Ahron Soloveichik that whatever the status of the obligation to pray with a *minyan*, there is no gender component involved, in Aryeh Frimer and Dov Frimer, "Women's Prayer Services – Theory and Practice," *Tradition* 32:2 (1998), footnote 85.

attend communal *tefillah*, are not relevant for the question of who may *lead* such *tefillot*.

Summary

Praying with the community is an important social responsibility in which members of the community should make every effort to engage. It is also a personal desideratum, insofar as it improves the acceptability of one's individual prayer. If one focuses on the latter of these two elements, then women, being obligated to pray, also share an obligation to pray communally (and thus, the view of R. Ariel). If we focus on the former element – the responsibility to help make a *minyan* – then the proper location for the full examination of this question is the exploration of the question of women's inclusion in the *minyan* in contemporary contexts. Even for those who argue, however, that women do not count and that they therefore lack the social responsibility or the personal obligation to pray in a *minyan*, there is no basis to claim that this in any way affects women's fitness to serve as *Sha"tz*. Such a claim requires making three points in concert, each of which is far from self-evident in the sources:

1) There is an individual obligation to pray with a *minyan*. This notion is challenged by many *rishonim*.
2) There is a gender gap to that individual obligation. This is counterintuitive given women's equal obligation in *tefillah* and is unsupported by any evidence in the *rishonim*. It is most intelligible as a corollary of women's exclusion from *minyan*, which would then relegate this discussion to a subunit of the conversation around gender and the quorum required for public prayer. Even given this, many *Aḥaronim* explicitly describe the obligations around public prayer as being gender blind.
3) The assumed gender gap plays a role in one's ability to serve as *Sha"tz* – a point that makes little sense, given that an individual obligation in public prayer seems to be about *attending* public prayer, not leading it, and which seems to have no reflection in any source prior to the contemporary period.

Appendix C: The Relationship of *Zimmun* to Other Quorums of Ten

OUR main analysis of *minyan* above focused on the *minyan* required for aspects of public prayer. We only tangentially addressed sources regarding the required quorums for *zimmun*. In this appendix, we will aim to give a clearer picture of the history of the quorum of ten for *zimmun*, its gendered history, and the relationship of this quorum of ten to the quorums required for public prayer and Torah reading. In particular, do sources that ban the possibility of a *zimmun* of ten for women or groups of women and men necessarily clarify anything about other quorums of ten?

While classical rabbinic sources have nothing explicit and unambiguous to say about the role of gender in any quorum of ten, a number of sources do address the question about the role of gender in forming a *zimmun*.

Mishnah Berakhot 7:2 states concisely: נשים ועבדים וקטנים אין מזמנין עליהם; adult males (the presumed addressees of this Mishnah) may not form a *zimmun* with women, slaves and minors. A ***baraita*** on Berakhot 45b clarifies that women form their own *zimmun* and slaves form their own *zimmun*, but a group of women and slaves may not form a joint group. The gemara on **Arakhin 3a** cites a text of unclear provenance but of undisputed authority stating that women are obligated to form a *zimmun*. This is all the direct evidence that classical sources present on the question of women and *zimmun*.[1]

---

1. D. Koren has argued that the gemara in Arakhin also assumes that women and men may join together to form a *zimmun* and that this ought to be our understanding of Mishnah Berakhot 7:2 as well. According to her reading, the Mishnah only forbids *entire groups* of women, slaves *and* minors to form a minyan, but women's capacity to form a *zimmun* on their own or with adult men was never in question in the Tannaitic period and it was only the conceptual and literary creativity of Ravina on Talmud Bavli Berakhot 20b and the anonymous editor of Talmud Bavli Berakhot 47b that introduced the notion that *zimmun* was not a gender-blind practice. See above, Part Two, n8 and n15 for more on this argument and some of our concerns regarding it.

Regarding women's obligation in *birkat hamazon* more generally, **Mishnah Berakhot 3:3** clearly states that they are obligated. **Tosefta Berakhot 5:17**, as reflected in ms. Vienna and the first printing, however, exempts women (along with slaves and minors) from *birkat hamazon* and explains that they may not fulfill the obligations of others. It then adds that a woman may say *birkat hamazon* for her husband (and a slave may do so for his master and a son for his father): נשים ועבדים וקטנים פטורין ואין מוציאין את הרבים ידי חובתן באמת אמרו אשה מברכת לבעלה בן מברך לאביו עבד מברך לרבו. This then leaves unclear exactly what the status of women's obligation is. Is there indeed a gender gap with respect to obligation in *birkat hamazon*, while there was nonetheless, at least at one point, some tolerance for a woman saying *birkat hamazon* for her husband, at deviance with the usual rule that one can only fulfill the obligations of others if one is equally obligated?[2] Alternatively, should we conclude that a woman's ability to say *birkat hamazon* for her husband proves that women and men have an equal obligation in *birkat hamazon*, in which case we would have to say that the word פטורין is an error? Indeed, ms. Erfurt of the Tosefta here omits the word פטורין and simply states that women do not fulfill the obligations of others, which is possibly a statement that they are not *allowed* to do so, not that they are *unable* to do so.[3]

However we understand the Tosefta, the Mishnah's clear obligation of women in *birkat hamazon* seems to dominate subsequent discussion. On Berakhot 49a, **Rav** derives details about the essential core text of *birkat hamazon*

2. There is an even more intriguing possibility that should be considered here: Perhaps the phrase מוציאין את הרבים is *not* synonymous with the notion of להוציא את האחר. In other words, lack of obligation may not preclude one's ability to fulfill the obligations of another individual. Rather, it may be that a lack of obligation disqualifies one from serving in a *public* capacity to discharge the obligations of those assembled as a *group*. That would make perfect sense of this version of the Tosefta: Women, slaves and minors cannot lead a communal *birkat hamazon* for a group including men. However, on a one-to-one basis, the Tosefta may be telling us that there is no issue. This would also fit with the general pattern of the phrase באמת אמרו, which in no other place contradicts what comes before, but rather makes a qualifying statement consistent with the prior phrase, albeit counterintuitive or unexpected. While later sources clearly assume that sources like Mishnah Rosh Hashanah 3:8, כל שאינו מחוייב בדבר אינו מוציא את הרבים ידי חובתן, apply to individual interactions as well – a reading perhaps influenced by Mishnah Sukkah 3:10 – it might be that this Tosefta gives us a glimpse at a different approach to this question. Nonetheless, a later passage in Tosefta Berakhot 5 seems to apply concerns of obligation to even individual interactions: אנדרוגינוס מוציא את מינו ואינו מוציא את שאינו מינו – "A hermaphrodite can fulfill the obligations of another hermaphrodite, but not of a non-hermaphrodite."

3. S. Lieberman in Tosefta Kifshutah I:83 argues that ms. Erfurt preserves a more original and accurate reading here and points out that Tosafot and Tosafot Harosh on Sukkah 38a clearly had a text of the Tosefta that lacked the word פטורין. Meiri, in Beit Habeḥirah Megillah 4a emends a parallel text that reads פטורין ואין מוציאין to חייבין ואין מוציאין, and in Beit Habeḥirah Berakhot 20b he simply reports the text of our Tosefta as חייבין ואין מוציאין. Lieberman argues that that last report is a conscious correction and indicates that he had a text that read like ms. Vienna. It seems more likely to us that ms. Vienna is the original here and that all other versions are corrections in one way or another, but it is hard to make a solid case either way. See also קורן, "על שיטת ר' יהודה הכהן", מד–נ.

from the assumption that anything that does not apply to women cannot possibly be a core part of *birkat hamazon*, which seems to reflect an assumption that *birkat hamazon* is not gendered in any way. Therefore, Rav concludes, given that women are not circumcised nor commanded to study Torah, nor does the Davidic line flow through them, mentioning these themes in *birkat hamazon* must not be essential.

Nonetheless, possible echoes of a version of the Tosefta that spoke about exemption, along with the Mishnah's treatment of women as a separate and seemingly inferior class with respect to *zimmun* (the language of the Mishnah is *not* לא יזמן איש עם שתי נשים ולא תזמן אשה עם שני אנשים, following the structure of Mishnah Kiddushin 4:12) may have sown doubt as to whether the Mishnah's claim that women are obligated in *birkat hamazon* is unequivocal. Indeed, on Berakhot 20b, **Ravina** wonders if women's obligation in *birkat hamazon* might only be *derabbanan*. **Rava** responds by quoting the end of the Tosefta cited above, which seems to indicate a full-blown obligation for women, given that a wife is said to be able, in principle, to fulfill her husband's obligation in this regard. (Notably, this parallel omits the first part of the Tosefta as we have it, which states that women are exempt. It further adds a coda condemning any husband who would rely on his wife to perform such a task for him.) A final passage questions this interpretation, given that it seems to suggest that a minor can fulfill his father's obligation in *birkat hamazon*, even though the former's obligation is rabbinic, while the latter's is Biblical. Therefore, says the gemara, Rava's prooftext can be deflected as assuming women's obligation is rabbinic and that they (like minors) can only fulfill the obligations of adult males who have eaten so little that their obligation in *birkat hamazon* after that meal is rabbinic.

The impact of this final passage on the sugya's conclusion is an area of dispute. Most *Rishonim*, like **Ra'avad**, hold that this final section is a mere deflection devoid of halakhic weight and still assume that the sugya's conclusion follows Rava that women are Biblically obligated.[4] Some, like **Rambam**, take the deflection seriously and as the final legal word here: Ravina's question

4. Hasagot HaRa'avad letter *aleph* on Rif Berakhot 12a. These authorities address the problem of the child blessing for the father by saying that the father repeats the words of *birkat hamazon* after his son, following the resolution to this problem in Yerushalmi Berakhot 3:3, 6b. Alternatively, perhaps בן in the Bavli's version of the *baraita* means an adult son, who only presents a problem of social boundaries but not of an obligation gap. Regarding the last point, see Ramban, *Milhamot Hashem* on Rif Berakhot 12a, where he claims that the words וליטעמיך קטן בר חיובא הוא are a later addition to the base text, such that the gemara here never even took a stand on the notion of whether a minor is in play. We suggested above, n2, that the plain sense of the *baraita* may hark back to a time when obligation (and certainly equal obligation) was not a presumed prerequisite for discharging the obligations of others in more private settings.

is left unanswered and we do not know if women are Biblically obligated in *birkat hamazon* and therefore, we cannot allow them to fulfill the obligations of men in this regard.[5]

Returning to the question of women and *zimmun*, the gemara in Arakhin seems crystal clear that women are obligated to form their own *zimmun*. If one reads Mishnah Berakhot and the gemara in Arakhin as a pair, without engaging Ravina's question in the Bavli, one could easily conclude that *birkat hamazon* and *zimmun* are "separate but equal" rituals. Men and women share an obligation, but they must execute this obligation in gender-distinct groups. This approach can be found in various *Rishonim*. We noted above the *Rishonim* who say that women are Biblically obligated in *birkat hamazon*. **R. Yonah**[6] and **Rosh**,[7] even though they do not endorse a Biblical obligation in *birkat hamazon* for women, nonetheless obligate women in *zimmun* in the same way as men. Women and men, however, do not join together to form a *zimmun* but rather form groups on their own. This is a social concern; in the words of **Rashi as cited by R. Yonah:** אין חברתן נאה.[8] According to this view, there is something improper about a joint fellowship of men and women.[9] But as we noted above, the gender blindness of *birkat hamazon* does not seem to have been universally agreed upon throughout the rabbinic period, and this trend seems to have spilled over into the question of obligation in *zimmun*. **Rashi** already suggests that the reason men and women may not form a *zimmun* together is because women and men say different texts of *birkat hamazon*, with only men mentioning the concept of ברית/covenant-circumcision.[10] **Tosafot** also report that common practice – perhaps fueled by many women's ignorance of Hebrew – was for women *not* to ever lead a *zimmun* on their own. They therefore proposed a reading of the *baraita* on Berakhot 45b that only *allowed* three women to form a *zimmun*, but did not *require* them to do so.[11] In the face of the blatant evidence to the contrary in Arakhin, **R. Yitzḥak of Dampierre** explains that women are obligated in *zimmun* when they have eaten in the presence of three or more men and that this is the meaning of Arakhin 3a.[12] Note that this potentially shifts the discussion of a ban on mixed-gender

5. Rambam Hilkhot Berakhot 5:1.
6. R. Yonah on Rif Berakhot 33a s.v. *nashim* and s.v. *venir'eh*.
7. Rosh Berakhot 7:4.
8. R. Yonah on Rif Berakhot 33a s.v. *nashim*.
9. Note that this concern would apply even if there were three men and three women. They would seemingly be required to split into two groups. It is not clear if R. Yonah is specifically concerned about a meal-based environment, or if the problem is broader and goes to the question of any sort of mixed-gender group.
10. Rashi Arakhin 3a s.v. *mezamnot*.
11. Tosafot Berakhot 45b s.v. *shanei*.
12. Cited in Semag Positive Commandments #27 s.v. *tenan bivrakhot*. This is a forced inter-

zimmun from the realm of social policy to a problem regarding equality of obligation. More generally, the notion that perhaps groups of women are *not* obligated to have a *zimmun* plays a key role in later discussions of women and quorums in general.

The classical sources leave us with a few key ambiguities. Even if men and women may not join together to form a *zimmun* of three,[13] may men and women join to mention God's name in a *zimmun* of ten? We know that three women make a *zimmun* on their own. Does a group of ten women make a *zimmun* with God's name? Does one's stance on these questions affect whether ten women or mixed groups of ten can form other quorums, a topic not taken up explicitly in classical sources?

Above, we tracked the post-Talmudic history of the gendered nature of the quorum of ten required for *devarim shebikdushah*.[14] We saw how R. Sa'adiah Gaon seems to be the earliest source to make any explicit statement that a community of Jews for the purposes of public prayer consists of ten men. This statement is descriptive and almost instinctive, without any discussion of the basis for it or the reasons surrounding it. And most medieval sources maintain this sort of approach, either omitting any mention of gender when describing quorums of ten, or simply excluding women from them as a matter of fact without any need for comment. We analyzed above the few sources that do engage the question somewhat, either to uphold a strict male standard, or to open the possibility for female involvement.

Post-Talmudic discussions around the quorums of ten required for men-

---

pretation aimed at shoring up a practice that deviates from a central text. Note that it eviscerates any notion of impropriety just by dint of sharing a meal and then joining for *birkat hamazon*, such that, for Semag, it is obvious that three women can answer to the *zimmun* of three men and need not break off and make their own. This is not an obvious point and we will see sources below that fall on the other side of this question.

13. Since we are primarily interested here in quorums of ten, we will not address the unexpected position of R. Yehudah HaKohen, cited in Responsa of Maharam of Rothenberg IV:2227, who ruled that יכולה אשה לצרף בשלשה בברכת המזון. Later commentators struggle with how he reconciled this view with what they assume to be the Mishnah's ban on including women in a *zimmun*. Ḥiddushei Hagahot suggests that he thought the Mishnah only banned one man joining with two women, whereas Derishah thought he read the Mishnah as only banning creating groups of men, women, slaves, and minors all together. According to Ḥiddushei Hagahot, it seems R. Yehudah HaKohen would only have allowed *one* woman to count towards the 10 needed for *zimmun* with God's name, whereas Derishah would likely have him endorsing treating women as equals with respect to any *zimmun*, including *zimmun* with God's name together with men or on their own. See also Agur #289 and Bah OḤ 199. Maharam of Rothenberg argues against this view, in part appealing to his assumption that ten women cannot perform *zimmun* with God's name on their own, a view we will return to below. D. Koren tries to argue even more forcefully than Derishah that Mishnah Berakhot 7:2 never intended to ban a mixed-gender *zimmun*. See above, Part Two, n8 and n15. If she is correct – we are less sure than she – then the questions we ask here are even more open.

14. See Part Two, n20 and onward.

tioning God's name in *zimmun* and for the public reading of the *megillah* can help fill in the picture we described above. The question of women and these quorums of ten is first meaningfully engaged in the 12th century. **Rambam Berakhot 5:7** states that ten women may not make a *zimmun* with God's name, without providing any reason.[15] While he does not comment on the possibility of a mixed quorum of ten men and ten women for *zimmun*, it would seem that his citation of the Mishnah's language נשים ועבדים וקטנים אין מזמנין עליהן without exception is meant to endorse a ban on a mixed-gender *zimmun* encompassing the *zimmun* of ten as well.[16] **Ittur** (R. Yitzhak b. Abba Mari, Marseilles, 12th c.) argues that לכתחילה/ideally, women should not count towards the ten of *megillah*, just as they don't count towards the ten or the three of *zimmun*.[17] For him, the exclusion of women from *zimmun* is paradigmatic for excluding women from all mixed groups with men, albeit לכתחילה/ideally, suggesting that after the fact and/or in certain kinds of situations, such a mixed quorum does

15. The Frankel edition of Mishneh Torah Berakhot 5:7 reads as follows:

נשים ועבדים וקטנים אין מזמנין עליהם אבל מזמנין לעצמן, ולא תהא חבורה של נשים ועבדים וקטנים מפני הפריצות, אלא נשים לעצמן או עבדים לעצמן או קטנים לעצמן ובלבד שלא יזמנו בשם

One does not make a *zimmun* over women, slaves and minors, but they may make a *zimmun* on their own. There should not be a group of women, slaves and minors on account of [sexual] impropriety. Rather women on their own or slaves on their own or minors on their own, provided they do not make a *zimmun* with God's name.

The phrase או קטנים לעצמן is attested in a number of *rishonim*, including Tur OḤ 199. But other *rishonim* seem not to have had it and it was missing from the printed editions. See the notes in the Frankel edition. Note that while Rambam has always been read as forbidding 10 women from making a *zimmun* with God's name it is technically possible to read Rambam as only forbidding 10 slaves (or 10 minors) from engaging in this ritual. The gemara on Berakhot 47b cites R. Yehoshua b. Levi's view that 9 free people and one slave may join together. The immediate prior context is another ruling by R. Yehoshua b. Levi that an infant can be counted as an adjunct member of a *zimmun* of ten. This juxtaposition could easily lead one to assume that his ruling about a slave also applies to a case of a *zimmun* of ten. One might then infer that if the most lenient position only allowed counting a slave as a tenth (or a minor as an adjunct), then certainly a group of ten slaves (or ten minors) cannot form their own group of ten, despite their ability to form an independent group of three. This would then provide some more basis for Rambam's ruling here, which puzzled various authorities as devoid of any Talmudic source, and he would not be making a comment on women at all. In fact, Kesef Mishneh on Rambam Berakhot 5:7 only seems to explain the exclusion of slaves and minors from a *zimmun* with God's name and cross-references to chapter 8 of Hilkhot Tefillah, which does not engage the question of gender at all. But Beit Yosef OH 199 seems to throw gender into the mix as well when using the phrase **אנשים** גדולים ובני חורין. We have not, however, found any reader of Rambam who is explicit that his phrase ובלבד שלא יזמנו בשם does not apply to a group of ten women.

16. This is indeed how almost all later authorities understood Rambam. Note that D. Koren, who thinks that the language of the Mishnah itself does not preclude a mixed-gender *zimmun*, would make the same claim about Rambam's phrasing here. We do not find this to be a plausible reading of Rambam. If the first phrase – נשים ועבדים וקטנים אין מזמנין עליהם – means nothing more than a ban on groups of women, slaves and minors joining together to make a *zimmun*, the next phrase in Rambam becomes redundant.

17. Sefer HaIttur Aseret Hadiberot, Hilkhot Megillah 110a.

not compromise the integrity of the ritual. He says nothing about ten women reading the *megillah* on their own (or performing *zimmun* with God's name).

The next figure to contribute to this debate is **R. Meir b. Shimon HaMe'ili** (Provençe, 13th c.), who resists Rambam's ruling that ten women may not perform *zimmun* with God's name, suggesting that the statement that women form their own *zimmun* in the gemara is comprehensive and applies both to quorums of three and ten.[18] He offers two suggestions for the basis for Rambam's ruling:

1) He holds that women are permitted, but not obligated to form a *zimmun* and, therefore, consistent with his view that women do not say *berakhot* over *mitzvot* from which they are exempt, they may not mention God's name in an optional *zimmun*.[19]
2) A group of women lacks קביעות, the kind of social cohesion necessary to create a *zimmun*. Rambam felt that women and slaves do not generate a social center of gravity the way free men do, and perhaps this is the reason that they may not do *zimmun* with God's name.[20]

Despite these justifications, he argues that one should not stop groups of ten women who do *zimmun* with God's name, since there is no source in the gemara that opposes it.[21] He then goes further, however, actively permitting an adult male to lead a group of either ten minors or ten women in *zimmun* with God's name, revealing a rejection of Rambam's principle that a group of ten women or ten minors cannot mention God's name in the *zimmun*.[22]

---

18. Sefer Hameorot 45b.

19. According to this logic, communities that followed R. Tam and did permit women to say such *berakhot* would indeed allow 10 women to perform *zimmun* with God's name. Note that Sefer Hameorot's reading of Rambam here does not seem to be the plain sense of Rambam Berakhot 5:1, 7 (see Meiri's understanding of Rambam on this question), contradicts some versions of Rambam Hilkhot Berakhot 5:6 that explicitly obligate women in *zimmun* (see the Frankel edition) and is borrowed from the Tosafot's notion that women are exempt from *zimmun*. Likely for this reason, and out of a desire to understand how Rambam's ruling might apply to all communities, he suggests a second basis for the ruling here.

20. Sefer Hameorot's approach here seems to draw on the approach of Ra'avad in Temim De'im #1, where he lays out the idea that a lack of קביעות is the core of the problem with mixed-gender *zimmun*, arguing that a group of men and women never coheres into a single unit with its own single center of gravity. Sefer Hameorot extends this notion to suggest that women on their own have the same problem.

21. As we noted above, this sort of measured perspective would be welcome throughout the larger topic under discussion here, with Sefer Hameorot's principle applying to women's participation in the *minyan* for *devarim shebikdushah* as well.

22. Sefer Hameorot is thus likely the יש חולקין בכך cited in Meiri Berakhot 47b that supports 10 women performing a *zimmun* with God's name. The scenario of one adult male leading the *zimmun* with God's name for ten women is not intended to convey the notion that ten women cannot do this on their own, given that he otherwise rejects the notion that women join together

With respect to the Ittur's restrictive position on a mixed-gender group of ten for *megillah,* Sefer Hameorot echoes this view on Megillah 5a, saying that whenever ten are needed, men are required. In fact, this seems to go further than the Ittur, in that it suggests that ten women on their own are also ineligible to compose the ten for *megillah,* the first view to do so explicitly. This statement seems to reflect the kind of reflexive assumption that women are generally excluded from *minyanim* of ten that we saw above, extending this notion into the realm of *megillah.*[23]

At around the same time, **R. Simḥah of Speyer**, whose rulings we examined above,[24] also took for granted that at least one woman could count towards the ten of *zimmun.* We suggested above that he might have had an even bolder position, permitting women to function as equals in this quorum of ten, whether with or without men.[25] What is striking about R. Simḥah is that he carries

---

with men and the only reason to say God's name is thus the presence of ten women. Rather, he discusses the case of a man leading for ten women in order to argue the case – which he does in the next part of the passage – that there is never an issue of *peritzut* when free men lead rituals for women; that concern is limited to slaves and women joinging together for ritual performance. Though he also cites those who think that *peritzut* is a wide ranging problem in the context of meals, and that this would be a problem for allowing a man to lead a *zimmun* for women, he rejects this view. In the end, he therefore in principle endorses the notion that a woman would lead other women in a *zimmun* with God's name as well. Note also that R. Shmuel b. Meshullam Gerondi, in *Ohel Mo'ed* 107b, cites a view identical to that of Sefer Hameorot on this point in the name of R. Avraham, which may refer to Ra'avad. Given our citation of Ra'avad in Temim De'im above, Ohel Mo'ed seems to argue that if the problem with mixed-gender *zimmun* is the inability of men and women to cohere as a group, then there ought to be no issues with treating a group of women on its own identically to a group of men on its own. See Repsonsa Benei Banim 3:1. This view of Sefer Hameorot does not get much traction with later poskim and Meiri explicitly rejects him in his commentary on Berakhot 47b by echoing R. Manoah's claim – explored above, Part Two, n24 and onward – that *zimmun* with God's name requires a קהל, and ten women cannot form a קהל. [R. Ben Zion Lichtman, in Benei Tziyyon 199:6 struggles with this passage in the Meiri and suggests instead that perhaps Meiri had a different text on Megillah 23b that explicitly tied the requirement of ten for *zimmun* with God's name to the notion of קהל.] Most later authorities display no awareness of Sefer Hameorot's position. But note that Shiltei Hagibborim on Rif Berakhot 33a, letter *bet* cites Rosh as permitting women to count toward the *zimmun* of ten in language that sounds unrestricted.

23. Sefer Hameorot then offers a reason why women should not join with men towards the ten of *megillah,* Ittur's original point: such a mixed-gender group is a problem of *peritzut.* But, in light of his analysis on Berakhot 45a, where he suggests that free adults are not subject to such concerns, he comments here that the concern of *peritzut* could be easily dismissed. He thus seems to fall back on his first general statement that groups of ten are not the domain of women. This itself is a problematic statement, in that he is on record, as we saw, as permitting ten women to perform a *zimmun* with God's name. One might question whether his endorsement of the latter position also began to put into play the possibility of ten women reading the *megillah* on their own, a possibility not yet proposed in his day. It seems most reasonable to see Sefer Hameorot's inconsistency as emerging from the pioneering nature of much of his analysis.

24. See Part Two, n40 and onward.

25. Agur #289 reports that R. Simḥah agreed with R. Yehudah HaKohen that men and women could join towards the quorum of three. This strengthens the notion that R. Simhah might simply have said that any combination of ten adults is valid for *zimmun* with God's name. If this report is incorrect and R. Simhah only permitted women to count towards the quorum of ten, he maximally

the participation into the realm of the *minyan* of *tefillah*, something that no one before him did explicitly, even though the logic for doing so is similar to that of those, like Sefer Hameorot, who argued for the ability of ten women to form a *zimmun*. Nonetheless, as we saw above and will see again below, even those authorities entertaining including women in the ten of *zimmun* or *megillah* seem to have taken for granted their exclusion from the ten of *devarim shebikdushah* during communal prayer, for reasons we argued for elsewhere.[26]

The next voice to weigh in is that of **R. Aharon HaLevi of Barcelona**, who is cited in Ritva Megillah 4a. He argues there that women ought to be able to join with men towards the quorum of ten for *megillah*, directly rejecting the Ittur, and his logic makes clear that he would permit ten women on their own to count as a quorum for this purpose. He then attempts to distinguish the mixed-gender group he permits here from the one explicitly banned by the Mishnah. A *zimmun* constituted by men and women is problematic because an entirely new ritual (*zimmun*) is being added due to the joint participation of men and women, and this presents a concern of *peritzut*. Since neither the men on their own nor the women on their own could do this ritual, their joint participation is blatantly obvious, and thus problematic. In the case of *megillah*, however, the ritual looks the same irrespective of the size of the group, and therefore there is no issue of *peritzut*.[27]

As a summary of this topic, it is worth looking at a passage from the **Sefer Hamikhtam** (R. David b. Levi, Narbonne, 13th–14th c.), in which he tries to synthesize all of this various material regarding women and various quorums and to work through how controlling a paradigm the material on women and *zimmun* ought to be. He writes as follows:

ספר המכתם ברכות מה.

נשים ועבדים וקטנים אין מזמנין עליהן.

1) פי' דלאו בני חיובא נינהו כאנשים, ואע"פ שהנשים חייבות בבכרת המזון, ספק הוא אם חייבות מדאוריית' או מדרבנן, והאנשים חייבות מן התורה . . .

2) וכתב הרמ' דנשים אם מזמנות לעצמן לעולם אין מזמנות לעצמן בשם, אפי' ביותר מעשר.

3) ועוד מפרש בגמ' דנשים ועבדים אפי' אם רצו לזמן אין מזמנין משום פריצותא, כלומ' כדי להרחיק שלא לעשות מסיבה של נשים ועבדים.

4) ויש שאומ' דדוקא בעבדים שהם פרוצים, כדאמ' עבדא בהפקירא ניחא ליה, אבל בחבורה של נשים עם בני חורין הכשרין אין מפקירין.

would have permitted combinations of up to seven of one gender with three of the other, so as not to violate the Mishnah's ban on combining men and women to form the core *zimmun* of three.

26. See Part Two, n35 and onward.

27. We explored this view and some of its ramifications above, Part Two, n84–89.

5) אבל מכל מקום הנשים אינן מצטרפות עם האנשים, דסתמא דמתני' דנשי' ועבדים וקטנים אין מזמנין עליהן, ואפי' סניפין לעשרה אין עושין מהן.

6) ולא עוד אלא במה שמצטרפין הקטן היודע למי מברכין אין מצרפין אותן לענין זמון, דקטן אתי לכלל חיובא בגדול, אבל נשים לא.

7) ואע"ג דלענין מקרא מגילה מצטרפות לעשרה לדעת קצת הפוסקים, ומוציאות את האנשים אם היו יודעות לקרות, שאני התם דחיובן שוה לאנשים.

8) ואע"ג דאמרי' נמי אשה לא [תקרא] בתורה בציבור מפני כבוד [הציבור], דמשמע טעמא משום כבוד ציבור הוא דלא, הא לאו הכי שרי, התם נמי אפשר דקריאתה אינה עולה למנין השבעה, או אפילו תימא דעולה מ"מ איהי לא מצטרפא לעשרה דאין קורין בתורה בפחות מעשרה.

9) ויש שאומרי' דלהכי לא פסלינן נשים לספר תורה ולמקרא מגילה משום דלא נתמעטו נשים אלא מזימון, משום דבסעודה שכיחא שכרות ושחוק וקלות ראש וכל זה איננו שוה להכשירן לענין צירוף שלשה או עשרה אפי' בכשרים.

1) Sefer Hamikhtam begins here by explaining why it is, in his view, that women and men do not join together to make a *zimmun*: They may lack equal obligation to men. Even though they are obligated, once the gemara on Berakhot 20b raises a doubt as to whether their obligation is Biblical, they are no longer necessarily on the same plane as men with regard to *zimmun* and may not join them.[28]

2) He notes that Rambam says ten women may not do *zimmun* with God's name.

3) The gemara clarifies that women and slaves may not form a joint group for *zimmun*, because of concerns of sexual impropriety. There should never be a joint meal of women and slaves.[29]

4) The above logic would seem to ban men and women from ever having a joint *zimmun* or meal, so Sefer Hamikhtam now cites the view of Sefer Hameorot that there is no fear of [sexual] impropriety with regard to free men and women. Therefore, three men and three women may participate in the same *zimmun*.[30]

---

28. Sefer Hamikhtam here follows Rambam Hilkhot Berakhot 5:1. As we noted above, this is a highly disputed point; most *rishonim* thought that women were Biblically obligated in *birkat hamazon* just like men.

29. Note that the logic here applies even if the women and slaves are not relying on one another for a quorum. In other words, when the *baraita* on Berakhot 45b forbids women and slaves from mixing together because of פריצותא, the plain sense is that even three women and three slaves cannot combine to the same *zimmun*. This coerced separation is intended to prevent their inappropriate cohesion as a group. See above, n12, our comment regarding the question of whether three men and three women may join together to form a *zimmun*; based on Sefer Hamikhtam's understanding here, we would not permit in such a case if we felt there was a problem of פריצותא in a mixed-gender group of free adults.

30. Note that one who did not accept Sefer Hameorot's distinction, or who felt that other problematic social issues arose from a mixed-gender meal, might reject this permission. Indeed, this seems to be the view of Rashi cited by R. Yonah that we cited above, who says that women do

5) Nonetheless, even if free men and women present no problem of [sexual] impropriety, such that they can participate in the same *zimmun*, they still may not join together to form a quorum of three or ten; the Mishnah's ban must minimally prevent these sorts of joint quorums [even if it might still allow for joint participation in a *zimmun* formed by a single-gender quorum]. Even nine men and one woman may not perform *zimmun* with God's name.[31]
6) You might object that the Mishnah also forbids including minors in a *zimmun* and, yet, voices in the gemara legitimate counting at least one minor.[32] Why shouldn't at least one woman be allowed to count towards the ten required for *zimmun* with God's name? He deflects this problem by insisting that minors are different, since they will eventually be fully obligated in *birkat hamazon* as adults, whereas women's obligation will never be on par with men's.[33]

---

not join with men because אין חברתם נאה, a concern that would apply to any kind of joint *zimmun*, whether or not the men need the women to attain the quorum. While Beit Yosef 199:8–9 rejects this view in favor of the Semag cited above, he agrees that this is the proper reading of R. Yonah, and this section of Sefer Hamikhtam confirms the plausibility of such a position.

31. Obviously, R. Simḥah read the Mishnah differently. See also Part Two, n8 and n15 for D. Koren's even bolder alternate reading of the Mishnah.

32. This is a reference to the idea that a minor who is sufficiently intelligent to understand the notion of blessing God for the food one has eaten may indeed help form the *zimmun*. R. Naḥman rules this way on Berakhot 48a and the gemara on Arakhin 3a endorses this view as normative. This then leads to a Geonic gloss that creeps into the text of Berakhot 48a affirming R. Naḥman's statement as consensus law.

33. The logic of distinguishing minors from other categories of people via the claim אתי לכלל חיובא – their eventual status as free, adult Jewish males renders them more similar to the latter group than others outside of that category – was an innovation of Tosafistic circles. In fact, the almost certain referent here is a passage that appears in two parallel Tosafot (on Eruvin 96b and Rosh Hashanah 33a) that discuss the question of whether women are allowed to say berakhot over the voluntary performance of *mitzvot* from which they are exempt. After citing R. Tam's support for this position, Tosafot deflect several suggested proofs for this view (even though they do not challenge the validity of R. Tam's view itself). The end of the Tosafot reads as follows: ומקטן דמברך ברכת המזון אף על פי שהוא פטור אין ראיה לאשה דקטן בא לכלל חיוב וחייב לחנכו ואינו מוזהר על לא תשא. The potential argument here is that Mishnah Berakhot 3:3 (which we looked at above), rules (according to Rashi and Tosafot's interpretation of that text) that minors say *birkat hamazon*. Given that minors are exempt and yet allowed to say these blessings, one might argue that women, even though exempt, can say blessings over *mitzvot* that they voluntarily perform. Tosafot reject this potential argument by suggesting that we would more readily let a minor bless than an exempt adult: Minors will eventually become obligated and must be educated; moreover, they are not yet culpable for taking God's name in vain. Tosafot's claim here seems to be that because the minor will eventually be obligated in these *mitzvot*, there is a value in educating him to perform them. This is supported by Tosafot on Nazir 57b, where they consider it a forced suggestion that one would be stricter in the case of a minor simply because he will eventually become obligated in the absence of educational concerns. Sefer Hamikhtam borrows that concept here to claim that we are more invested in including minors in a *zimmun* as part of their training to become adults. Therefore, our leniencies with them have no implications for women.

7) Given the blanket ban Sefer Hamikhtam argues for on men and women forming a joint quorum for *zimmun*, you might be surprised by those authorities (like Ra'ah), who permit women and men to join for the ten of *megillah*. Shouldn't women and men be banned from ever forming a joint quorum, based on the model of *zimmun*? Sefer Hamikhtam argues that *megillah* is different from *zimmun*, because women's obligation in *megillah* is equal to that of men, whereas this is not [at least clearly] the case, in his view, with regard to *birkat hamazon*.
8) Given the blanket ban Sefer Hamikhtam argues for on men and women forming a joint quorum for *zimmun*, you might be surprised that the *baraita* on Megillah 23b makes it sound like a woman can be among the quorum of seven readers for the Torah [assuming we control for the concern of *kevod tzibbur*]. Sefer Hamikhtam offers two ways of explaining how women are indeed not really joining together with men to form a Torah reading quorum. First of all, some say that her reading cannot count towards the count of seven.[34] And even if one follows the plain sense of the *baraita*, which poses no objections to women's *'aliyot* other than *kevod hatzibbur*,[35] women are still excluded from the quorum of ten required to enable the reading to happen in the first place.[36] Therefore, even if men and women can join to form the quorum of seven, we still see a disability analogous to the ban on a joint *zimmun* in the context of the ritual of Torah reading as well. In short, Torah reading in fact conforms to the ban on a mixed-gender *zimmun* quorum in one way or another.
9) Alternatively, there is another way of explaining why men and women might not jointly create a quorum for *zimmun* even though they can join for the ten required for the *megillah* and the seven required for Torah

34. This very likely refers to the view that women were only ever allowed to read when they did not have to make a berakhah over the reading, since originally only the first and last reader did so. Once each person coming to the Torah was required to make a blessing, women, who were classically exempt from Torah study, were no longer eligible to participate in Torah reading at all. This view is first suggested as a deflection in Tosafot Rosh Hashanah 33a and is later picked up as an actual ruling by later authorities, such as R. David Kokhavi, in Sefer Habatim, Sha'arei Keriat Hatorah 2:6, and R. Menahem HaMeiri, in Beit Habeḥirah Megillah 23a. See above (Part One, n117, towards the end).

35. This is likely not just a theoretical point raised here in Sefer Hamikhtam. The author was likely aware of rulings like the one cited in Sefer Habatim – which we discussed above, Part One, n106 and onward – permitting women to read Torah in a private home where *kevod hatzibbur* might be said not to apply.

36. This fact is asserted as obvious by simply appealing to the text of the Mishnah. Obviously, Sefer Hamikhtam here is subject to the same analysis we offered earlier in our discussion of all such statements in the rishonim, and he is another good example of the phenomenon of asserting this assumption of religious practice.

> reading:[37] *Zimmun* presents a serious problem for mixed gender activity, because mealtimes are prone to alcoholic consumption and inappropriate levity and gaity; *zimmun* is not paradigmatic for other rituals that lack this quality, such as Torah reading and *megillah*. Therefore, one might entertain including women with men in the latter rituals while maintaining an ironclad ban on allowing even free men and women to jointly form the quorums of three and ten for *zimmun*. [This is the view cited by Sefer Hameorot on Berakhot 45a, though he rejects it.]

Even though almost every one of his points is substantively disputed by some medieval authority, Sefer Hamikhtam is a good place to end our discussion because of his fairly comprehensive survey of the material we have covered.[38] He also demonstrates the deeply embedded assumption of so many *Rishonim* that women are excluded from the ten required for *devarim shebikdushah*. This exclusion, for many *Rishonim*, is a truth in need of no justification, even as some of those same *Rishonim* entertain including women in other quorums of ten. We examined this pattern and its significance above. Finally, this source, along with the others we have explored in this appendix, demonstrates how the thin record on women and quorums in classical sources can be taken in a variety of directions with respect to a variety of rituals. Whether one views *zimmun* as paradigmatic or exceptional ultimately reflects what each authority understood to be the principles underlying the gendering of that practice. This should help put in perspective our analysis of the underlying principles of the gendering of the ten required for *devarim shebikdushah* and how one might apply that information in different religious times and places.

---

37. In other words, this is another effort to justify the rulings permitting women and men to combine for the ten of *megillah* (Ra'ah) and permitting women to read Torah (Sefer Habatim) without running afoul of the Mishnah's opposition to mixed-gender groups in the context of *zimmun*.

38. Meiri on Berakhot 47b essentially cites Sefer Hamikhtam here, almost verbatim. His main contribution is to add a brief discussion on the question of whether ten women can perform *zimmun* with God's name, citing Sefer Hameorot's opposing view to that of Rambam, though ultimately rejecting it.